JACQUELINE LAMBA

The Forgotten Surrealist

Salomon Grimberg

JACQUELINE LAMBA
The Forgotten Surrealist

MERRELL
LONDON · NEW YORK

By my kiss I make you eternally mine.
You shall be beautiful as I am beautiful.
You shall love what I love and what loves me:
water, clouds, silence and the night;
the green unfathomable sea;
water without form and multiform;
the place where you are not;
the lover you will never know;
monstrous flowers; delirious perfume;
languorous cats who lie on pianos and moan like women
with sweet and husky voices!

Charles Baudelaire
Translated from the French by Louise Varèse

for Dolorès Vanetti

Contents

Prelude

To an American friend, Jacqueline Lamba wrote a one-line letter on Wednesday, June 12, 1954. He had asked, "Why the long silence? ... Are you angry?" "Absolutely not," she replied, "I am simply empty and insatiable."[1] Having split from her second husband, David Hare, two years previously, Jacqueline had returned to France from the United States, and their separation was taking its toll. Light, the emotional source in her painting, had started to fade.[2]

In quiet moments, Jacqueline's thoughts would often turn to the memory of her father. Her older sister, Huguette, explained: "She used to say that the only thing she recalled about my father was that one day, when she was enraged, he took her in his arms, walked to a balcony, where there were many flowers, picked one and gave it to her. That calmed her anger."[3]

Their father died when Jacqueline was only three and a half years old (pl. 3), and her continued yearning for more time with him gave rise to her belief that her life would have been different had he lived. This early memory became the cornerstone of her emotional life. A friend remembered: "Right before her death, Jacqueline spoke about his [her father's] death as the great tragedy of her life because he really had loved her."[4] To the outside observer, the life of Jacqueline Lamba may seem simply extraordinary, but her belief that it was tragic suggests that, in spite of appearances, she lived in pain. To soothe herself, she often tried building lives with others who might fill the void left by the loss of her father at such a young age. She had been certain that a life of poetry with André Breton would do it. When that failed, she turned to Hare's unbridled passion. On both accounts, she was mistaken. Another friend would later summarize: "André wrote *Mad Love* for her. David showed her it [mad love]."[5] But neither man could demonstrate his love for her as convincingly as her father had with the gift of the flower that quelled her rage.

Walking on the street with Huguette one summer afternoon, Jacqueline suddenly asked her sister: "What do you want? I really don't want to get with a third man. Two are enough. Men want women for only one thing—they just want us to sew their buttons. I am done."

Days later, the doorbell rang. Jacqueline was living on 46 rue Gay-Lussac, Paris, in a sixth-floor walk-up. When she opened her door, Alberto Giacometti was climbing the stairs, muttering, "Ah! I'm fed up! This is going to fall." He was holding his abdomen with both hands. Jacqueline had known him since her early twenties, when he and Pablo Picasso adopted her as their little sister.

"Are you ill?" she asked him.

"No, the top button popped off my pants, and the string I was using has broken. Will you sew a button for me?"[6]

Sewing Giacometti's button felt natural to Jacqueline; he was not like other men. He knew who he was, and did not need encouragement or approval. "When I first met Giacometti," a friend explained, "it was during a season when André Breton, Surrealism's central personage, had decreed that so far as possible everything he and his colleagues ate or drank should be green ... But Giacometti ordered something orange. Clearly, he was destined for a lonely path. His association with Surrealism was brief. Afterward, he never subscribed to any group of artists. Instead, he worked for many years alone in his studio on 46 rue Hippolyte-Maindron in the 14th *arrondissement* [neighborhood], cordial to visitors but giving the impression of profound isolation within the art and activities of his time.[7] Perhaps that was why his closest friend was the painter Balthus, like himself a confirmed solitary, shying away from movements and manifestoes, gatherings and programs, working in seclusion to reassert the validity of the maverick against artists."[8]

Jacqueline, even toward the end of her life, could still recall one December evening in 1934 as if it were yesterday. When Giacometti told André he had stopped making Surrealist art and would be devoting himself to developing his personal iconography, André became livid over losing control of him, and before a gathering of co-religionists was ready to pounce on him. But "Giacometti was not easily intimidated, especially when his ongoing purpose in life was opposed ... 'Don't bother,' said Alberto, 'I'm going.' He went without ceremony. Behind, he left a room full of former friends and an important period in his life ... Men who had been his friends refused to speak to him, turning their backs in the street. The power of the Surrealist leader was certainly great."[9]

That evening was just one example of "this ascendancy, indeed, of one man over the judgment and conduct of others, who happened to be among the most gifted and intelligent of his generation."[10] Jacqueline took note at the time but only subsequently understood why the memory stayed with her.

Jacqueline's first marriage, to Breton, ended bitterly, each blaming the other for its failure. Despite both wanting the union to work, neither had the flexibility, wherewithal or practicality to adapt. Both were intransigent, willful and rigid. Both wanted it their way; and neither had steady work. Until then, their lives had been intellectual exercises rather than actual day-to-day living. To Mark Polizzotti, Breton's biographer, Jacqueline explained: "He saw in me what he wanted to see, but he really didn't see me."[11] Yet she would not acknowledge her own contribution; she too saw in him only what she wanted to see.

Early in the marriage, Jacqueline found out that the gas company would not accept poetry in lieu of payment. And André, surprised that the bill had not remained the same after Jacqueline moved in, blamed her for the increase. It was the first of their many fights.[12] André did not earn a regular living, yet he found ways to build an art collection coveted by museums. Until then, Jacqueline had barely covered her expenses by doing various jobs—as a taxi girl, a salesperson, a model, and a nude swimmer in a glass pool at the Coliséum nightclub, where André first laid eyes on her. Once married, she stopped working, assuming Breton would provide her with freedom to do what she wanted: to make art full-time. The British Surrealist Eileen Agar told it like it was: "Among the European Surrealists, double standards seem to have proliferated, and the women came off worst. As Breton's wife, Jacqueline was expected to behave as the great man's muse, not to have an active creative existence of her own. In fact, she was a painter of considerable ability, but Breton never mentioned her work."[13]

David Hare took an interest in Jacqueline as a person, which filled this gap, at least at first. While pregnant with her second child, though, she sensed that David was having an affair—the first of many—turning her dream marriage into a nightmare. Her suspicion first arose at a party when he introduced her as "my wife" and someone blurted out, "Which one?"[14] Feeling humiliated, Jacqueline began to think she had been deluding herself; this was not a relationship that made her feel prized. Others could see that she was alone, too: "A friend noticed her at a gathering looking very conservative and subdued—something in her life had changed, she was completely altered. After she left David, something was lost."[15] David told Therry Frey, his fourth wife, that when he and Jacqueline were living together, "She became impossible, almost always very angry; they fought about everything, there was no peace."[16]

Dolorès Vanetti, godmother to the Hares' son Merlin, believed Jacqueline "was very courageous to leave David. She went back to nothing. She was married, she had a house, she was being taken care of, she went back to Paris [from the United States] to what? Disappointment. She was brave to move back with a child and nothing else."[17] Jacqueline hoped that David would follow her. He did, but not for long. During the next four years—until 1954—he shifted back and forth between New York, which he missed, and France, which he disliked. He and Jacqueline shared a mutual untruth. Although they recognized their conflict, neither dared discuss it: he, too unwilling to take responsibility; she, too proud to ask, and fearful that confronting him would frighten him away. The end came suddenly in 1957. Eager to marry Denise Browne, his third wife, David flew to Mexico for a quick divorce—without telling Jacqueline—and mailed the document to her from there. Jacqueline had given her best to the relationship but now discovered that it had not been enough. Nonetheless, "She never gave up on David," a friend recalled: another wound that did not heal.[18]

Childhood

Jacqueline Mathilde Lamba was born on November 17, 1910, in Saint Mandé, Seine, a suburb of Paris, the younger of two girls from the marriage of Jeanette (Jane) Adele Pinon and Joseph (José) Lamba.[19] To her parents, her birth was an open disappointment, and she developed her sense of self "seething inside that her parents wanted a boy and not a girl."[20] José sent Jane on ahead to the maternity facility in Paris because he was unable to get away from work. Toward the end of her pregnancy, on October 15, José wrote an enthusiastic postcard to his wife about the forthcoming "birth of my son," whom he intended to name Jacob:

> *My Dear Little Wife,*
>
> *I am writing you a couple of words in order not to let the mail go without sending you my thoughts ... Go for the regular [dry] nurse from La Varenne if your mother thinks she will be able to do her job. Tell your father that I thank him for taking care of dealing with the best doctor who will take care of the operation. I will not, unfortunately, be present. I hope however to be in Paris to receive my son and I ask you to tell him to wait quietly for me in his maternal sleep.*
>
> *I kiss you tenderly*

Tellingly, Jacqueline later added "birth" to gloss "the operation" and underlined "my son," adding "*abhorée*" (loathed). They named her Jacqueline but referred to her as Jacquot, a variant of Jacob, and dressed her as a boy.

Personalizing her parents' disappointment, Jacqueline grew up believing that women were destined for lives of insubordination: "Men win—not because they are better—it's because they are men."[21] Women were naturally relegated to a losing place, defeated before starting.

Jacqueline grew up a tomboy, often reminded that she was "*un garçon manqué*," "an incomplete boy." Huguette remembered: "Jacqueline used to say, 'You know, they wanted a boy and I came along.' So she felt our parents' disappointment. She suffered a little because of this, since she didn't have an easy personality, but that's the way it is. She preferred that she be loved as a little girl, but she had a personality which resembled closely our father's dynamic one. She carried on like a boy, so we used to say she was a regular tomboy. She was always stirring things up."[22]

In adolescence, Jacqueline embraced the identity given to her, wearing men's clothes and going by the name Jack. Marianne Clouzot, her friend and art school classmate, kept a diary in which she drew several portraits of Jacqueline labeled "Jack" wearing rolled-up knickerbockers, like her father had worn, with Scottish stockings and a boy's haircut (pl. 5). Even her mother referred to her as "Jack."[23]

Jacqueline saved a letter from her mother in which she refers to her as "Jack" and explains why "he" and the family did not have to think alike:

> *This Sunday*
> *My Dear Little One* ["*mon petit*," the masculine form],
> *What a week I've had. First of all, such palpitations and heart pain that I had to see a doctor. It was great fatigue and today is going better, but a stomach pain had me howling for 99 minutes, then a tooth abscess that hasn't gone away for two days. Hey, that's nice, I must admit that it is a bit much for a woman alone for a whole week, and I would wish that a merciful God would stop treating me like a second Job. Let's say that, with His grace, we would have been able, me, you and Hug*[uette], *to spend our day at the cinema whereas I have not left my bed of ailing. Jack, you must love your family which loves you and which is so kind. So what if your ideas are not in agreement* [with ours]. *What importance next to the heart, but I'm tired. Tender kisses, my little one* [again using the masculine form].
> *Maman*[24]

Before Jacqueline was born, the Lambas had been living in Egypt, but they came home to France for the birth. Afterward, they returned to Egypt, "leaving her in Paris, in the care of a nursemaid," Huguette explained, "but Grandmother took Jacqueline [back] since the woman did not nurse as expected. And she stayed at least a year and a half with Grandmother before leaving for Egypt."[25]

A bonding failure during these first two and a half years contributed to Jacqueline's chronic anger and difficult personality. At least, that's how it seemed to Aube, Jacqueline's daughter, who grew up to become a social worker for children. Her earliest recollection of Jacqueline was her self-absorption: "She was a narcissist, used to being admired for her beauty. I remember her sitting at her vanity table looking into the mirror. I have the feeling of her presence, but I don't have the feeling of a motherly presence. I have the feeling, in a confused way, of the presence of a very beautiful woman—quite narcissistic [although] I did not know what that meant at the time. She was much more preoccupied with herself than with the child that I was. I have a lot of memories of my father, since he was more often with me than Jacqueline was."[26]

Once, Aunt Lucy (Jane's younger sister) noticed Huguette observing her reflection and warned: "If you look at yourself in the mirror, you'll see the Devil."[27] Aunt Lucy was warning against vanity, but Huguette took her literally—imagining the Devil she had seen in illustrations, with horns and a tail—and avoided mirrors thereafter. Had Aunt Lucy warned Jacqueline, her response would have been the opposite; Jacqueline would have wanted to see what the Devil looked like. In 1927, Jacqueline portrayed the androgynous angel Heurtebise in a painting influenced by Jean Cocteau's play *Orpheus* (1926). The image reveals how, already at an early age, she was attuned to her intuition, developing a relationship to her reflection in the mirror and her gender identity. In the myth, Heurtebise obeys a higher order that allows it to slip in and out of the mirror and transform itself at will from human form into pure energy. Jacqueline's Heurtebise observes the viewer from the other side of the mirror, hands pressed to the glass. Its otherworldly, sexually ambiguous body is male, but its made-up face and golden ringlets are female. The pastel anticipates by seven years Jacqueline's future as a nude underwater dancer in a glass pool, and her bisexuality.

Huguette Lamba, three years older than her sister, remained in Egypt with her parents during Jacqueline's infancy and fondly recalled summers when the family returned to France: "Our father took us to Cannes, he himself liking the light and heat. Jacqueline had our father's love of drawing, and drawing well, and the love of plants. She always liked flowers a lot."[28] Jacqueline kept a drawing by José of the Grand Canal's luminous expanse in Venice, as fine as anything by Whistler. Once they were all in Egypt, the family lived in a small house and the girls shared a room with Henriette, a governess who cared for all their needs: "We didn't even eat at our parents' table because my father was very busy. Marzouk, the Arab cook, served us in our room. Well, our mother took care of us too, but we were somewhat separated from our father, who was very busy, except of course during vacation. Our father came to join us in France when we were on holiday in Royan. And there he was a father just like any other. He was nice to us."[29]

Jacqueline was given the middle name Mathilde after José's older sister, the mother of André Delons—her first cousin, first love, and guiding light in adolescence. Henri Lamba, José's older brother, taught law in Egypt. He was "a bit of a snob and wanted it known that they were descended from Italians," Huguette mused. "He claimed that Lamba Doria was their original name," like the Italian admiral from the Republic of Genoa, "but this was never proved. For me in Cairo," she added, "my father was a mythical personage with an affectionate look and tender gestures. But long conversations were rare. He did not have time."[30] A photograph of José shows him reading in his sitting room: slender, handsome, hair cropped short, sporting a trimmed beard, handlebar mustache, and a pipe. While vacationing at Oberhofen, Austria, in 1904, he was photographed in the garden of the pension where the couple stayed, smiling for the camera, fashionably dressed in straw fedora, linen suit, and knickerbockers rolled to the knee (pl. 1).

In Egypt, José was the agricultural engineer in charge of a plantation in Lower Egypt at El Qattah. He published scientific articles in specialized journals on Mediterranean roses, diseases of banana trees, artificial cotton, and related subjects.[31] In recognition of his contributions to agronomy, the French government honored him with a medal from the Société nationale d'encouragement à l'agriculture.

In 1905, José was commissioned by the Nile Land and Agricultural Company to create Garden City, an exclusive neighborhood for Cairo's elite. He cleverly planned it like a maze, laying out "a series of narrow winding roads outlining ill-defined triangles and curvy rectangles. Three times out of four, you end up where you started. Even as one traveled down a single road, it erratically changed names at vague intervals."[32] The villas, inspired by the natural world in the Art Nouveau style, had small gardens and plant-like embellishments. In the center, one major garden took the shape of a giant fish, its head pointing west toward the Nile.

One Friday, on February 27, 1914, José was involved in a fatal accident when driving in Heliopolis with Pierre Jouget, an Egyptologist colleague from Lille. As the cart in front of him made a turn, a loose beam slipped, impaling José's windshield and abdomen, causing him to suffer a double intestinal perforation. He died on March 1.[33] It was largely José's death, Huguette believed, that caused Jacqueline, then aged three, to develop a cynical, no-nonsense attitude at such an early age. For example, one Christmas while Huguette was writing her wish list to Père Noël, she urged Jacqueline to do the same, but Jacqueline "refused and looked disapprovingly, adding, 'It's not worth it.'"[34]

Huguette described her mother's side of the family as "simple people, peasants."[35] Grandfather Edouard had come to Paris on a scholarship to finish his studies and became Administrator of the Hôpital de la Pitié. Grandmother Juliette, a pious Catholic, was respectful of the rest of the household, all of whom were non-believers. She was a loving woman who cared for Jacqueline, even indulged her, but Jacqueline remembered her as difficult to talk to, owing to her conservative views. Not Grandfather, though, who, having retired from hospital work, wrote serialized novels (romans-feuilletons) for newspapers and magazines. He doted on his granddaughters, and they loved their time together. He was fun, teaching them word games and taking them on promenades to the Bois de Vincennes, a park near their home where they could explore the artificial lakes, grottoes, footpaths, and zoo.

In 1914, a month before the start of World War I, the newly widowed Jane Lamba, her sister Lucy, the girls, and their governess sailed back to France. They settled in Saint Mandé, at the home of their maternal grandparents at 3 rue Cart, remaining there until 1918, when they moved into an apartment on Avenue de Suffren, near the formal garden Champ de Mars. A photograph from 1907 of Jane in their Cairo house, inscribed "*La siesta*," shows a pretty woman lounging on the living-room sofa, hair and dress in the fashionable Edwardian style. Before marrying, Jane (pl. 2) had been a librarian, and she always valued education. Huguette noted: "Our mother was one of the first to read Marcel Proust, and she encouraged us to read a lot. She was a very cultivated woman. She wanted us to know everything. She did everything she could for us, right up to her death."[36] Curiously, when Marianne Clouzot spoke of Jane, she recalled a perceived resemblance between her and Odette de Crecy, Charles Swann's love interest in Proust's *Swann's Way*.[37] Jane had initially planned to enter medical school but was dissuaded by a family friend, a physician, who warned that medicine was no profession for women and urged her to follow the more traditional path of marriage and homemaking. She took that advice but continued her independent education and remained an avid reader.

Upon returning from Egypt, following José's tragic death, Jane sought to be alone in order to gain clarity about her new life and prospects. Leaving the girls (pl. 4) with her parents, she traveled to England to teach French as governess to an upper-class family. She returned with refined mannerisms, such as taking afternoon tea.[38] Clouzot also recalled that Jane's conversation was peppered with English words.[39]

Admiring Jane as a "*grande dame*" who had taught French and spoke English fluently, Jacqueline recalled her intellect: "My mother was anti-Catholic. She had rather broad ideas. Spotting a book by Cocteau in my pocket, she once said, 'Well you are reading horrible things.' She had an excellent library, and she read. She knew who he was."[40] Jacqueline identified with the intellectual side of Jane, whom she greatly admired, and became a voracious reader, also learning English and teaching French abroad.

During the last year of the war, the girls, aged seven and ten, were sent to a non-religious boarding school in Neuilly-sur-Seine, a suburb just west of Paris. The girls were popular and chosen to appear together in plays, including Pierre Wolff's *Les Deux Amants*, the story of two girls, one born very rich and one very poor. Jacqueline liked it there and amusedly told a friend some twenty-five years later that whenever families came to inspect the school, exploring the possibility of enrolling their child, she was presented as their typical student.[41] She loved it. Jacqueline, always her own person, knew she had never been typical of anything, but apparently she looked the part. With golden curls, large hazel eyes, and rosy cheeks, she was showing signs of the great beauty that would attract attention throughout her life but also become problematic. In her seventies, looking back, she insightfully acknowledged to art historian Martica Sawin: "If I had been less beautiful, I would have been a better painter."[42] Time spent preoccupied with her looks sapped energy from the creative force she might have used to make art and develop her artistic career earlier. Admiration, once it came, was experienced as finally receiving the attention missed early on, but she became addicted to it, needing it in order to feel right about herself. Such dependency later became isolating as her looks gave way to aging.[43]

Jacqueline's art education began early, with frequent visits to the Louvre accompanied by her sister and mother, and often Clouzot, who was two years her senior. Marianne's older sister Marie-Rose was about the same age as Huguette, and their mothers had been friends for years. Marianne's father, Henri Clouzot, was a librarian at Bibliothèque Forney and later, in 1920, Conservator at the Musée Galliera (now the Musée de la Mode de la Ville de Paris), where the family lived in an apartment. At their home, Jacqueline saw for the first time African and Oceanic art, which Clouzot *père* collected, exhibited, and wrote about. At the Musée Galliera, he curated four exhibitions a year of decorative art, printed fabrics, and painted paper that proved influential in Jacqueline's development as a visual artist.[44]

One can learn a great deal about the Lamba girls' childhood from Marianne's diary, particularly about Jacqueline. Huguette, mild-mannered and easy to get along with, was scarcely mentioned; not so Jacqueline, who constantly misbehaved, threw tantrums, and was often slapped by Jane or sent out of the room. Marianne remembered:

> *Huguette was something sweet, a little button, obedient. I don't have many good memories of Jacqueline. She was really somebody. She was a little girl, obstinate, not easy. Her mother was very conventional, very goody-goody, and Jacqueline was not goody-goody. She really had a hard character, very hard ... I wrote in my diary that I was lunching at the Lambas', the mother slapped her throughout the whole meal ... I tell that Madeleine enters the room, wants to sit down, Jacquot pulls away the chair, Madeleine falls and Jacquot kicks her, Madeleine begins to cry. We are furious and send Jacquot to time out because she had done it on purpose ... We placed her in time out. But the whole time it was tricks like that.[45]*

Adolescence

In the summer of Jacqueline's fourteenth year, Jane and the girls were vacationing on the English Channel, at Le Portel near Boulogne-sur-Mer. Other than Jacqueline winning a compass in a sandcastle-building contest, their stay at the beach was uneventful. Perhaps too quiet, Jane thought. She began to suspect something was amiss when she noticed that Jacqueline and Marianne Clouzot had exchanged fifteen letters in just two months. The explanation was in Clouzot's diary:

> *September 1924*
>
> *Living on a beach filled with youth, she [Jacqueline] was very excited and her letters were such as to raise the hair on one's neck. I replied in a more prudent way since the life we were leading at La Chaste Abondance did not allow for such things, but I did comment on what she had written. Now Jane Lamba, worried about the frequency of our correspondence, took two of my letters from her [Jacqueline's] drawer and caused such a scene! ... So, realizing that the whole family was intercepting my correspondence, I wrote her my last letter in "Huguette" style, writing only about rain, the sun, drawing, about her "big sister," etc. And this morning I received a letter full of insults for "cretinism going beyond the permitted limit." Poor Jack, she is nice and her style is more licentious than her actions. She tells me about "nights of orgies in the dirtiest areas of Le Portel," about smoking on the beach in the moonlight with a boy, dancing until 4 in the morning in a "bogue," which, according to accepted information, was the fanciest dance spot in Le Portel! She's only 14 years old!*[46]

Adolescence hit Jacqueline with enough force to launch her fiercely out of childhood. Huguette recalled that her younger sister would often disappear without telling anyone. Coming and going without explanation—who could stop her? Jane would not dare slap her anymore. Jacqueline had secretly joined the French Communist Party, inspired by Communism's "promise of equality and to win every man's right not only to bread but to poetry."[47] Later, in her seventies, while speaking with filmmaker Teri Wehn Damisch, she described the private world she kept to herself during those years:

*I was already alert at an early age. I was in the Communist Party,
which is a world, and I was fifteen years old. I joined, attended
meetings, and I listened to speeches. I was not signed up because
I hate being signed up in whatever the thing might be. I was in
agreement. It was a time when the Communists were still proper.
And then later, it's not that they became dirty right away, but
I found them downright annoying. The speakers had absolutely no
talent. One got bored. It's not what one should be saying anyway.
I was just impossible. I am a severe judge.*[48]

But there was also a man, "B," at the meetings, who took special interest in
her, another reason for attending: "Well, I went all the time. There were gifts
there. He liked me a lot so I went there. I didn't have a dime, but I managed."[49]

Three young painters—Jacqueline Lamba, Marianne Clouzot, and
Theodora Markovitch—formed a group apart. The last named, as Dora Maar,
became a Surrealist photographer and painter, and later Picasso's lover and
model for many portraits, including the "weeping women" after the German
bombing of Guernica. Even as a girl, Maar was known for her elegant dress,
studied mannerisms, and aloof demeanor. At the Clouzots' dance parties, for
example, she avoided mingling and condescendingly referred to the boys and
girls as "frivolous." Clouzot recalled: "When she left us, she would say, 'I'm off
to see some people,'" leaving them to wonder how she perceived them, if not as
people. In Clouzot's several portraits of Maar dating from 1927, she is impeccably
coiffed or wearing cloche hats, headbands, fur stoles, scarves, and gloves. In one,
La Femme Chic, she sits beside the Eiffel Tower surrounded by exciting action: a
red Bugatti races by and a Black man sings of love. For the handsome young man
in the top right-hand corner, however, the source of the excitement is Maar.[50]

Jacqueline's creative imagination manifested itself early. For Clouzot,
strictly educated in a conservative milieu, Jacqueline's freedom was awe-inspiring.
She wrote in her diary:

*I adore Jack ... This kid is terrific, ruthless, stubborn, [has]
reprehensible ideas and nature, but what willingness, intelligence,
temperament! To have developed so, all alone—it's magical. With
her, one enters a world of genius, modern, active, really another
world. We are not two students but two artists (brilliant of course),
judging, discussing. Cocteau accompanies us. Claudel precedes us.
I am still under the spell of the Angel Heurtebise. I cannot forget
him, neither Orphée. We went together to see the Picasso show
The Painter with Fairy Fingers.*

I have just spent an hour with Jack, reading to her Eurydice
Twice Lost by Paul Drouot. God, it's beautiful! She understands
and vibrates with ardor equal to mine. Like me, she adores this
sentence from Rimbaud's Farewell [A Season in Hell]: "And at
dawn, armed with burning patience, we will enter splendid cities."[51]

How can one work on a major opus with this whirlwind and
this tumult of friends at my window ... Ah! Jack has discovered the
place and the formula, she deserves her genius—not I.

Art School

Most children eventually stop drawing, but Jacqueline continued into adolescence and her talent blossomed (pl. 6). At fourteen, she and Clouzot left the Lycée Victor-Duruy to enter Lucien Simon's atelier. A respected exponent of Gustave Courbet's realistic style, Simon was a founding member of the prestigious Académie de la Grande Chaumière, where a long list of influential teachers taught students who went on to make history. Clouzot described Simon as "a good teacher," saying, "I went there regularly for one or two years. He was serious, had me copy his own works, which I thought was a little funny. He couldn't find better, it appears."[52] At eighteen, she was hired as a designer by the Galeries Lafayette and started to earn a living; she had built a strong foundation on Simon's atelier.

Although Jane Lamba was not against Jacqueline making art, she advised against a profession that would bring little economic security. Understanding her mother's concern, Jacqueline compromised. From October 1926 through June 1929, she attended the École de l'Union Centrale des Arts Décoratifs on rue Beethoven, Paris, graduating "with full satisfaction due to the quality of her work."[53] Jacqueline started creating book designs and advertising, including fabric and paper for such large stores as Bon Marché and Trois Quartiers. She also did decorating of all types for homes. Eventually, however, she parted ways with the department stores over creative differences. "Well, my decorations were annoying everyone," she said. "I took on any kind of work so as to avoid doing decorations and advertisements, because I was having my ideas corrected. They were too advanced, of course."[54] Meanwhile, her yearning to paint continued unabated, and she began visiting artists' studios.

When Maar began to study with André Lhote, who was known for his teaching, cutting-edge art, and individuality, Jacqueline visited his studio. Under his influence, she created her earliest professional work. Three works remain from that period: a luminescent watercolor drawn in the manner of Paul Cézanne (a painter whom Lhote prized), and two pastels. In one of the latter images, *Self-Portrait* (1927), Jacqueline's face fills the page in warm earth tones. It brings to life her carefree smile and bobbed auburn hair, engaging the viewer with a gleam in her large hazel eyes, showing a playful desire to cause trouble. She built the composition on Maurice Denis's *Elle était plus belle que les rêves* (She Was More Beautiful than Dreams), a lithograph from his album *Amour* (Love, 1899). The other pastel is a portrait of Cocteau's mysterious *L'Ange Heurtebise* (The Angel Heurtebise, 1927). In gratitude for introducing her to Cocteau's writings, Jacqueline gifted Clouzot both pastels and Cocteau's book, illustrated on the frontispiece with a rayogram by Man Ray, his visualization of the angel.

In her early painting, Jacqueline embraced the mystic-religious approach to Symbolist art, with its spiritual debt to Baudelaire and particularly Rimbaud, from whom she learned to "avoid using the direct personal, above all in states of the soul, especially intimate feelings if they are tragic."[55] She identified with Baudelaire's vision of life, which he developed too as a young child: "I felt in my heart two contrary emotions: the horror of life and the ecstasy of life." Torn between the sacred and the profane, Jacqueline twice drew his portrait and explained, "I am Baudelaire."[56] She built her mindset on these early lessons. The painter, writer, and decorative artist she admired was Maurice Denis, theoretician of the Nabis—a name derived from *navi*, Hebrew for "prophets." Key to the transition from Impressionism to Modern art, the group included Pierre Bonnard, Aristide Maillol, Odilon Redon, Ker-Xavier Roussel, Félix Vallotton, and Édouard Vuillard. The painting style that attracted Jacqueline was a decorative expressionism defining the subject's inner life, with planes of color tending toward abstraction, contoured by sinuous lines of intertwining rhythms. She continued to apply Denis's lasting influence after 1941, when she painted abstract Surrealism, and after 1947, when she painted non-objective art.

Lhote's interest in photography as a new mode of artistic expression opened Jacqueline's and Dora's eyes, and he encouraged them to explore the medium, which Dora did professionally. Jacqueline's didactic exercises, made spontaneously, gravitated toward light as a source of emotion. André Delons, her cousin and a regular contributor to the periodical *Du Cinéma*, brought her photographs to the attention of publisher José Corti, who used them to complement two articles—her earliest reproduced work. *Still Life* (ca. 1928), a metaphysical composition illustrating Louis Chavance's *Le Décorateur et le métier* (The Decorator and the Profession), shows a Roman bust of a youth, its blind gaze turned toward bands of light that slide through half-open shutters.[57] Delons's *Chronique des films perdus* (Chronicle of Lost Films, ca. 1928) is illustrated with *Aux Lèvres de vermouth* (With Vermouth Lips, ca. 1928), a flat wooden cut-out of a waiter holding the aperitif Saint Raphaël on a tray.[58] Photographed at an oblique angle against a background of trees, the silhouette is like that of a giant carrying a bottle of the fortified wine through the woods. These images, inspired and influenced by Robert Delaunay's paintings of the Eiffel Tower and Giorgio de Chirico's Metaphysical Painting, a cornerstone of Surrealism, are imbued with a sense of poetry.

Jacqueline's interest in light is also evident in her abstract photographs of Paris's bridges and the Eiffel Tower, details of steelwork that twists and turns, emphasizing movement and the interplay between dark and light. In *Swimmer* (ca. 1928), a scene from life, the viewer remains unclear whether the figure in the water is a person or a mannequin, male or female. *Dreamer* (ca. 1928) is pure Surrealism. A cane lies as if it were a person on a metal bed, its arched neck craning forward, away from the pillow. Under the bed, an archway created by a double exposure opens through shadow into a passageway where a burst of light draws the eye. In *Fountain* (ca. 1928), a simple close-up of a sculpture renders a sea monster emerging. In *Lit Room* (ca. 1928), a patch of light slips through an open window, casting warmth into an otherwise dark room. In *The Sea* (ca. 1928), a rippling moonlit seascape anticipates the last work that Jacqueline will paint fifty years later. Her photographs are technically less than perfect, but their emotional content is captivating.

Jane Dies

In January 1927, Jane Lamba succumbed to tuberculosis at the young age of forty-seven. It is likely that she returned infected from her stay in England. Jacqueline was seventeen. Clouzot's diary reads:

> *Jane Lamba is dead. Now here is Jack, an orphan, head of the family and responsible for her unhappy sister. Poor little Jack, so courageous, so pitiful, in a mourning veil, thin as a rake in her mourning dress, her poor small face, no make-up, but pale, surrounding her large doe-like eyes. She's talking about earning*

her living, about owing nothing to anyone, to keep Huguette with
her, fighting for this privilege despite all the advice of the family.
What pluck she has! She has looked after her suffering mother,
now dead, taken care of everything, bluffed right up to the end so
as not to worry her and even now forbids herself to cry in public.
She has only me, I have to be her support, her distraction, her
encouragement and her tenderness.[59]

It was an impossible time for Jacqueline, but she pressed on without complaint. During her second year of decorative arts school she had been caring for her mother while also looking after Huguette, who at fifteen had become "catatonic" as a result of walking in on her mother and her mother's lover, "Uncle" Leon, with whom the Lambas had been friends and who had a daughter the same age as Jacqueline.[60] Recommended by Delons, Dr. René Allendy, a founding member of the Société Psychanalytique de Paris, was making no progress in her treatment. Clouzot recalled: "She was fed by hand in a clinic ... she was totally inanimate, her head, her brain at zero. Completely depressed. And when their mother died, Jacqueline said, 'Me, I'm going to have her [at home], and I will cure her.' She had just read Freud, she had 'figured it out.' She had no doubt surmised the cause, and she cured her. That's one of the best things she did in her life, and because of that, she is in Paradise. She was hateful with Huguette, but she saved her. She took responsibility in this rescue, which was almost unthinkable at that time. Because Freud—there were not many people familiar with him. It was so remarkable, to have done this, and yet not to have shouted this from the rooftops. She kept this to herself. I find this all extraordinary."[61]

When Jacqueline brought Huguette home, she knew that her sister's catatonic state prevented her from speaking but not from hearing, so she spoke to her. When Jacqueline said, *"Maman est morte"* (Mama is dead), Huguette came to as if surfacing from a deep sleep, and that was the beginning of her full recovery: "When Huguette woke up, three years had passed. She did not know how to do anything. She had no diploma. She knew a little music. She became a piano teacher, but ... Jacqueline helped her often."[62]

Jane's death added a layer of hardness to the premature cynicism Jacqueline developed in the wake of her father's demise, catapulting her overnight into pseudo-maturity, using her looks as currency. Early loss and the double-edged sword of great beauty sliced through her life, awakening a sense of justice that expressed itself in a desire to change the world. When compared to the self-portrait Jacqueline painted months earlier, Clouzot's portrait of her after the transformation is of another woman: an exquisite beauty steeped in sadness. Carefully made up, short hair dyed blonde and tightly permed, her eyes the color of honey, she looks inward, oblivious to the viewer. She is dressed to the nines in a low-cut Art Deco top. Parallel rows of navy stripes shape the square collar, and a fabric corsage of bright flowers adorns the left shoulder.

Once Huguette regained her footing, Jacqueline moved her in with cousins and took a room, on Dora's recommendation, in the Saint Germain-des-Prés convent on rue de l'Abbaye. This "home for young women," run by nuns, was inexpensive, and Jacqueline could afford to pay for her stay with her meager earnings from design work. Naturally, she gave the nuns hell. Clouzot recalled that Jacqueline was unhappy there: "The good nuns hated her. They were scared to death of her. She was terrible, and I believe things went very badly. She disregarded the hour when she had to be in. She talked back. She was not allowed to smoke, but did anyway. Her manner was completely outrageous. She did everything to make her room modern, literary, and artistic. It was not in the style of the good sisters." But she did not rebel so much at first; Clouzot continued:

> Today, I went to see Jack at the St Germain-des-Prés convent. A room that is very Francis Jammes [the poet] ... A simple bed, white iron paint, a large ornamental wardrobe, a pedestal table decorated with a simple bouquet of violets, and a low-set window where one can sit and which one can step over to reach the balcony. From there, one can see the horse chestnut trees and the little children playing in the garden. To the right, the flying buttresses of the Abbey and its bell tower. On the windowsill, two pots of china-asters [reine marguerites], and in the room, she herself [Jacqueline], a solitary child, withdrawn, stubborn, stunning. She has done three pastels exhibiting a marvelous harmony; she has a sense of color that makes me die of shame ...
>
> As one enters this ordinary, standard room, one sees nothing of note, but if we open one of the firmly closed drawers, there! Cocteau, Claudel, Radiguet, Stevenson, Cendrars! ... and on, Michelangelo, Picasso, Foujita ... It really takes you aback. We conversed from 4 until 7:30 pm and improvised a charming snack, using white china cups on a tablecloth with yellow checks, sitting in front of the window, whence the shouts of children merged into the old sky filled with swallows.
>
> This was the period when I was with them [Jacqueline and Dora] more often, and when she [Jacqueline] was painting a lot. At that time she was doing pastels, like me. We got along marvelously, we got enthusiastic over poems ... She must have been

17, I believe ... when we communed together. And right after, as soon as she stepped inside Les Deux Magots [the Paris café] and met the Surrealists, she had what she wanted, and I lost complete sight of her. With Dora, it was the same[;] from the moment she was with Picasso, we were no longer in communication. Jacqueline erased me from her life. She was unrecognizable, dress and hair like Antinea [heroine] of Pierre Benoit's novel L'Atlantide, with completely dyed blonde hair with little shells around her head, made up, dressed head to foot in red, wearing sandals, though it was freezing outside.[63] She was hard to believe. It was Surrealism in fable form.[64]

In December 1936, Jacqueline felt compelled to see Yvonne Clouzot, Marianne's mother. She had been married to André Breton two years and four months, and Aube (born December 20) was exactly a year old. Marianne recorded the visit:

Last event of the year and not one of the least = Goodbye to Jacqueline Lamba
   A vision of ecstasy = a blonde creature, molded into a crimson red crêpe-de-chine dress, bare legs (it's 7°C [44°F]), red/purple beret, her golden eyes ringed in black, a bitter mouth, eyelashes like fine wire, half-skeletal, half-sinuous body, but rich in noble manners. Still insolent, odious, with willing wickedness oozing from every pore. She stayed two hours: "You are beautiful, Yvonne," she said icily to mother, the latter blushing dumbfounded ...[65]

Jacqueline and Marianne agreed to meet again in the afternoon. Seeking an independent view of Jacqueline, Marianne came with a friend:

Not wishing to remain alone to enjoy this spectacle of choice, I invited [Pedro] Pruna[66] to come to see her at the Coupole at 2 pm. He came, listened with astonishment to this avalanche of sarcasm that poured forth like hail from this weary and disgusting mouth—after a while he said to her: "Are you really nasty or is it a pose, a mask that one wears over a tender heart? It's quite in fashion this year."
   "Ha! Ha! I don't believe in a tender heart! Are you a painter, Monsieur?"
   "Yes, Mademoiselle, a great painter."
   "Ah ... and you know what Marianne is doing?"

"Yes."

"What do you think of it?"

"She should continue."

"In the same direction?"

"Yes."

"However, what she is doing now is decoration. Painting should express something else ... Max Ernst, for example ..."

Quite disgusted, Pruna gave up. The next day, he was still in a towering rage, and the most pleasant summary I can come up with regarding his thoughts about her is: "She's dead and rotten, she already smells bad, and I forbid you to see a whore like that. In my opinion, she is beyond salvation, completely unbalanced both intellectually and sexually, intoxicated by Surrealism, having killed in herself the most elementary modicum of humanity, and the only thing to be done is to let her have it ..."[67]

Pruna had been right the first time. Behind Jacqueline's transparent theatrics, a scared girl was protecting her tender heart, ashamed to be seen as vulnerable. Although she would not admit it, Jacqueline missed Jane, which was why she "casually" paid occasional visits to Marianne's mother. Marianne said: "She liked my mother very much. She used to say to her, 'You are very nice, Yvonne,' speaking in a superior fashion, and my mother, quite intimidated by her, was left with her mouth open." In her diary, Clouzot also described her own grief at the loss of her treasured friend: "I had given her all that I had to give—poetry ... it was finished. And I was not on her list. It didn't please me. And then, we did not see each other at all."[68]

When speaking of her youth, Jacqueline generally glossed over the years she lived abroad. She mentioned teaching French in England in 1932 and in Greece in 1933, but rarely elaborated. What little we know of this period comes from Dolorès Vanetti.

Jacqueline fell in love with Vasilis, a Greek boy, and, pregnant, followed him to Greece.[69] They likely met at a Communist Party meeting, for in Greece she not only taught French but also worked at the Party's office.[70] They arrived in Athens at a politically active time. The previous year the KKE, the Marxist–Leninist political party, had established collaboration with other Communist parties to oppose the rise of fascism in Europe. The party would also play a significant role in the Greek resistance during World War II, and later during the Greek Civil War of 1946–49. Not surprisingly, as Jacqueline had done before and would do again, she caused havoc, although this time, since she was not a Greek citizen, it got her expelled from the country: "I taught French in Greece.

26

I did some work at Nouvelle Communist, so I was escorted by the gendarmes right to the boat. I was involved in life. I knew what I wanted, and I really did it, a lot. I was quite silly. I was fired up with all that. I would read a lot, writers who were not yet known at the time, who later became famous."[71]

Fresh off the boat in France, the memory of Greece behind her, Jacqueline was ready for her next adventure. In May 1934, while living at the Hôtel Medical on rue du Faubourg-Saint-Jacques (another boarding house, its name taken from the physical therapy gym on the ground floor), her life took a dramatic turn when she met André Breton. A year earlier, in February 1933, Delons—who suggested that Allendy treat Huguette—had introduced her to Breton's writing. She was blown away:

> *I had a cousin, André Delons, an ex-Grand Jeu member, who was older than me by about three years. So one day he said to me, "You should read Breton." I had heard about him but buying expensive books* [was beyond my means] *... So, he lent me some, and I was just astonished. It was not Surrealism that interested me. It was what Breton was saying, because he was saying things that affected me, exactly what I was thinking, and I had no doubt that we were going to meet, one way or another.*[72]

Le Grand Jeu (The Great Game) was a radical group of writers close to Surrealism who attacked the perception of reality through anesthesia, narcotics, and near-death experiences, with the intention of transcending the individual ego and reconnecting with the collective mind. Delons warned against accepting received opinions unquestioningly:

> *2 February '33*
>
> *My dear Jacqueline,*
>
> *... As for me, I would confirm to you that the struggle is difficult, and by searching for a long time I am able today to know certainties. It was inevitable. Life comes at its price. But I assure you that it is worth it to have gone that way; and that certain moments that I have already experienced, namely, when we catch, for example, the clear look of a worker, when one can sense the deep brotherhood that links you to this look, these are the unforgettable and decisive ones. They are stronger than those of lassitude, discouragements, anger that one can still moreover experience too much. The tremendous joy of being with men, and having left or unmasked cowards,*

is one of those that does not mistake the truth of the action in which one is engaged.

I return to those questions you put to me. Go in the direction you have decided. I believe it is excellent for you. I am suggesting that you read André Breton's book [Les Vases communicants; Communicating Vessels]. I was asked the other night to publish the text of my talk. I could perhaps send you a copy. But don't accept anything out of it as dogma: look for yourself.

I hope you will send me your address.

And, of course, be the happiest that you can be.

Affectionately yours,

André[73]

In Breton, Jacqueline found a kindred spirit. Looking back, she told an interviewer:

I was fifteen years old in 1925. As was true of so many others at the time, my very nature, as well as my involvement in painting and poetry, had brought me to a state of mind of anarchistic revolt against the bourgeois society around me. Nonetheless, it was only in 1927 that I really became aware of the October Revolution in Russia. Despite my real desire, however, to somehow take part in this revolutionary ferment, I was unable to make up my mind to become a militant. The leftist meetings I attended seemed to me utterly routine in character, elementary and gray. My expectations were usually deceived. They turned me off. And then, in 1929, I learned of the Surrealist Movement and particularly of the writings of André Breton, which were, for me and for many others at the time, a revelation.

These writings offered a definitive response to certain problems that are exceptionally difficult to resolve individually, problems regarding the relation between the poetic and artistic sensibility, and a revolutionary consciousness, militant or otherwise, applied to all levels of existence. The thoroughgoing, exalting, unique spirit of Breton and his friends, their whole approach to life and the world, and the tone of certainty and supreme defiance that accompanied it; all this fulfilled me, liberated me, and instilled in me a joy such as I suspect young people today can hardly grasp ...[74]

André Breton

André Robert Breton was born in Tinchebray, in the Normandy region of northwestern France, on February 19, 1896. He was the only child of struggling parents: Louis Breton, the administrator at the local police station, and Marguerite Le Gouguès, a seamstress. Aube recalled her grandparents:

> He [Louis] *was an adorable man, nothing but tenderness, who liked me very much. There is nothing much else to say ... he did everything he could to please me. He was just only love and infinite love for André as well. I have very bad memories of my grandmother. I had no contact with her because I had the feeling that she was a very hard person. She told me "You know, Elisa* [André's third wife] *is your stepmother so you should hate her." But she didn't love any of André's wives. She was jealous of them. She wasn't intelligent, that woman.*
>
> *I asked André why he didn't talk to anyone about his childhood. "As for my father," André replied, "I adored him, he was a marvelous man, but my mother was horrible throughout my whole childhood; throughout my whole life." I asked why. He replied: "All the humiliations that a mother can impose on her son, I bore them all." So I asked, "What kind, for instance?" It was then he related an episode that was quite personal. He never related things like these to me but he told me how he'd been humiliated. "One day," he said, "I must have been I don't know how old"—and he was still bedwetting, very late, like many children who are not loved—"Mother was outside with some friends, holding me by the hand. She was talking and suddenly said to her friends, 'Just imagine, he's nine years old and still doing pee-pee in bed.'"* [75]

To overcome a childhood marked by humiliation, André developed a craving for supremacy that became his modus operandi, eventually earning him the sobriquet "The Pope of Surrealism." Although he did not create the Surrealist Movement alone, because of his attitude, people began deferring to him as the main authority, and he started expecting deference. Should someone else be deferred to, he would take offense and forbid it.

Feeling emasculated was part of the problem, for it also expressed itself sexually. Breton confided in Jean-Paul Sartre: "I should be ashamed to appear naked before a woman without an erection."[76] In fact, André was so inhibited that in the nine years of his marriage to Jacqueline, she never saw him naked. Aube continued:

> *There was also that famous matter when he completed three years of medical studies. For parents, people of modest means, to have a son who was going to be a doctor or an attorney justified and validated them, for a mother, especially. They were sending him money to pursue his medical studies, but very little since they didn't have much. It must have taken great courage to inform his parents that he would be not completing his medical school training—considering his fear of Marguerite. When André said, "I am not continuing my medical studies; it's not what I want, I want to be a poet," his mother replied, "I would have preferred it if you had been killed in the war."[77]*

At a loss for what to do, Louis and Marguerite naïvely wrote to poet Paul Valéry, whom André had idolized since adolescence, asking that he intervene to dissuade their son from his chosen path.[78] In those years, André's favorite book was Valéry's *La Soirée avec monsieur Teste* (The Evening with Monsieur Teste). When André, a sign-seeker, learned that the book had been published in the year of his birth, he interpreted it as a *hasard objectif*, a fortunate coincidence, and practically learned it by heart: "Breton personally identified Valéry with M. Teste, an imaginary character who did not read or write, who only thought eternal thoughts which he communicated, once in a while, to some privileged witness."[79]

As in the unconscious, the juxtaposition of opposites, such as day and night, or male and female, is present in Surrealist iconography. Such a binary system in André embodied his parents' opposite personalities. But he lived torn, inhibited as a result of struggling to balance extremes: affectionate and cold, accepting and judgmental, supportive and neglectful. That was why he was overly cautious about how he presented himself, always in control, fearful of being singled out for making a mistake. A simple observation could wound him deeply, humiliating him, even if that was never intended. Thus, he kept vigilant to avoid making himself vulnerable. Belittled by his mother while growing up made him hypersensitive to criticism, particularly from women, another reason why he often placed them on a pedestal. Although this might have seemed like admiration, it was an attempt to control, to keep them at a distance, to anticipate and inhibit any wrong word or behavior and be prepared to respond; it imprisoned women such that the expression of their needs was limited by his demands. Helena Holzer, wife of André's friend the artist Wifredo Lam, saw through this tendency and felt sympathy for André because she knew he was suffering. To her, it was obvious that, although misguided at times, he was a thoughtful man who meant well and wanted to do the right thing, "but walking into a room where everything had to stop because there were ten women whose hands he had to kiss first—before people could get on—was too much."[80]

From Louis, André inherited a tender, childlike, loving side. Leonora Carrington, who joined the Surrealist Movement in 1937, escaping a family where art-making was considered a disease, was received by André with open arms. She never forgot that he expressed interest in her painting before anyone.[81] This was his attitude toward the creative process, whether it was art made by professionals, untrained people, or forms created by nature. That, plus the ability to bring people together and help them to transform their inner reality into art, was at the root of his success. With a brilliant intellect, characterized by depth and understanding, André evoked awe and affection that could distract from his controlling personality, and he used this to shield himself from feeling rejected. "André had a great intellectual integrity and expected the same from those around him; he did not accept any artist who received a prize. It was intellectual prostitution," recalled Aube.[82] Should anyone do so, that person would immediately pay, becoming a target of his unforgiving rage and being ostracized and excommunicated forever from his life.

André learned from the best: Marguerite. His poetry was spun out of his damaged sense of self, as was his focus on aesthetics, by striving to remold his pain into poetry.

During World War I, André worked as a physician's assistant with shell-shocked soldiers from the Battle of Verdun at the military Val de Grâce hospital near the Sorbonne. Having learned about the unconscious from Sigmund Freud's *The Interpretation of Dreams* (1899), André witnessed the effects of psychological trauma on the protective shield that kept the unconscious sealed off to prevent it from contaminating the conscious mind and thus potentially causing psychosis. Fascinated, Breton wondered about ways of drawing out unconscious conflict—without experiencing trauma—and transforming it into poetry. The idea was among his contributions to Surrealism, which was initially a literary movement.

A Fortunate Coincidence

Jacqueline planned carefully her accidental encounter with André for 7:30 in the evening of May 29, 1934, at the Café de la Place Blanche in Paris. She was twenty-four. He was thirty-nine. During the day she made art. At night, she survived financially by swimming nude in the glass pool of Le Coliséum nightclub at 65 rue de Rochechouart. Photos of her performance taken by Rogi André are in the collection of the Bibliothèque Nationale de France (pl. 7). Breton watched her swim nude, with her petite, impeccable figure. When the voice of the dishwasher suddenly announced "*Ici l'on dîne*" (Here one dines), a mesmerized André heard "*Ici l'ondine*" (Here, the water sprite).

Jacqueline, just over five feet tall, was described by a friend as having an extraordinary body, "since she loved the sun, golden all over and very well groomed. She swam like a fish; naturally she looked better naked than dressed."[83] She exercised, worked out on a trapeze, and took care with her diet. She was riveting, whether nude or coiffed in a "towering headdress worn by one of Louis XIV's unofficial mistresses, Marie de Fontanges."[84] Her garments belonged stylistically to the past, whether folkloric or city elegant. They were often made of decorating materials, upholstery silks or velvet, and combined with unusual jewelry. Her looks were striking. She had a commanding presence, was well read, and expressed herself with educated opinions. She also had a temper that earned her the nickname "Bastille Day" from a co-worker.[85]

Her presence was noted at the Café Flore by Simone de Beauvoir, who often spent evenings there with Sartre: "This place had become a regular rendezvous for film people, ranging from directors and actors to script girls and [film] cutters. There were also some extremely attractive girls to be seen there. Sometimes, Jacqueline Breton put in an appearance, shell pendants in her ears, eyelashes painted with mascara, bracelets jangling as she waved her hands to show off those long, alluring fingernails."[86]

Following their first meeting, André wrote Jacqueline the first love letter:

> *Ondine and Paradise! I wasn't at all ready to wake up when they came to bring me the most beautiful letter of all, and that's just the way it should have been. It was still very dark, you could just see one of those pallid skies we've had since you left, today breaking all the records, and I saw you lengthily without seeing anything. You were there, I was waiting for you, and I imagined a thousand things, each more dreadful than the others; I was reading again,*

already knowing them by heart, certain sentences answering so clearly the desires I expressed to you yesterday and I was fascinated by the appearance of words of such a soft violet cloth ... I LOVE YOU so much, I am so unaware that we are still on this earth. I would like to disperse myself for you in the water, in the sun and in the wind. Don't forget that I am waiting for you again tonight, think tomorrow that at 11 I shall have knelt for you, I adore this prayer.

... I have just made the acquaintance of someone very special.[87] He's a doctor to various consuls, with whom, after dining with René Char, I spent the end of the evening the night before last in a rather exhilarated state and all last evening. In an instant we had, he and I, the impression of sharing some extraordinary affinities on rather unusual points, how can I put it, of possessing complementary views on certain very difficult things. He's the former head of a clinic in the University of Paris, that is clearly someone at the top of his profession, and he is also extremely learned in occultism. As I was tempted to talk to him almost immediately about what so moves me in the passage of the fictional to the real marked by the events of [Breton's poem] "Sunflower," he mentioned right away some extremely impressive things about it (discovering for example that I had certainly "Jupiter in the ninth house"). He got so excited about this happening that he begged me to allow us to examine it together in great depth. I am absolutely convinced that our discovery of each other is endowed with the highest magnetism, and he is absolutely convinced likewise. In the evening he had no sooner looked around the studio and said a few words about the magic and "black" character of the assembly of objects than the lamps went out, which happened several times in analogous circumstances, about which [Paul] Éluard can bear witness, as Giacometti can bear witness to our collective disturbance during yesterday's very short eclipse.

My lovely Demon ... this to show you that I am still in the good graces of the demon. My beautiful liquid Element, I drown in you. Will there be heaths gray enough, rocks tormented enough, forests hollow enough for our flight together tonight? One more word, but let it be at least carried by my voice: I love you.
André[88]

André immortalized the night of their first meeting in *L'Amour Fou* (*Mad Love*, 1937), a book about their affair: "This woman was scandalously beautiful. From the first moments, a quite vague intuition had encouraged me to imagine that the fate of that young woman could someday, no matter how tentatively, be entwined with mine."[89] Jacqueline entered first his dreams, then his writings, and then—once he evicted his lover Marcelle ("Lila") Ferry—his double studio at 42 rue Fontaine.

Initially, Jacqueline relished the role of muse to the poet leader of the Surrealist Movement. She enjoyed André's attention, his adoration, and the recognition it brought her. After pairing up with André, she dropped her friends from the past, whom she now described as "silly," except for Maar. Feeling like a woman of the world, Jacqueline entered Breton's life and, like a star, reached the highest heaven of Surrealism, propelled by the belief that she had found a perfect lover who lived for the arts, a political system that matched her beliefs, and an artistic realm where she could thrive as a person and come into her own as a painter. Two and a half months after meeting, they married. Going against the grain, naturally, the bride wore black and did not invite family.[90] Witnesses were Giacometti and Paul Éluard. Man Ray photographed the group at the Courthouse (pl. 9), and afterward they traveled to the countryside, where he photographed the couples, André and Jacqueline, and Paul and Nusch (who were married the following week), re-creating Édouard Manet's *Le Déjeuner sur l'herbe* (Luncheon on the Grass, 1863), with the brides nude. To André's consternation, after moving into rue Fontaine, Jacqueline interspersed these photographs among his art collection.

On September 3, 1934, *Comoedia Illustré*, the leading cultural newspaper in France, printed a notice announcing the double marriage:

> *SURREALIST MARRIAGES*
> *We received yesterday two announcements in only one envelope.*
> *The first, printed in green on Bristol white, carries the words:*
> *Tuesday 21 August 1934*
> *Maria Benz*
> *Paul Éluard*
> *are pleased to inform you of their marriage.*
> *On the second, printed in white on Bristol green, we read:*
> *Tuesday 14 August 1934*
> *Jacqueline Lamba*
> *André Breton*
> *are pleased to inform you of their marriage.*

In later years, Jacqueline would claim that she had produced Surrealist art only to please André, since he would have it no other way, and that she left him in order to paint differently. The truth was more complex, however. Nourished by Rimbaud's dictum, "We must change life," she was attuned to the mindset of the Surrealists. Both believed one had to oppose the establishment in order to achieve change, so she took to the Movement as a fish takes to water. The fact was that Jacqueline did what Jacqueline wanted; no one could make her paint what she did not wish to paint, or do anything else she did not wish to do. Unasked, she acknowledged, "I am a Surrealist."[91] Early examples of her personal style show her transitioning from Symbolism's expressions of emotions and ideas through symbolic representation, to Surrealism's exploration of the unconscious in dreams, the illogical and the irrational—while retaining an interest in both. "One's style is determined by one's nature, which one does not choose," she explained, and her nature made her gravitate toward "poetic awe."[92] Her painting emerged from darkness into light under the influence of Surrealism. And, after immigrating to the United States, she abandoned traditional Surrealist iconography to paint abstract Surrealism.

Following her separation from David Hare in 1952, Jacqueline was forced to accept that she had lost her way. Light became secondary to her art. Living in France without the man she loved left her ungrounded. She stopped painting non-objective art, which she had painted while living with David, and began painting conventional subjects influenced by Henri Matisse's Fauvist style of uncontrolled color without basis in nature—a market, a country circus, an artist's studio, a woman contemplating the stars, still lifes—what might have been described as decorative subjects. Perhaps the narrative behind one unusually disturbing still life Jacqueline painted after separating from David spoke of his betrayal. In a dark room, kitchen objects rest on a flat surface: a metal French drip Biggin coffee pot, an apple, two oranges, a white mortar and pestle, and a sourdough boule stabbed with a knife. The pierced loaf recalls a similar detail in a still life from 1937 by Balthus that Jacqueline would have known, since they were friends when he painted it. In fact, he and Giacometti were among the old friends she visited after returning to France, when she painted the work.

Strangely, most of Jacqueline's early paintings produced soon after she joined the Surrealist Movement suffered a tragic end.[93] Of those painted in France between 1934 and 1940, only *Portrait of André Breton as Saint-Just* (1937; pl. 11) survived. Jacqueline gave the *Portrait* to Huguette for safekeeping before departing, but during the war, in a hungry moment, she sold it to collector Edmond Bomsel. For a time, the portrait disappeared from view, since its new owner would not lend it. Jacqueline explained that after André returned to France, to punish her for leaving him, he destroyed her letters as well as the paintings she left at rue Fontaine. She had not tried to retrieve them: "I didn't even give a thought about my paintings. I was into a different type of painting."[94] After André's death, Jacqueline contacted his widow, Elisa, who invited her to Breton's office to check if there was anything of hers there, but when she went she found nothing. The poet Antonin Artaud had described Jacqueline as "the face of the sun," a source of light and truth, and wrote for her two protective incantations while he was interned at Rodez; those, she found in André's holdings at the Jacques Doucet Library. The first was:

> *Spell for Jacqueline Breton 17 September 1937*
>> *I'm sending a Spell to the First One who will dare touch you. I'll crush his braggart little snooty to pulp. I'll spank him in front of 100,000 people! HIS PAINTINGS WHICH NEVER WERE THAT GREAT HAVE DEFINITELY BECOME LOUSY. HE'S GOT TOO UGLY A VOICE. HE'S THE ANTICHRIST.*[95]

This was followed by a second, two months later, in November 1937:

> *You will be avenged, dear Jacqueline, and also the superior being of whom you are the predestined spouse.*
>> *You are a noble heart, a brave spirit, and a generous soul. You believe yourself evil, and you are mistaken, it's your imagination that creates in you a false external evil, purely external, but is not your nature.*
>> *I will reveal Mysteries to your Husband, and I will reveal to him what is the Sublime Rank that he occupies in the order of Spirits creators of the World.*
>> *He is [an] active intelligence of Brahma, the Father, represented in the symbolism of the Middle Ages by Angel Gabriel. It is the manifestation of pure Spirit, the visible Nature and the 4 Elements.*[96]

The last time Jacqueline heard from Artaud, on April 7, 1939, he wrote from Ville-Évrard, the psychiatric hospital, asking for help with his release.[97] "I am a fanatic not a madman," he explained.[98]

Privately owned paintings—such as *Les Heures* (The Hours, 1936; pl. 18) and *Le Cantonnier* (The Roadmender; n.d.)—were also lost. Among the abstract Surrealist works Jacqueline produced between 1942 and 1944, only two paintings—*Malgré tout, le printemps* (In Spite of Everything, Spring, 1942; Private collection) and *Derrière le Soleil* (Behind the Sun, 1943; pl. 30)—and three drawings survived. Jacqueline destroyed the rest on an impulse, which she later regretted. Fortunately, the paintings had been acquired by painter-critic Rudi Blesh, a friend of Jimmy Ernst—through the Norlyst Gallery, run by Ernst and his partner, Eleanor Lust—during Jacqueline's solo show in 1944; one drawing was sold and the other two she gifted.

Jacqueline recalled the moment she destroyed the works: "I did quite a few, in fact, I always do canvases. You see, I was still into Surrealism. One day, [Roberto] Matta showed up—I will explain why I am a little stupid myself. Matta saw my work, he showed up just like that. Well, I asked him if he wanted to see what I was doing. Matta was already riding high. He looked and said to me: 'It's just like what I'm doing.' So I destroyed everything."[99] Unfortunately, most of these works had not been photographed. Some are identified from reproductions in periodicals or catalogues. Others appear in the background of a photo of Jacqueline taken by David in their Bleecker Street apartment (pl. 31).

Long after Jacqueline divorced André, she would look back on their years together and recall how each day with him brought her into contact with people who were making history. Her desire to educate herself—studying continued to be paramount—kept her motivated. "That is why I stayed," she explained, "why I miss living with him."[100] As an afterthought, she added, "André is a genius, so he's handsome."[101] But she was ready to leave him earlier, she explained. In fact, not long after they married, she began spending long periods away, mostly with Maar and Picasso (pl. 23), who, between 1934 and 1939, used the two women as models for several paintings, alone or together. Some of Picasso's portraits of Jacqueline done during those years are mistakenly believed to be of his muse Marie-Thérèse Walter. *Girl Writing* or *Reading at a Table* (1934; Metropolitan Museum of Art) is of the former, not the latter. The women in *Interior with a Girl Drawing* (1935; pl. 15) are Jacqueline and Dora, not Marie-Thérèse and Dora. It is also Jacqueline and Dora in *Two Women* (1935; MAM de la Ville de Paris). And Jacqueline is the *Woman Reading* (1935; Picasso Museum, Paris). In the etching *Minotauromachy* (1935), Dora and Jacqueline are the two women at the window in the upper left. There are photographs of Jacqueline at Picasso's wearing a camisole, sitting nude on his bed, and lathering herself in his tub. In one photo of the two women together, Dora is wearing the crown of flowers she wears in the double portrait *Interior with a Girl Drawing*.[102] As Picasso took the photo, his shadow appears on the wall (pl. 14).

Jacqueline never regretted leaving André. Both his unwillingness to reconcile expectations of having her perform as housewife and mother—for they soon had Aube—and his lack of interest in her need to make art were demeaning to her. That was not what she signed on for when she married him. He knew she was a painter before they married, and nothing would change that. One might think that, after having Aube, life at his apartment in rue Fontaine would have been easier if she had accessed her maternal instinct. But Jacqueline was not mature enough. An infant needs attention twenty-four hours a day, seven days a week. Having a child means putting one's own needs aside. Aube's neediness frightened Jacqueline; it hit too close to home. She, too, was needy and demanding. Had André made any effort to help, she might have been more accessible. But he—a child himself—spent more than he could wisely afford in flea markets, buying what he did not need, rather than trying to make his marriage work. Even when broke, he still met friends for evening aperitifs, and they paid, naturally.

In André, Jacqueline married a man who she hoped would make up for the love she had missed from her father. Once she brought Aube into the world, she realized that would never happen. She would be competing with Aube for André's love, and would never win. Jacqueline never forgave Aube for this, as if she were to blame. For craving—and not receiving—Breton's acknowledgment as a painter, while witnessing his encouragement of others' creativity, she made him pay by neglecting Aube and refusing to acknowledge her needs. Long after Jacqueline and André had forgotten the source of their conflict—if they ever were aware of it—the cycle of resentment between them, with Aube as target, had become habit. Dismissively of both, Dolorès recalled: "André and Jacqueline were monsters of selfishness. Aube was the only good thing that came from them."[103]

The problem was simple and had a practical solution, but both were stuck. When Jacqueline questioned André's "pathologic" collecting of priceless objects while struggling to meet basic expenses, he could offer little by way of explanation.[104] Still, he adored her, so shortly after their marriage he sacrificed, as best he could, by selling to the poet Joë Bousquet a Kandinsky watercolor and a sanguine drawing by André Derain.

Breton, who had previously sworn off ever having children, was ecstatic at the news that Jacqueline was expecting, and treasured his daughter, who was born December 20, 1935 (pl. 13). He named her Aube (Dawn), after the title of a miniature watercolor of daybreak by Victor Hugo; containing the word AUBE suspended in the sky, it hung on the wall behind the desk in André's studio. He chose Solange (Sun Angel) as her middle name because together Aube Solange meant "Sun, Angel of Daybreak." When Éluard tried to register Aube's birth, the clerk balked at the name and refused to issue the birth certificate until he pointed out that Aurore, a name often used for girls, also meant dawn; then the clerk issued it.

Shortly before Aube's birth, André relented and sold to Alfred Barr, director of the Museum of Modern Art in New York, two paintings by Yves Tanguy and various Surrealist documents, and to Pierre Matisse the crown jewel of his collection, de Chirico's *The Enigma of a Day* (1914). Jacqueline was not appeased—they were still living in poverty. Further sporadic sales could neither satisfy her nor undo her displeasure with Breton's mounting pressure that she accept as primary the roles he demanded of her and relegate her painting to a secondary place. Feeling imprisoned, she ran off more than once for weeks, sometimes months, leaving Aube with André, who naturally panicked since he did not even know how to prepare a feeding bottle.

On September 15, 1936, Éluard wrote to his ex-wife Gala: "Jacqueline left Breton, for good I think. She found work in Algeria. Breton is alone with the child. Breton's parents have lost interest in him."[105] Fortunately for Aube, Breton found Marguerite Thévenet Rosmer to care for the child while Jacqueline was gone.[106] Marguerite well understood Breton's predicament when he brought Aube to her; she, too, had been abandoned by her mother in infancy and raised by her father. André begged Jacqueline to return, each time promising that she would be able to make art, that things would be different, but in the event nothing changed. Each time she returned, he slipped back into complacency, eventually with disastrous consequences for the marriage.

During their years together—until the end—Jacqueline and André's involvement with each other was all-consuming, and their work, often a dialogue between them, revealed intimate details about their relationship. In his writing, she was the recurring theme; and, based on extant works from this period, he, too, was on her mind. Ambivalence tore at Jacqueline with competing roles as wife, mother, and painter. She loved Aube, but resented that her care took time and energy away from making art; similarly, she loved and admired Breton, but he expected her to be subservient to him as his wife; she remained nameless, referred to as "her," as "the woman who inspired ...," or simply as "Breton's wife." She soon grew tired. Jacqueline was not ready to be married, certainly not to Breton; much less was she ready to be a mother.

For *Portrait of André Breton as Saint-Just* (1937), Jacqueline used as her model an iconic portrait of the "wild, handsome and transgressive" leader of the Jacobins to reflect both admiration for the personage and resentment of the man. She could have used any number of André's heroes as her model, but she chose the French revolutionary Louis-Antoine Léon de Saint-Just, who, despite his brilliance and heroism, was guillotined. Massacres and public executions were taking place during the overthrow of the Girondists, and Saint-Just, advocate of the Reign of Terror, remarked: "One does not rule innocently."[107]

André and Jacqueline had been married for two and a half years when, on February 2, 1937, Gallimard published *Mad Love*, the book in which André described each step of the *hasard objectif*, the fortunate coincidence that foretold his imminent meeting with Jacqueline, his love interest. In her portrait of André, Jacqueline established a visual dialogue while referring to symbols that he employed in the text. Curiously, it was painted on a misshapen canvas—an uneven rectangle that Jacqueline transformed into a Surrealist object.

Elegantly dressed in a period black suit, André wears a white shirt, a ribbon tied in a bow at the neck. Like a wraith with gray skin and pink lips, he gazes furtively at something within the painterly space. In *Mad Love*, André parallels his view of what brings together art, a human life, and the quartz crystal he holds in his right hand: "The work of art, just like any fragment of human life, considered in its deepest meaning, seems to me devoid of value if it does not offer the hardness, the rigidity, the regularity, the luster on every interior and exterior facet of the crystal."[108]

Jacqueline represents herself as a glass-wing butterfly on André's shoulder, its transparent wings blending into the sky—"the soul and unconscious attraction toward light."[109] Adding to the strangeness of the scene is her placement of a nighttime event inside the room while a window shows daylight outside. The Tour Saint Jacques, what remained of the sixteenth-century church Saint-Jacques-de-la-Boucherie, illuminated in the distance, stands out against the night as it did on their first evening together, when they strolled along rue de Rivoli and Jacqueline pointed out the Gothic tower where alchemist Nicolas Flamel is buried, "the world's greatest monument to the occult."[110] Flamel and his wife, Perenelle, had been church patrons. While he achieved immortality for discovering the philosopher's stone, she was gifted with the ability to understand nature. At the base of the tower stood a sculpted bust of philosopher Blaise Pascal, who offered, "The heart has reasons which reason knows nothing of ... We know the truth not only by reason but by heart." And as a physicist, he explained the weight of air that André references in "*L'Air de l'eau*" (The Air of Water), a chapter in *Mad Love* that describes Jacqueline swimming like a water sprite.

André's access to the sublime, the source of his poetic power, he used to soothe himself. But it did not work every time. Jacqueline recalled that he lived mired: "He just couldn't be alone ... he was an anguished being, and it prevented him from achieving. He was filled with anxiety, and stayed (stuck) in the same place. He required so much help. He used to go out into the street, just to relieve his anxiety and to meet people, anyone, women of course in particular, but going no further, simply to give her a rose, you see, and to suddenly feel wonderment and awe."[111] Momentarily, distraction effaced his anxiety and lifted him out of loneliness.

André and Jacqueline had been married seven months when she left to visit her grandmother in the country for Huguette's birthday celebration. In a letter to her, André describes his separation anxiety, explaining that before writing, he panicked, thinking he had lost her address. He expresses how lonely he is, and repeatedly brings up examples of their moments together. But toward the end, he warns prophetically that one day she may regret having chosen him:

Monday, April 22, 1935

My great Love, I just got scared because I suddenly could not find your address. I am very lonely here in Paris[;] as for you, you do not need to leave this city to find yourself covered in primroses up to your neck, you are a bunch of flowers and I wonder what I have done to deserve to be brought back to this long moment when I was waiting for you to get married ... I like to think that I married you, like in fairytales. Yesterday afternoon must have lasted at least eight to nine days. I don't understand how I could live waiting for you so many years.

I wish I could kiss you right now. I have lost all means to get adjusted to solitude and if I sometimes must break your defense and go in another room just to look at you and make sure that this light stays awake around your forehead, that your shoulders flow with their water so fast and so smooth and that it is me you are tirelessly smiling at, that it is with me that you play like, as you say, you have never played before and that the future is here within its exact parameters, within these proportions that are harmony itself, in this relationship of hues that immediately reveal what, for me, is alive and beautiful. How do you want me, since yesterday and until tomorrow, not to fly around and throw myself against the walls. And nobody will tell me that you, if you missed me a little as it seems you did when I was in Brussels, is that true?

My dear beautiful Love, I also think of you with all the gravity I am capable of because of what we spoke about not long ago lying down in bed. I ignore why that conversation takes me back to that morning at the Hôtel Medical where it was suddenly decided that we would live for each other without any fear, it was so beautiful ... You were fixing your hair and you turned toward me only a few times. A significant decisive move, something like star conjunction, must have taken place and I found myself in front of you for a long time, leaning on the window from where I thought I saw something very certain, very new, very big that I wouldn't have dared to foresee. It became difficult for me to leave that window, the footlight itself where happiness thrust. And it was also something that overflowed my heart, and before which I felt so weak, like when trying to hold back and not say: it's too much ...

One day you may have some regrets, and I cannot be responsible for that. Your beauty, your intelligence, everything that emanates from you then enters in me, how could I put it, a triumphant mind that is something that mustn't be deviated from, frustrated. It is not the present that is involved, but what is to be. It is over my future that you, the whole you, rule. Under those conditions, I do not believe that it would be worthy of me to let any material concern stop me (money, suffering, this last word is so hard for me to write. I tell you in spite of myself in a triumphant light).

I am waiting for you—I smile at the lovely childish question you asked me a little bit before you left. Don't forget to telegraph me the time of your arrival. For me, it is always so wonderful to see that little fairy from the thirteenth floor on whom the under bushes, the canals, the meadows have lost their color, boldly moving forward on the train station platform (without mentioning the anachronism of the cigarette). I adore you and my arms are open as I think of you from afar, like a picture ...

All my affection to your grandmother and my most sincere congratulations to Huguette.

The lips of my treasure[112]

Surrealism

The Surrealist Movement, having initially been dismissed as a minor and outlandish expression of the human psyche, was by the early 1930s being reconsidered for its historical significance. It was also gaining popularity with young people. Each exhibition was more comprehensive than the one before. In 1932, the first (unofficial) Surrealist exhibit was mounted in Prague by the Mánes Gallery. The first official show, the *International Kunstudstilling Kubisme: Surrealisme*, co-curated by Breton and Vilhelm Bjerke-Petersen, in Copenhagen at Den Frie Udstilling Center of Contemporary Art, January 15–28, 1935, was hardly noticed. Breton himself did not attend. Finally, in the spring of 1935, André, with Jacqueline and Éluard, traveled to meet the Czech Surrealists. André was elated; in three months, he sold 800 copies of *Communicating Vessels*.

Of the Prague meeting, Jacqueline recalled "the particularly warm reactions which they raised in us. The welcome and hospitality to the point of luxury to which we were little accustomed. André, Eluard, and me ... at the mercy of precarious finances that the Czech Surrealists had available, and the *Front Rouge* [Red Front] comrades; the view of this town that André took upon himself to speak about, as only he could speak about certain places."[113]

Almost immediately after returning from Prague, André, Jacqueline and poet Benjamin Péret traveled to the *Exposición Internacional del Surrealismo* held at the Ateneo de Santa Cruz, Tenerife, in the Canary Islands, curated by painter Óscar Domínguez, May 14–27, 1935 (pl. 17). Jacqueline was represented by two paintings, although neither her name nor the titles of the works appeared on the checklist.[114] She also went uncredited for designing the catalogue's bright pink cover, with "peeled off" areas exposing information about the exhibition: title, place, dates, time of vernissage, and names of organizers. The exhibit attracted many visitors, which the artists and organizers loved; unfortunately, none of the works—all of which were for sale—sold. And Luis Buñuel's film *L'Âge d'or* (The Golden Age), which was part of the exhibition—about the questionable values of the Church, the insanity of modern life, and bourgeois society's hypocritical sexual mores—was banned as immoral. The producers, having expected to recoup expenses through ticket sales, were disappointed. Nevertheless, enthusiasts rose to the occasion and paid for the insurance and transportation of the works, including the restoration of Picasso's painting, gashed in transit, that André arranged to have fixed in Paris. From the Tenerife experience, Breton wrote "The Starry Castle," a chapter he added to the forthcoming *Mad Love*. While in the Canary Islands, Jacqueline was often photographed by the critic Eduardo Westerdahl, who convinced Breton to present the show. Two months pregnant with Aube, Jacqueline had never looked so radiant. For once, she looked happy.

Valentine Hugo's *L'Esprit du tournesol* (The Spirit of the Sunflower, 1934; Private collection) hung in the exhibition. For a time, Valentine and Breton were involved in a one-sided romantic relationship. She had been serious about him, but he was uncaring about her and treated her dismissively. When he and Jacqueline married, Valentine expressed her pent-up resentment toward him in a painting, wishing him a bad marriage. Its title is drawn from André's text *The Night of the Sunflower* (1937), in which he foretells meeting Jacqueline. Valentine curses Breton's home address, 42 rue Fontaine, where he and Jacqueline will be living. *L'Esprit du tournesol* portrays this malediction on André and Jacqueline's union. The single wedding band hanging from a nail dripping blood predicts that only one member of the couple will commit to the marriage. A glass filled with liquid holds a thistle on which sit two *Parnassius* nocturnal moths, their abdomens joined. On the ground lie cocoons that cannot survive without being attached to a host plant. In Genesis 3:17–18, God says to Adam and Eve after they have eaten the forbidden fruit, "cursed is the ground for thy sake; in sorrow shalt thou eat of it all the days of thy life … Thorns also and thistles shall it bring forth to thee." Valentine, unable to conceive, wished the same for André and Jacqueline. Following the exhibition, Valentine sold the painting to Lise Deharme, a flame of André's during his marriage to Simone Kahn, his first wife.

Regardless of whether André supported her art-making, or whether she was able to afford art supplies, Jacqueline was determined to participate in Surrealist activities and contribute to the creation of exquisite corpses, making collages, decalcomanias, objects, and paintings, and exhibiting with the group.[115] Less than a year after their marriage, as Jacqueline Breton, she participated in the *Surrealist Exhibition of Objects* at the Charles Ratton Gallery in Paris, curated by André, May 22–29, 1936.

One object showed the depth of her creative power, cleverly bringing together Surrealism's dark humor and mystery. She transformed a black gauze scarf into a butterfly—for its head, an African Krobo bead painted with eyes, and eleven tiny beads to hold down the strings that articulated the polyhedron skeleton, its six wings spread unevenly against the flat background to which the body was pinned—and gifted it to Man Ray. If, after looking at the object, spectators still wondered about it, they could read *"Pour la Poche"* ("For the Pocket," 1935; pl. 16) in the upper right of the mount and realize, "Of course, it's a handkerchief!" Jacqueline gave Éluard one of her works, *La Femme blonde* (The Blonde Woman, 1936; lost), a symbolic reference to herself, comprising a small cabinet where, through the glass door, tassels and metal spheres, in harmony, dangle from rods.[116] Her collaboration with Breton produced two objects: *Le Grand Paranoïac* (The Great Paranoiac, 1936; lost), a bottle rack holding a feather, a necklace, eyeglasses, a candle, and a drinking glass; and *Le Petit Mimétique* (The Little Bureaucrat, 1936; Centre Pompidou)—an ironic reference to the Bretons' troubled relationship—a box containing a dry praying mantis, pinned through the thorax to a signature of leaves. In captivity, these predators eat their young, and the female devours the male after copulating, lest he escape. With these objects, Breton intended to show disdain for the bourgeois or social realist. Photographer Claude Cahun explained: "In our present society not all of us are always able to make ourselves ductile, good conductors of liberating forces, and sometimes we are surprised that we have a closer resemblance to the little bureaucrat than to the great paranoiac."[117]

Éluard, despite being a lender, did not attend the show. Trouble was quietly brewing between him and Breton: the calm before the storm.

Surrealism in London

In June 1936, Jacqueline and André traveled to London for the vernissage and ancillary events of the *International Surrealist Exhibition* at the New Burlington Galleries, programmed from June 11 to July 4, 1936 (pl. 19). Earlier, Paul Éluard had asked the organizers to arrange his schedule so as to avoid coinciding with the Bretons. The show had been co-curated by Roland Penrose, who chose the English Surrealists, while Éluard and André, Man Ray and Georges Hugnet chose work by other artists. Éluard intentionally made communication difficult since he would speak with André only by telephone. To provoke him further, Éluard tried securing—without success—Salvador Dalí's portrait *Lenin with a Big Ass*, which two years earlier had nearly gotten Dalí expelled from the group. On June 11, André officially opened the exhibition, and on June 16 he presented his lecture *Surrealism without Borders*, "all clad in green and smoking a green pipe, a gift from [Scottish poet] Ruthven Todd [secretary to the exhibition]. He was accompanied by his wife whose long hair was also green."[118] Assuming André would be pleased, Jacqueline dyed her hair green as Baudelaire before her. "Baudelaire, nothing," he snapped. "You wash that off now or I'll divorce you."[119]

Jacqueline washed it out, but by then newspapers had picked up the story, which, in twisted ways, became legendary.[120] A typical review read: "One of the leading members of the group which has promoted the forthcoming International Surrealist Exhibition in London, by name André Breton, is described by an admirer in the following terms: 'I read in a Fleet Street gossip column that the leader of the Surrealist Movement and his wife "are both passionate about green." She has green eyes, with which she wears green eyelashes and eyebrows, and he wears green suits, smokes a green pipe, and drinks a very green aperitif.'" Another reviewer attributed to Breton the "hallmarks of genius": "He drinks an aperitif called *oxygène*, which is a beautiful clear emerald green. Who could doubt M. Breton's genius after such evidence?" Another wrote: "M. Breton has a wife who on the same showing would appear to be a genius, too. She has a marvelous figure, hair the color of half-burnt toast and pale green eyes. She affects green eyelashes and often wears green nail varnish. But I suspect Madame Breton is not so green as she looks."[121]

Following the official opening, Sheila Legge, the Surrealist Phantom clad by Dalí, wandered in, dressed in a white satin gown and black gauze gloves, her head and face concealed by a mask of blue hydrangeas. She held a lamb chop in one hand and—to echo her name—an artificial leg filled with red roses in the other; because of the heat, though, she disposed of the chop after a while.

Two thousand guests were invited, and more than twenty thousand visitors came. On June 24, Éluard's lecture *Poetic Evidence* described Surrealism as a spiritual state. On July 1, after making an entrance with two Borzoi dogs on a leash, and wearing a diving suit and helmet with a jeweled dagger in his belt, Dalí spoke on *The Authentic Paranoid Phantoms*, but with the helmet covering his head, no one could hear a word he said. After it grew too hot, with great effort, he removed the helmet and spoke, but his accent was so thick that, again, no one understood him. Todd said Dalí's lecture "combined paranoia and claustrophobia."[122] The critic of *The Times* accused the Surrealists of a kind of artistic dishonesty, of consciously using "'interesting hints of supernormal capacity' to make an effect."[123] But the most virulent and perhaps also the most stupid attack on Surrealism came from Raymond Mortimer, who reviewed the exhibition for *The Listener* (June 17, 1936). He explained the origins of the movement in Paris bohemianism as "would-be writers and painters, with a lot of artistic temperament and very little talent ... Drink, drugs, sexuality in its most psychopathic forms, were the ostentatious relaxations ... of this heterogeneous mob."[124]

The only thing more stupid than giving a lecture, Dalí offered during his lecture, was listening to one. He poured milk into his boot, pulled an omelet from his pocket, and plopped it on a woman's head. Despite often being referred to in the newspapers, neither Jacqueline nor André appeared in any of the official photographs, although someone managed to photograph them posing next to de Chirico's *The Child's Brain*, a work from Breton's collection.

In London, Jacqueline exhibited *Les Heures*—lent to Lise Deharme, then lost after her death—and two unidentified objects. Photographs of the installation show the painting displayed in the main gallery. Francis Picabia's *Spanish Night* (1922), of two standing persons, was strategically centered between two works depicting women in repose, Jacqueline's *Les Heures* on the left and Picasso's *Reclining Woman* (1924) on the right. Jacqueline's oval canvas portrays an isolated queen conch shell lying on its back on the ocean floor.[125] Her treatment of the shell suggests a self-portrait shaped by her relationship with André. Jacqueline transformed the dormant shell, with its thick, pink flaring lip, into a vulva, alluding to her role as sexual object. If André was the king of Surrealism, Jacqueline was the queen. For the delicately painted work, she reshaped the protruding nodules of the conch's whorl into a spiral crown, adding a vacantly staring eye and a slender leg that ended in a small, high-heeled slipper. This tiny shoe refers to the Cinderella slipper, the *trouvaille*, that André wrote about for Jacqueline in *Mad Love*: "I have wanted to see some very special object constructed in response to some poetic fantasy." He then described the wooden spoon that he, with Giacometti, acquired in a flea market.[126] Much to his joy, after placing it on the table at home, he discovered that "from the side, at a certain height, the little wood spoon coming out of its handle, took on, with the help of a curvature of the handle, the aspect of a heel and the whole object presented the silhouette of a slipper on tiptoe like those of dancers. Cinderella was certainly returning to the ball."[127] To marry the prince, he might have added.

Les Heures emphasized the underlying intimacy between Jacqueline's painting and André's writing. Here, she represented herself as a beautiful sexual trouvaille linked to the Archangel of Terror who overthrew the Girondists. However, her embraced identity as a passive object foretold trouble before she realized its implications or considered its consequences; willingly, she identified herself as a sexual object to be admired and used for the needs of others, with few alternatives, while Breton did as he pleased, even participating in heroic activities by contributing to the betterment of the world. The reality of her self-created isolation hit her as she began sensing the piper coming nearer, demanding to be paid. Only then did she begin shifting attention from herself to making art.

Meanwhile, André and Éluard's seventeen-year friendship had reached a bitter end. Unlike Éluard, Breton "preferred his truth to friendship, ideas to flesh-and-blood humans."[128] It was evident during World War I, while André worked as a physician's assistant, that his interest in patients was intellectual, not driven by compassion. Overlooking the fact that psychosis is a debilitating mental illness, Breton found the experience to be a poetic source. His sense of the creative process became his mixed legacy, his contribution and his failure. Éluard had been tolerant of André's demands in the beginning, but he lost patience over time with conflicts caused by the latter's growing authoritarianism and demanding ways, preferring "the Breton behind the mask of leader and legislator, the secret Breton, the human, the emotional, the vulnerable, the sometimes unhappy poet."[129] Once open and trusting, their friendship had soured by the time the London exhibition began; but Éluard, on good terms with everyone else, knew it would be better to stay than to walk out at the last moment.

Both friends knew what contributed to the break-up, although neither would come forward with specifics, which meant neither wanted the truth out. Silence encouraged speculation. Politics became the official story; André believed in Trotsky's Communism; Éluard in Stalin's. But Hugnet, treasurer of the FIARI (Manifesto for an Independent Revolutionary Art), knew something. André had confided in him that he was expelling Éluard for being partousard (polyamorous)—for casually having several sexual partners. And he demanded that Hugnet discontinue his friendship with Éluard for having recently published a poem in L'Humanité, the newspaper of the French Communist Party.[130] Hugnet refused. It seemed hypocritical that Breton was condemning Éluard's sexual practices while flying the banner of the Marquis de Sade, who pursued any carnal experience he pleased, including "sexual pleasures that each choose depending upon one's nature or tastes. What about free love as extolled by the Surrealists?"[131] Dressed in Mexican garb, Jacqueline and Frida Kahlo witnessed Breton humiliate Hugnet in front of his friends for disobeying him; André knew that Jacqueline had been instrumental in his and Éluard's break-up, but was making their political differences the ostensible reason. And at that moment Jacqueline was also having an affair with Kahlo (pl. 21).

The event that triggered the Breton–Éluard conflict was Breton's jealousy after learning of Jacqueline's dalliance with Paul. André knew when he married Jacqueline that she was sexually uninhibited and that their marriage would not change that. Although he disapproved, and it angered him, he accepted it grudgingly, for there was nothing he could do. But Paul, his best friend? André would not show himself vulnerable by admitting jealousy. Being discreet, Éluard said nothing, but Jacqueline kissed and told—"delicious" was how she described him.[132] Unabashedly, she had made for him the vitrine *La Femme blonde* (The Blonde Woman), a reference to herself, and gave him a nude photo inscribed "To Paul Éluard my friend, the Great Polar Butterfly Jacqueline Breton."[133] It was a Man Ray portrait made in 1934, the year she married Breton (pl. 12).[134] Powerless to confront Jacqueline over the real cause of his hurt, André's anger had to go somewhere and Éluard made a good target.

The following year, the group held its first exhibition in Japan, *Surrealism*, at the Nippon Salon in Ginza, Tokyo (June 9–14, 1937). The show was curated by Shūzō Takiguchi, artist, critic, poet, and the prominent Japanese exponent of the Movement. Jacqueline exhibited *Le Cantonnier* (The Roadmender, 1937; lost) and her collaboration with André on *Le Petit Mimétique*, lent the previous year to Charles Ratton's exhibition of Surrealist objects. Jacqueline's titles were often drawn from poetry, and *Le Cantonnier* was drawn from Symbolist Stéphane Mallarmé's reflection on his workday:

> You level those pebbles
> and being a troubadour,
> I too must crack open
> a cube of brains each day.[135]

Drawn with ink in *grattage* (a technique that involves scraping fresh paint), a sphere formed by a welter of interconnected lines suggests a harlequin trapped at the bottom of a construction, its body a lattice of elongated diamonds.

That same year, Hugnet published *La Carte Surréaliste*, a portfolio of twenty-one collotype postcards reproducing works by various artists. Jacqueline's contribution was *Pont de demi sommeil* (Bridge of Drowsiness, 1937), a sequence of three rose stems wrapped in tissue paper that gradually vanish from under their protective cover, leaving their imprint on the ground. In 1968, Bulgarian artist Christo, best known for wrapping buildings, took Jacqueline's idea a step further and produced *Wrapped Roses* in a limited edition. Copies of three plastic roses wrapped with polyethylene, staples, and twine, signed and numbered, entered the collections of several museums, including that of the MoMA.

Despite their being handed a golden opportunity to earn a salary from steady work, the Bretons' financial situation did not improve in 1937 when Louis Bomsel, a notary from Versailles, put up funds to open Gradiva Gallery at 31 rue de Seine.[136] Breton as director and Jacqueline as attendant were expected to take consignments, do shows, and sell primitive and Surrealist works, including art from Bomsel's collection. Breton named the gallery after Wilhelm Jensen's nineteenth-century novella about an archaeologist who falls in love and becomes obsessed with a bas-relief of a walking woman, eventually realizing that she represents his childhood sweetheart. The glass door, a design by Marcel Duchamp, shows a large male and a small female merged into a single silhouette. The enterprise did not do well. André had neither the patience to sell art nor the desire to pay commission to Bomsel for property sold from his collection; he could only be a poet, and Jacqueline, as impractical, could only paint. This inability to do anything else would eventually be an undoing of their marriage. Éluard predicted its failure: "His store isn't coming along. Breton is not cut out for this kind of business. Neither is Jacqueline."[137] By March 1939, the gallery had closed.

In Breton's anthology *La Trajectoire du rêve* (The Trajectory of the Dream), the "Dream" issue, published by Cahiers GLM in March 1938, Jacqueline illustrated with a binary black-and-white *grattage* Benjamin Péret's "Durruti's Egg Will Bloom" narrative about the assassination of Spanish insurrectionary anarchist and military commander José Buenaventura Durruti Dumange.[138] *Veilleuse* (Night Light, ca. 1938; Jenna Segal collection), titled after a poem by Paul Verlaine about the beauty of a moonlit night, represents Dream and Wakefulness. In the Dream part, a tiny person flies an enormous kite in the pitch dark. In Wakefulness, a nightlight hanging from a white brick wall offers safety from the dark.

Surrealism in Paris

"Not everybody approved—but everybody felt the impact," wrote Guy Cruzete for *La Grande Revue* about the *Exposition Internationale du Surréalisme* at the Galerie Beaux-Arts, Paris, in 1938, a slap in the face of the Nazi regime's four-year traveling exhibition *Degenerate Art*, which had opened in Munich the previous July. Inexplicably, the photograph reproduced in German newspapers of the vernissage shows Hitler standing by *La Belle Jardinière* (The Beautiful Gardener), a life-size painting by German Surrealist Max Ernst.

Fascist bombs were falling in Spain during the week prior to the opening of the French exhibition, but the Surrealists refused to bend. Jacqueline did not tire of repeating that the Surrealists were going to go on, that freedom belongs to everyone, that no one has a right to steal it. The *International Surrealist Exhibition*, a Surrealist experience in itself, would have made the Führer rage—to the joy of many. It summarized a Movement, broke ground, and joined the annals of art history, along with Impressionism, Fauvism, and Cubism.

On January 19, 1938, Surrealism stopped shocking and became amusing—even boring to some—but interesting to many. The *Dictionnaire abrégé du surréalisme*, the illustrated catalogue of the show, edited by André Breton and Paul Éluard, contained information about more than sixty artists and poets from sixteen countries. The entry for the letter "J" consists of two lines drawn from André's poem *"L'Air de l'eau"*:

> *Jacqueline,*
> *When the hand of Jacqueline X,*
> *Opens like a casement window onto a nocturnal garden*

And reproduced on page 46 is Jacqueline's vitrine *La Femme blonde*, her sole contribution to the exhibition.

Despite being overseen by two poets, Breton and Éluard, the show's emphasis was no longer on poetry, Surrealism's original focus. This time, it was visual, with the intention of re-creating a dream environment with alternate contexts by using everyday objects, with disturbing, sexualized imagery, represented through brutally frank assemblages, paintings, and sculpture.

Initially, viewers entered a courtyard where Dalí's rainy taxi—a system of pipes caused it to rain on the vehicle—received them with two mannequins inside, a driver and a "rotting" female wearing an evening dress, with tousled hair, lettuce and chicory growing under her, and live snails crawling over her naked body. After entering the *rue Surréaliste*, lined with sixteen female mannequins, each created by a different artist, visitors were handed flashlights by Man Ray to light the main hall designed by Wolfgang Paalen and Marcel Duchamp, and the dark rooms where miniature retrospective exhibitions of particular painters hung on revolving doors. From the ceiling were suspended fifteen hundred sacks of coal. German military music played in the background as a phonograph sang hysterically, non-stop. The *act manqué*, or unconsummated act, was performed by naked dancer Hélène Vanel on a pink satin bed.

Surrealism was more than an art movement. It was an obsession, a state of mind.

Mexico

On March 30, 1938, André and Jacqueline sailed—without Aube—for Mexico out of Cherbourg on the MS *Orinoco*, making landfall in Veracruz on April 18. On that date, and for the next four months, the Bretons experienced one surprise after another. Although the trip had been arranged by the French Ministry of Foreign Affairs, provision had not been made for their three-month stay, which ended up lasting four months.[139] Jacqueline explained:

> *At the time, poet Saint-John Perse was at the Quai d'Orsay, and Dr. Henri Laugier in the Recherche Scientifique. We were in a particularly difficult financial situation. Those two persons managed to send André and me on a cultural mission to Mexico, to present conferences on poetry and painting. Naturally, we thought that our lodging had been arranged. Otherwise, we would have canceled the trip. On landing, an embassy secretary was waiting to receive us, but there was no speech or official presentation. We had money to live on for about eight days. With our return tickets in our pockets, André decided to take the next boat home, immediately. He was about to notify the secretary when [Diego] Rivera presented himself, transmitting an invitation from Lev Davidovich [Leon Trotsky] to meet two days later, and offered us hospitality in his house, in San Angel, for a stay of three to four months.[140]*

While the Bretons considered alternatives, Rivera arrived to save the day. His talent for painting was comparable to his talent for diplomacy and seizing opportunities—often without considering the possible consequences. Rivera, the great operator, had been responsible for convincing President Lázaro Cárdenas to grant asylum to Trotsky when no other country dared, fearful of Stalin's far-reaching tentacles, giving assurance that Trotsky would be in Mexico only as Rivera's guest. Bringing together Breton and Trotsky would add insult to injury, further poking Stalin's beehive.

Initially, André and Jacqueline stayed at Calle Tampico 6 in the Condesa neighborhood of Mexico City, at the apartment of Lupe Marín, Rivera's ex-wife, before moving to one of Frida Kahlo and Diego Rivera's houses, Villa Obregón on Altavista and Palmas. Jacqueline continued:

> *Diego and Frida Rivera lived in one of the most modern houses from the period: two white cubes, half glass, united by an external staircase without ramp and a catwalk at the top reserved for us. An Indian [Indigenous] woman, the guardian, cooked familiar food on coals in the garden; open under the trees, and completely free, an anteater. This last, André took as a favorable sign, for his ex-libris, drawn by Dalí, was an anteater.*
>
> > *On the threshold, Frida Kahlo de Rivera, the exceptional, dressed like the women from the Tehuantepec region. And while the unexpected kept happening, we learned she was a Surrealist painter. Her canvases around her, and like her, tragic and splendid.[141]*

The Bretons made trips with Trotsky and his second wife, Natalia Sedova, to Puebla and Cholula. In Monterrey, the Bretons visited the Military Zone. Following their return to Mexico City, all three couples traveled to Cuernavaca, Morelia, the Tarascan island of Pátzcuaro, Teotihuacan, and Xochicalco. Jacqueline observed the interaction between Breton, Rivera, and Trotsky as the FIARI developed, and took note. Thirty-nine years after the event, her sharp memory recalled this historic moment to Arturo Schwarz in detail, including what she saw and heard, as well as her conversations with André after his meetings with Trotsky and Rivera (pl. 20).[142]

As so often, André had a profound effect on the people around him. On this trip, his influence was transformative, not just for Jacqueline and Frida, but also, arguably, for the state of Mexico. The Bretons arrived in a country in turmoil. Conflict caused by Trotsky's political asylum continued throughout their stay. Cárdenas had expropriated oil from the United States, and students were killed in university conflicts under Dean Luis Chico Goerne. But life went on. Six days after their arrival, on April 24, the Bretons attended the vernissage of Francisco Gutiérrez's Surrealist exhibition at the Galería de Arte de la Universidad, where André spoke publicly for the first time in Mexico, and Jacqueline, as usual, drew attention in the press for her looks and dress. The next day, hostile reviews began, with one critic explaining that Surrealism is better understood by users of the hallucinogenic peyote.

Breton's meeting with Trotsky proved damaging to the artist and to Surrealism, and being a guest of Rivera made him a target of hostile barbs in Stalinist publications. These attacks, naturally, let up once he departed. Officially, Breton had planned to present four lectures on French literature and art. On May 13, he delivered the first, *Modern Transformations in Art and Surrealism*, at the university. On May 17, after he introduced the première of Buñuel's *Un Chien Andalou* at the Palacio de Bellas Artes, the press killed his program, his sponsor resigned, and the French consulate, powerless to help, did nothing. Only a few trial proofs of *The Communicating Vessels*, Rivera's poster for his talk, were ever printed. Breton was attacked in many publications, but only positive reviews were shown to him. *Letras de México*, which covered much of his visit, wrote, "Surrealism equals zero."[143]

Breton arrived in Mexico believing he brought Surrealism with him. What he brought was a theoretical framework for artists of a similar mindset to understand and give free rein to their creativity as an organized group. But Mexico's mindset, which existed in a transitional space where separate realities overlapped and transformational shifts took place, made Surrealism jump out at him wherever he went. The pine bookcase built from a sketch that Breton made for a carpenter, for example, followed the forced perspective of his drawing. Permeated with black humor, Mexican art cut directly to the psyche, where such opposites as life and death coexisted naturally side by side. Mexicans, innate surrealists, slipped into and out of invisible realms without thinking. In Mexico, Surrealism was a state of mind, existing without a name or self-awareness.[144]

Upon visiting Kahlo's studio, André was taken aback by her self-portrait *What the Water Gave Me* (1934), in which she and the viewer sit together in the bathtub, observing her life afloat above her outstretched legs. Her work resonated with the phrase from his book *Nadja*: "I am the thought of bathing in the mirrorless room," and he welcomed her as a daughter of Surrealism.[145] To journalist Rafael Heliodoro Valle, André described Mexico as "The Surrealist place *par excellence*."[146] On having its sense of identity reframed, Mexico responded with unexpected enthusiasm. Before Breton pointed out that they were leading surrealist lives, Mexicans simply saw themselves without a label.

Earlier in the year, American art dealer Julien Levy had written to Rivera proposing an exhibition in his New York gallery. Kahlo, who handled her husband's correspondence, explained that he had no new work to show and no time to prepare for the proposed date.[147] In response, Levy suggested a show of her painting, and she discussed the idea with Rivera. Traveling to New York appealed to her, although she needed to be discreet, since she had become infatuated with photographer Nickolas Muray, who lived there. Breton also proposed that the show travel to Paris, agreeing to make the arrangements. Enthused by the idea, Rivera saw it as an opportunity to take advantage. It would be good for Frida, for her painting, a way to gain autonomy.

But in Kahlo's mind, pressure to be autonomous felt like abandonment. It had been a year since she and Diego reconciled following his affair with her sister Cristina, and she did not trust him. During that first separation, they discussed divorce, and she contemplated suicide. Out of that experience, she painted *What the Water Gave Me*—the self-portrait about what her life had been.[148] But she knew when to fight Diego and when to concede. This was a time for the latter. She became angry with André for proposing that the show should travel to Paris, and with Diego for agreeing—anger she would not dare express—and displaced it toward André. As Frida's relationship with Jacqueline developed, they opened up about their marriages. Dependency enslaved both women to their husbands. Frida lived in fear that if she were not as Diego wanted, he would abandon her, and she would be unable to survive without his protection; Jacqueline feared leaving André since she lacked the ability to survive on her own with Aube. Yet both were aware that their sacrifices brought certain benefits. By the time Jacqueline and André returned to France, he had fallen in love with Mexico, and she with Frida.

For Stendhal, Jacqueline's bedside reading, passion was the finest form of love. And Jacqueline's letters to Frida confirm that they had fallen passionately in love. Although Jacqueline had likely participated in *ménages à trois* with Paul and Nusch Éluard, and with Picasso and Maar, those trysts were merely sexual. It is unknown whether she had previous romantic interest in other women. There are photographs of Jacqueline nude or in undergarments taken while she was staying with Picasso and Maar. But, by Stendhal's definition, such sexual moments were purely physical, a social game. What Jacqueline and Frida had was love.

Among the gifts that Jacqueline received from Frida prior to her departure was a miniature self-portrait inscribed "28 Julio 1938 México," with one of Frida's typical coded messages. Frida had made a connection with Jacqueline and was conflicted about her departure. The self-portrait foresees the effect their separation will have on her. Strings around her neck pull at her every which way, suggesting that Frida is helpless against external forces and associating her predicament with the imminent death of the plant tied to one of the strings, uprooted and separated from its source of nourishment.

On August 15, 1938, following their departure from Mexico, André wrote in French from the SS *Iberia*, Hamburg–America Line:

> *Frida, Diego, beloved,*
> *Here the sea is rapidly turning dirty because it's an evening when we touch Europe: just happy to dump trash in Lisbon, a dozen fascists who paraded themselves in blue shirts with daggers and pistols on the bridge.*

After outlining his views on the Russo-Japanese War, André devotes the letter mostly to business, some PR, and mentions that they saw a priest on the boat, which made them want to vomit. "Jacqueline was in a sordid costume dance and won second place in her Tehuana dress. First [place] went to a woman dressed as a yellow turkey in a tablecloth." He apologizes to "Fridacita" for still not having written the introduction for her show at Levy's in "these miserable conditions," then asks her to send him the date of the opening. He adds in closing that the miniature self-portrait in the butterfly frame she had gifted him and Jacqueline is hanging on the wall of the cabin and, at night, when it makes a metallic noise, it wakes him, and he remembers it is she.

For "My Dear Diego," André has a list of requests. First, he asks for the original document of the FIARI and photos taken by Fritz Bach, and that Diego please "remember me to him [Bach] with affection." Then, he asks Rivera to send the *Mexican Folkways* issues that writer and anthropologist Frances Toor had promised him, the article for *Minotaure* (his and Trotsky's), a photo from Roberto Montenegro of the anonymous painting that is inscribed (probably *Así es la vida*), and more. He also writes to "L.D." (Lev Davidovich Trotsky) and adds, "Fridacita don't frown your swallow eyebrows." Jacqueline closes the letter with a promise: "Frida darling I will write to you on arrival. Don't forget me. Embrace Diego tenderly with both arms around his neck."[149] Back in Paris, a smitten Jacqueline writes Frida a first long letter in red ink in English:

> *6 September 1938*
> *4 o'clock*
>
> MY FRIDA.
>
> *André received your letter this morning; finally you exist once again for me or me for you (I have decided that it is the same thing) but <u>I doubt, I do not believe anymore anything from you,</u> sorry.*
>
> *I told myself this morning when André opened your letter— why <u>he</u>? Does she ever want to talk to me ... and there are other things, then I have reread your letter 7 times, I keep it near me to begin once again, you write French like an angel—*

She explains about André and his preface, and continues:

Darling I write you once again ... it seems to me it has been a century since I have been on my bed—they operated on me <u>you know of what,</u> those damn stories of women, but when they put me to sleep it was so beautiful, I thought of you intensely—how many times had they performed on you the ceremony of the mask—I ask myself if that pleased you, I said to myself; often, <u>certainly,</u> but not because of those circumstances.[150] Then I thought once again of you in a pure way, simply because you are dear to me, for example to give me the strength because I have an idiotic, appalling fear that gives me an incredible appearance of calm.

Good—Aube sleeps very deeply near me after declaring that she would do nothing and that she will sing all the time in her bed—I truly love her very much, she gives me some kicks, bites, and hugs as easily, when she feels like it.

I interrupted myself from writing because I felt unwell. Aube is full of humor and her gestures are very funny ... very sweet ...

Frida, you tell me not to forget you; will you feel the same way when you receive this letter? ...

This morning, one or two hours after your letter to André arrived, I read a story by Franz Kafka called "The Judgment" where they speak of a young woman named FRIEDA ... I rush into the pleasure of writing, and with the certainty that promises you will hear me even if you never receive this letter ...

Once again interrupted, they have come to see me, ordinary people, always ordinary people. Yet, [Yves] Tanguy, he knows you a little now ... I love to speak of you, show your [self-]portrait, precisely even to ordinary people and that English woman that came and found you very beautiful and [spoke] about the Mexican exhibition in London after the one in Paris, would you like that? That would take place one month after, we all might go ...

I can go on a long time if I am not afraid of boring the <u>real</u> creature that you are and now <u>I see you well</u> once again, <u>as you are,</u> from everything I know of you, in one second I see it, and that is what I love, don't forget that which I loved first.

7:30

Jacqueline

Looping around the kiss at the bottom, Jacqueline adds: "I also would like your physical news."

On September 9, Jacqueline writes once more to Frida. After some comments on the preface comes a heartfelt:

> *Frida darling, I have still not received a line from you, other than the letter for André, but ... I always wait, I sleep as little as possible, life seems like a corridor, a bit narrow but it surely leads to the doors full of surprises and you are waiting behind one of the doors there, the one that remains the most desired.*
>
> *Do not leave me alone as long as you're alone,*
> *Jacqueline*

Frida in New York

Diego's encouragement that Frida should attend both shows, in New York and Paris, she predictably interpreted as a form of rejection; she wrote reminding him that she would return at his asking.[151] She did not trust him around other women, although she trusted his judgment to take advantage of opportunities that otherwise might not have presented themselves, so she decided to enjoy the experience to the full; it was in her best professional interest. Before she left Mexico for New York, Diego wrote letters of introduction to persons who could help her. The letter to his old buddy Walter Pach, art advisor to the Rockefellers, became particularly important, for Pach bought *Survivor* on opening night, paving the way for other sales.

The exhibition at Julien Levy's was a success and Frida was eagerly sought out. While she was wined and dined, she juggled her affair with Nickolas Muray with a momentary fling with Levy. Nick was passionately in love, vulnerable, eating out of her hand. Mesmerized, he had taken photographs of Frida before, but none like the portraits he took before her departure. There are variants of her wearing her magenta *rebozo*, in which a nimbus lights her from head to waist. In one, her back against the wall, her right hand covers her left, and her face is turned toward the viewer. Nick sent a black-and-white print to André, who had requested it while in Mexico.

In a letter bearing the date November 12, 1938, Jacqueline wrote to "Frida darling":

We have received many catalogues from Levy. Your exhibition is nearly finished. I was hoping all the time for your success, it must be a great one. Now André wants to know <u>exactly</u> if you are coming or not in order to settle everything for you here. I mean the gallery, the catalogue and so on. And then, he wants to have some photographs of your pictures better than the ones we already have (not the one of the bath) ...

> *I don't think you were pleased about André's introduction. I ask you in a very LOUD voice to reply ... <u>to those questions</u> ...*
> <u>*If you are coming don't forget that there is room for you here, my friendship and the pleasure of everybody to see you.*</u>
> <u>*Jacqueline*</u>
> *Sorry for my bad English.*

At the foot of the letter was appended:

I am also very very sorry and I kiss your hands.
> *André*

Following the opening in New York, Jacqueline wrote again to Frida:

Bravo Frida, it is a great success without exaggeration. We are very glad, and now you have to come in January very soon or better at the end of December, because the same Mexican exhibition is already settled down in London at the beginning of February ... [the next page(s) of the letter are missing] *... I am waiting for your real letter or its phantom.*

> *And the very very end I give you a real kiss.*
> *Jacqueline*

Frida in Paris

After leaving New York, Frida arrived in Paris on January 19, 1939. She did not want to be there. She had been dreading the trip, feeling homesick before leaving Mexico, missing Diego and feeling the need to keep an eye on him. She also missed Nick's personality, his spontaneity, his passion, and those whose fascination with her kept her in balance. A problem was Frida's chronic alienation and illnesses, for which she needed constant coddling from those who, drawn by her helplessness, surrounded her wherever she went. People do for the ill and the helpless what they will not do for others, and Frida, often ill and helpless, always had someone to watch over her. In France, she knew only Jacqueline, who could do little. The problem was compounded by the language barrier; her inability to speak French kept her from communicating freely. Naturally, she feared she would run into problems that she could not handle.

Frida's resentment toward André began during his visit to Mexico the previous year and grew until she blamed him for what went wrong in Paris, much of which could have been avoided had he been more conscientious. It began with his tardiness in delivering the introduction for the exhibition brochure catalogue at Levy's gallery, leaving no time for it to be translated into English. The photographs of Frida's paintings taken by Nick were of only fair quality. Moreover, André had not secured a gallery or completed the paperwork to release the paintings from customs. He complained about having to pay for storage at the train station, from December 28 through February 14, for Frida's luggage that could not fit in his apartment. The Bretons gave up their bed for Frida, but she had to share it with Aube and sleep by the three-year-old's chamberpot; she had no place to bathe or to hang her clothes. Fed up, she described this and more to Diego in her first letter, dated January 28, 1939:

> *My pretty child, my love,*
>
> *I wanted to write from the ship to mail the letter in Le Havre but imagine that I had a trip of the pure <u>fuck</u> and the last four days I hardly left the cabin because there were such storms that one could not walk on account of how the ship was moving, there were wounded, and three poor men broke their ribs and arms. I was so afraid that I cried without consolation because I was certain that the ship was sinking. Even the newspapers gave notice of the trip, and they say the captain did not sleep two days because in five years there had not been such bad weather, and most of all, that the ship is*

a shit because it's old and fucked up, and it cannot make the trip in five days as before but in eight, so you see they could not even pass the storm quickly. I came screwed up with the bad foot so imagine that when I had a cold in New York one night I placed a hot-water bottle on my feet and, without feeling, I burned a toe. [Dr.] *David* [Glusker] *took care of me but the last day before leaving did not want me to embark again because the dirty burn got infected, he took me to another doctor to ask his opinion and after much thinking between them they let me come, the parting day, it was David himself who went to talk to the ship's doctor and gave him indications how to cure my foot, every day, twice a day.*

So you can imagine in what conditions I came. The ship's doctor spoke perfect Spanish, and he behaved very well with me, he did not let me move at all and most of all those days of the terrible storms. Mary [Sklar, sister of art historian Meyer Schapiro] *referred me to two gringos who came on the ship and helped me very much. Imagine that the large trunks in my cabin moved from one side to another as if they were trash, at midnight they came over at me, against the bed with such strength, even if I tied them up with ropes, the knots burst and I thought I was going to die squished like a bedbug. The old women screamed all night, loud shrieks as the lights went out constantly and there was an alarm signal because the kitchen began catching fire. You can't imagine my anguish and as much as I wanted to make myself strong, sadness was taking me away. Two black men who came here to dance in a cabaret were walking day and night with their life jackets on as if in a movie. Now I see it with calm, but I was already sure that it was a short time before I went to the other world. We finally arrived at Plymouth. People were unable to disembark because it was intolerable to reach the port and even less to go down on another small boat, so they pulled in to Le Havre. We arrived eighteen hours late. Jacqueline went to Le Havre for me with Dora Mar* [sic], *the girl who lives with Picasso. Poor Jacqueline and Dora had arrived earlier that morning but the ship did not arrive until six in the afternoon and they had to wait until seven p.m. until the passengers were able to disembark, an hour later than scheduled. Finally, we arrived in Paris at eleven thirty in the night. On the train I met a so-called Munguia, Mexican ... supposedly from the League of Nations, he knows you well but one can see he's a son of a ... like all his sort. Because not all the people from the ship were able to buy train tickets or anything, since there was so much confusion that one could barely move, Jacqueline, Dora, and me did not find room, and that Munguia offered us his compartment to sit down, so there was no more remedy than to accept because I was dying of fatigue with my leg and standing more than an hour in customs, so even if Stalin would offer me his seat I would have accepted with pleasure. In the station André was waiting for us—at those times—nearly dead I had to climb the damn five stories of Breton's house, carrying two suitcases because there was not a soul to help me. I arrived so tired and nervous that I did not sleep a single instant all night. Plus, they put me to sleep in the room of the girl and every three hours she had to pee and I had to sit her on the potty. I tell you that in my life I have never gone through anything like this and now I am so angry because I have not told you the main things.*

Breton's house consists of two rooms, the lousiest you can imagine, packed with surrealist things, from the ceiling to the last corner. So I would be comfortable, they gave me their bed, which is where the girl sleeps ... In each detail I felt I was in the way, but they truly were making an effort ... they wanted me to be comfortable. The large trunks did not fit in the house and were returned to the station. I used that as a pretext to take a room in a hotel because there was no way to stay without clothes to wear. They searched for a hotel sort of bourgeois to be safe and I didn't last more than three days in the home of the Bretons and I came flying to the hotel (it is called Hotel Regina, 2 Place de Pyramides)[;] it's in front of the Louvre and the fucking statue of Joan of Arc. I have a regular room and a bathroom which is what I dreamed of having ... The little Breton Girl is a marvel of intelligence ... She adores me and from the first moment she became my friend. She tells me at every moment Frida tu est belle, tu est belle!! A doll of a girl and smart like few ...

All this I am telling you is <u>nothing</u> in comparison to how I have been throwing fits with the exhibition. As I told you the last telegram of André that I received in New York it read literally it was urgent the paintings [arrive] by January 1. Levy sent them immediately and they arrived in France on December 28. I arrived with the certainty that everything was arranged and then André comes up with the paintings are in customs still because they demand a permit. He had not arranged with one gallery because he insists on putting in Mexican things and the portraits of XIX century with my paintings ....[152]

Again, Diego, the magician, saved the day through Pach, who contacted Marcel Duchamp, who again made things right and arranged for the show to be held at the Galerie Renou et Colle. But André moved the date of the exhibition forward, changing its focus completely and angering Frida further. It would no longer be a one-woman show, but rather *MEXIQUE*, an exhibition that brought together pre-Hispanic art, photographs by Manuel Álvarez Bravo, nineteenth-century portraits that had to be restored (for 200 dollars borrowed from Frida, a fact that infuriated Diego), popular crafts, and her paintings.

In Mexico, André's behavior had been obsequious. In Paris, he was impatient, demanding, and quick to anger. One evening he snapped at Frida over drawings she refused to give him for a project he intended to work on. Afterward, he wrote her an apology; but she had had enough.

The move to the hotel made all the difference. Frida enjoyed her privacy, and Jacqueline showed her a Paris that she would not have seen on her own. They spent time with Maar, who drew Frida's portrait and photographed her, and she met Picasso, among other luminaries. Mary Reynolds, Duchamp's companion, watched over Frida. When she came down with a kidney infection, Reynolds arranged for her admission to the American Hospital and paid her hotel and hospital bills. And, while Reynolds stayed in the countryside, she let Frida and Michel Petitjean, assistant director at Charles Ratton's gallery—with whom Frida began an affair—stay at her house.[153] When Frida left France, she gifted *The Heart* (1937) to a smitten Petitjean, a self-portrait crying, her heart eviscerated. He was left broken-hearted; she never replied to his letters.

During Frida's exhibition, *The Frame* (1938), a self-portrait in a decorated frame from Juquila, a region of Oaxaca, was acquired by the Galerie Nationale du Jeu de Paume. Jacqueline wrote Diego: "Everyone agrees and recognizes that her [Frida's] paintings are the best by a woman to date."[154]

The following are some of the letters of the period, all originally in French:

16 February [1939]

Frida Darling
    André opened this letter this morning believing it was for him, he was not fully awake—but he did not read it. I taped it [the envelope] *back to send by pneumatique* [message conveyor] *so you can receive it fast.*
        Jacqueline and Aube
        [sealed with lipstick kisses]

Sunday 3 o'clock [March 12, 1939]

Cherished Frida,
I was a bully with you yesterday.
You don't have to pay attention.
It is only I who knows how I love you.
In reality:
I am always close to you
But life pisses me off
My dear love, so long,
Jacqueline

Monday, 13 March 1939

Frida my darling,

I remain very sad about what happened last evening, very sad also that you are not coming back to this house where I live, or rather where I love you often. You did not telephone me this morning. I called you, but too late. I did not wish to wake you up, it's why I telephoned only close to midday.

You don't have to love me today, March 13, too bad ... I love you intensely. You have to think well that I only love you. Aube sleeps, I think of yesterday in the taxi and I cry with rage—I dreamed that I was in my school, the one I showed you, as boarder, it was like a hotel, with the most refined comfort, I was wounded, professors of incredible politeness showed me every corner, I lost blood but marvelous, all the young girls looked like you, each was you but as soon as possible, one had your eyes, the other your neck, the other your mouth, your smile, like that, gradually to infinity, I was walking. In the dressing room behind the curtains, all your dresses were hanging, waiting for me, where are you?

Last evening, I was thinking, as I was falling asleep from tiredness at Dora's home, aren't you sick after all that alcohol? Last evening, I was a bit uncomfortable but happy to hear you laugh and I found <u>you alone</u> drawing.

I have never hated André more than yesterday—and I never will again. In these eyes it's badly written, isn't it, will you be able to read it? Otherwise, my writing becomes totally that of a baby, and a sad baby, it's silly, don't you find it so? With all these years of rage, of love, of dreams I never did that, and swim I would love to swim for you, you would look at me through a glass. I would dance for you, all that you say you would understand me better and you would love me. Frida I have terrible need of you,

you need to know, it is three o'clock, I kiss your two breasts and your mouth, I feel the closest possible to you.

André followed Jacqueline's with a letter to Frida:

Dear little Frida,

I behaved very meanly and very stupidly the evening before yesterday: I beg you to forgive me. I am totally sad at the thought of having hurt you and yet nothing was more the opposite to my intention. The most stupid [thing] is that all my disappointment was because I was counting on your collaboration to do something awesome with the drawings ... My behavior was completely childish. I also committed a blunder toward you and toward the friend [Petitjean] who accompanied you: very humbly, I recognize my mistakes. I have only as excuse that I was very tired at that moment, overcome by a great crisis of pessimism.

Nevertheless, very dear Frida, you must understand, do not be overly harsh [with me] ... My deplorable moment of impatience must be for you something without future: allow that I ask you on my knees to forget it. Nevertheless, you must well know that I admire and love you with all my heart.
André

Jacqueline soon wrote again:

20 March 1939

Frida darling,

I am in a little café very near the flea market—I did not find your bracelet—the two old ladies were absent, sorry—(too frozen, no doubt). I am waiting for the booksellers to arrive this evening. They promised me, except if they missed the publisher, we would have to wait two days. I would have many dreams to write you about, but I no longer know if they are true or false. I would like also that you did not drink so much ... so you can return standing before you go home. Pay attention to the first page of the little book that you have in your bag. I didn't open it yesterday, only that page, to love you, DO NOT ERASE IT—not EVER, if you can.

I greet all of you,
J.

Once settled, Frida summed up her stay in a letter in English to Muray:

Paris, Feb. 16, 1939

My adorable Nick. Mi Niño—

I am writing you in my bed in the American Hospital—yesterday it was the first day I didn't have fever and they aloud [sic] me to eat a little, so I feel better. Two weeks ago I was so ill that they brought me here in an ambulance because I couldn't even walk. You know that I don't know why or how I got the colibacilus [sic] through the intestines, and I had such an inflammation and pains that I thought I was going to die. They took several X rays of the kidneys and it seems that they are infected with those damn colibacilus. Now <u>I am better</u> and next Monday I will be out of this rotten hospital. I can't go to the hotel, because I would be all alone, so the wife of Marcel Duchamp invited me to stay with her for a week while I recover a little. Your telegram arrived this morning and I cried very much—of happiness, and because I miss you with all my heart and my blood ... Your letter, my sweet, came yesterday, it is so beautiful, so tender, that I have no words to tell you what a joy it gave me. I adore you my love, believe me, like I never loved anyone—only Diego will be in my heart as you—always. I haven't tell Diego a word about all this troubles of being ill—because he will worry too much—and I think in a few days I will be all-right again, so isn't it worthwhile to alarm him. Don't you think so?

Besides this damn sickness I had the lousiest luck since I arrived. In first place the question of the exhibition is all a damn mess. Until I came, the paintings were still in the custum house, because the s. of a. b. of Breton didn't take the trouble to get them out. The photographs which you sent <u>ages ago, he never received</u> So he says—the gallery was not arranged for the exhibit <u>at all</u> and Breton has not had a gallery of his own long ago. So I had to wait days and days just like an idiot till I met Marcel Duchamp (a marvelous painter), who is the only one who has his feet on the earth, among all these bunch of cuckoo lunatic sons of bitches of the surrealists. He immediately got my paintings out and tried to find a gallery. Finally there was a gallery called "Pierre Colle" which accepted the damn exhibition. Now, Breton wants to exhibit together with my paintings 14 portraits of the XIX century (Mexicans), about 32 photographs of Alvarez Bravo, and lots of popular objects he bought on the markets of Mexico—<u>all this junk,</u>

can you beat that? By the 15 of March the gallery supose [sic] to be ready. But the 14 oils of the XIX century must be <u>restored</u> and the damn restoration takes a whole month. I had to lend Breton 200 bucks (Dlls) for the restoration because he doesn't have a penny. (I sent a cable to Diego telling him the situation and telling him that I lended to Breton that money—he was furious, but now is <u>done</u> and I have nothing to do about it). I still have money to stay here till the beginning of March, so I don't have to worry so much.

Well, after things were more or less settled as I told you, a few days ago Breton told me that the associate of Pierre Colle, an old bastard and son of a bitch, saw my paintings and found that only <u>two</u> were possible to be shown because the rest are too "<u>shocking</u>" for the public!! I could of kill that guy and eaten it afterwards, but I am so sick and tired of the <u>whole affair</u> that I decided to send everything to hell, and scram from this rotten Paris before I get nuts myself. You have no idea the kind of bitches these people are. They make me vomit. They are so damn "intellectual" and rotten that I can't stand them any more. It is really too much for my character[;] I rather sit on the floor in the market of Toluca and sell tortillas than have any thing to do with these "artistic" bitches of Paris.

They sit for hours in the "cafés" warming their precious behinds, and talk without stop about "culture," "art," "revolution" and so on and so forth, thinking themselves the gods of the world, dreaming the most fantastic nonsenses, and poisoning the air with theories and theories that never come true. Next morning—they don't have anything to eat in their houses because <u>none of them work</u>, and they live like parasites off the bunch of rich bitches who admire their "genius" of "artists." <u>Shit</u> and only <u>shit</u> is what they are. I have never seen Diego or you wasting time on stupid gossip and "intellectual" discussions that is why you are real <u>men</u> and not lousy "artists" Gee whiz! It was worthwhile to come here only to see why Europe is rottening. Why all these people—good for nothing—are the cause of all the Hitlers and Mussolinis. I bet you my life I will hate this place and its people as long as I live. There is something so false and unreal about them that they drive me nuts.

I am just hoping to get well soon and scram from here.

My ticket will last for a long time, but I already have accommodations for "Isle de France" on the 8 of March. I hope I can take this boat. In any case I won't stay here any longer than

the 15 of March. To hell with the exhibition in London. To hell with
everything concerning Breton and this whole lousy place. I want to
go back to you. I miss every movement of your being, your voice,
your eyes, your hands, your beautiful mouth, your laugh so clear
and honest, YOU. I love you, my Nick. I am so happy to think I love
you—to think you wait for me—you love me ...

> *For you, my heart full of tenderness and caresses, one*
special kiss on your neck.
> > *your Xóchitl—[155]*

On Saturday, March 25, Jacqueline and Frida traveled to Le Havre, where the latter was to embark on the SS *Normandie* the following day for a five-day trip to New York. After two intense months, it was a quiet goodbye. Jacqueline presented Frida with a photograph of herself with the imprint of a kiss with pink lipstick, inscribed to *XOCHITL 25 Marzo 39. HAVRE*, and a white ruffle lace skirt with an antique blouse.[156] Frida gifted Jacqueline a purplish-red *huipil* (tunic). What else was there to say?

Through the ship's porthole, each watched the other disappear. On April 7, Jacqueline wrote Frida on a lace-trimmed paper doily, "Some of these days you'll miss me, honey," and drew another oval, framing their lives together; within the doily, she added, "The face of Frida in my dreams" and connected three ovals: the porthole, the self-portrait Frida painted for her, and *Les Heures*, the crowned queen conch that Jacqueline painted prior to their meeting (pl. 22). Much later, in December 1944, after living in Frida's home for several months, Jacqueline returned to the United States. Then, Kahlo wrote in her diary recalling their goodbye in Le Havre, when she left Jacqueline and France behind:

> *I have wanted to explain to you that I cannot break away from the*
> *days, to another time. I have not forgotten you—the nights are*
> *long and difficult ... You also know that everything that my eyes*
> *see and touch with my Self, from everything far away, is Diego ...*
> *You felt it, that is why you allowed the ship to bring me* [back]
> *from Le Havre where you never said goodbye to me.[157]*

Back in Paris, built-up tension between Jacqueline and André, over problems during Frida's visit that should have been avoided, exploded into a quarrel. Jacqueline, feeling stuck in the relationship, blamed André for making her ill. Exactly one month to the day after Frida's departure, on April 25, with Aube, Jacqueline left to visit Claude Cahun and Marcel Moore on the island of Jersey, where they stayed until May 26. To Maar she wrote, "I am interested in Claude Cahun, and I like talking with her ... She has a great sensitivity and intelligence."[158] She described how "on the beach they looked for porcelains, a thousand times more interesting than shells that surround the granite tiles on the way to the beach."[159]

At Cahun's, Jacqueline also wrote Frida a letter that begins casually but turns into a description of her helplessness and death wishes:

> I am here again about ten days and my skin is the same color [as] when you saw me the first time; that color gives me pleasure. I am smoking marvelous cigarettes and picking up the small broken shells polished by the sea—of the same kind as the one I placed for you in the green and violet box among other objects. Do you still have it?
>
> ... I am writing to you [while] sunbathing nude, facing the sea. I am in Jersey, the English island. I come from being very ill in Paris shortly after your departure. I had to leave, to rest "in the countryside." I chose this place because it's unknown, and I could no longer stay with André. He contributed a lot to this illness that came from the mental depression where I was. I came to a place where I desired nothing more than to find myself far from him, from his word and from his observations, which I received with such reluctance and dramatic fear that I would have wanted one of us to die right away—sometimes I wish HIS DEATH—other times mine, most often that.
>
> When I got up from my bed, my hair was so tangled that two teeth of the comb—that you gave me in Mexico, that I use to untangle my hair—broke off. I was in such a rage, a few days later, two of my teeth hurt me while brushing them. I imagined I would have to rip them off, then all would fall into place. But the dentist explained that it was nothing, a small accident with the gums that had become very thin in that place. But I still do not believe it's a coincidence, but a conflict I put on that comb in that state to resemble a punishment I would have liked to inflict on myself.
>
> I told André when I left that I don't love him anymore; he does not want TO BELIEVE IT—who can I tell except Dora, they all don't want to believe it—the little girl [Aube] is with me—I am again in great physical weakness, and I cannot fall asleep until morning. I am with two friends that you saw the last time ... One heals me, the other speaks to me—why aren't you here—everything would fade away—you could do anything without causing yourself

any harm. I heal quickly. The grass trembles with desire. Let others come, but I would never be done with you. I do not think I see you exactly as you are, but I know I see you better than everyone else, what is most precious in you—I see it in the most acute way and, as an "initiate" in the most ancient cults, I have that power, and you cannot ... same as if you cannot understand exactly what I want to say but you end up understanding after all. I believe I do not have any power to create, but "to look," that is power to re-create. Therefore, I cannot say what spiritual state you will be in when reading this letter, that I cannot do, naturally. Leave it if it bores you; or if it makes you smile, you will end up reading it with your hand clasped in mine.

Apparently, this is a letter of great sentimental triviality. Paris has flowed. "Le Normandie" as expected will also flow. I go so far as possible with you "this morning."

Jacqueline goes on to describe a dream that

takes place on a boat. I was already on the way, thus, I arrived yesterday in Mexico ... I leave this letter to reach you, then I will send a telegram simply with my name [on it]—if you behave well, you reply to me the same way, [with] "your name." Simply, and the same day if that is possible—if you are ill, send the telegram with another word, also unique. I'll be waiting in Paris around the same moment in 20 days. I don't miss doing it because you will receive that telegram and that you <u>cannot do otherwise</u> than reply in the same manner. You will do that or I will never believe in <u>anything</u>. Do you understand my handwriting? I practiced well, I assure you[;] I also tried to arrange the ill-written words that distracted. I write here a lot and receive letters, brought canvases to paint but I don't know what to paint [and] by the way I do not know what I will paint.

I regret a bit of not having shown you my canvases, perhaps you would have found something that would have pleased you! There is a very old one on the wall of the room, but I did not care to show it to you. Above all forget, forget very strongly the moments when I was unpleasant to you or if you cannot forgive me it's that I was badly awakened, that's it.

Remember that you made me give you a whole afternoon. That is enough. I love you.
Jacqueline

Chémilieu

In 1939, painter Gordon Onslow Ford recalled: "Paris became so powerful, [with] so many conflicts, differences of opinion, noise, trouble, that for me it became impossible to work there." That triggered his decision to look for a quiet place in the countryside for the summer.

In the spring, Onslow Ford, Roberto Matta, and painter Esteban Francés made a whirlwind trip, visiting several places. At the suggestion of Gertrude Stein—who spent summers in Bilignin, a farming community near the town of Belley in eastern France—Matta and Onslow Ford rented the Château de Chémilieu in Ain, near the Swiss border. This castle, usually empty, had for a time been rented by Balthus.[160] The owners occupied it for about three weeks of the year, only for the grape harvest. For a small sum, Onslow Ford and Matta rented it for the whole summer. With Matta's wife, Anne (known as *"Pajarito,"* little bird), and Francés, they settled there, inviting friends to join them. André arrived first, followed by Tanguy and poet/artist Kay Sage (who were by then involved), although Sage stayed at the nearby Château de Bourdeau, also in Ain. At different times, they were visited by Ithell Colquhoun, Dr. Pierre Mabille, Marcel Jean, and Onslow Ford's sister Elisabeth, as well as by Stein and Alice Toklas. Peggy Guggenheim, who had been one of Tanguy's lovers and was still interested, asked to join the party, but Tanguy—having just left his wife, Jeannette, for Sage—didn't think it was a good idea. Onslow Ford told Guggenheim that there was no more room, but she, sensing she was being given the brush-off, never forgave him. Jacqueline and Aube came too, after staying with Cahun and Moore on Jersey. Each artist took two rooms, one for sleeping and one for making art.

Stein and Toklas visited Chémilieu with writer Thornton Wilder, who, Onslow Ford recalled, observed silently the whole time. When the group visited Stein and Toklas in Bilignin, Samuel Steward, an American literature professor-turned-tattoo artist and pornographer, recorded the experience:

> *"... let's talk about the Chémilieu crowd," said Gertrude. "There's some pointers I have to give you, they're a rather strange bunch. Separately, they are fine but together they make a, what do you call them, phalanx."*
>
> *"I'm listening."*
>
> *"Well," she said, "the first thing is André Breton, he's about as big as I am, and he's the leader and everybody has to kowtow to him, and certainly you must because he founded Surrealism,*

but don't genuflect. As for me, I won't kowtow, we meet as equals.
And there's Yves Tanguy, he's all tangled up but he's a nice person.
And Matta who comes from Chile and really can paint and he's
the handsomest of the lot. Then there will be Madame Breton or
at least that's what she is and they have a little girl—well, they'll
all be coming and who knows who else—and it'll be quite a crowd
and the Rops (Henri and Madeleine) will be here too. Oh my god,
I hate parties like this I really do, and people will be taking pictures
and spilling punch all over everything the drunker they get."

Sunday July 23, 1939

"I feel that we're waiting for the hurricane," I said. "The Party."

"Me too," Gertrude said. "That's an awful bunch of people
to be having."

"When are they arriving?"

"Oh, about two o'clock," Gertrude said. "If I had my way
there'd never be more than two people here at a time and one
would be better ..."

"Well, I think if you have any preparing to do, now's the
time," Gertrude said, and I went upstairs to wash my face.

Car by car I heard at the gate. There seemed to be five or
six automobiles. I looked out the front window and could see little
but the tops of heads—one balding, one with thick wavy black
hair, another with straight brown. The Breton child was easily
identifiable—a little golden-haired girl whose clothes were an exact
copy of her mother's. I finally went downstairs. The thick wavy black
hair was Matta, and he was very handsome, with cream-colored
skin; the taller one was Tanguy, and there were several new ones
Gertrude hadn't counted on. All of them were surréalistes. It was
good to see a familiar face in the crowd, and I made straight for
Henri and Madeleine Rops.

The punch was delicious, a wine and kirsch one, and
very strong. Madame Breton took a great deal of it. She and her
daughter wore pink gypsy dresses with yellow and orange flowers.
And Madame wore a necklace with hollow glass balls, large ones,
each one partly filled with colored water.

The party went on for several hours until Jacqueline took
Aube upstairs to the bathroom and Aube tripped on the stone stairs
splitting her lip. There was a flurry of cloths to catch the blood, and
toys to distract her, while Alice applied some mysterious herbal

concoction to stop the bleeding of the cut lip. At any rate that was the reason for ending the party—and there were apologies, farewells, and invitations for everyone to visit the house near Chamonix.

"Whew," Gertrude said. "I am really glad that's ended and as far as going to visit that menagerie, not on your life."[161]

Back in Chémilieu after visiting Stein and Toklas, Sage transcribed a dinner conversation during which everyone was interested in speaking their mind but not in hearing what others were saying. Onslow Ford recalled that Aube, at three, "was the most powerful of all of us at the table. She dominated the conversation very remarkably."[162]

CHÂTEAU DE CHÉMILIEU (1939)

Scene: Dining room Château de Chémilieu

Time: Dinner

Matta: I saw a laborer ...

Breton: The only thing that counts in life is death.

Matta: ... who was counting money.

Breton: I don't understand what you saw.

Matta: A laborer counting the money he earned ...

Francés: Do you know the story of the ...

Matta: ... with the sweat of his own brow.

Breton: I don't understand what you're saying.

Tanguy: For God's sake.

Aube (mouth full of potatoes, waving her fork): FOR GOD'S SAKE!

Matta: It did affect me a lot, in spite of myself.

Francés: The story of the two men with the cheeses.

Breton: It's anti-surrealistic.

(Pajarito says something but nobody listens to her)

Jacqueline: In any case, Gertrude Stein says what she thinks.

Kay: And thinks what she says.

Breton: But what you say is anti-Marxist.

Francés: I'm telling the story of the two men with the cheeses.

Jacqueline: What has she written anyway? Have you read anything?

Kay: Yes, she has written very important things.

Gordon: Personally, I feel my whole person reborn when I hear a whistle.

Kay: Gender, it's a bitch, it would be a bitch if it were not a non-bitch.

Aube (waving her fork): BITCH!

Tanguy: They can go to hell.

Aube: (waving her knife): They can go to hell!
Matta: All the same, this laborer.
Jacqueline: Personally, for instance, I can feel this in swimming, but I don't understand it in soccer.
Francés: They fought over cheeses, so one told the other ...
Breton: I can't hear what you are saying, but it's surely anti-surrealist.
Matta (very agitated): It might be anti-surrealist or whatever you want, but the laborer has affected me a lot—after all.
Francés: He said to the other—I am going to hide the cheeses in the back.
Breton: In the front.
Aube (waving her spoon): IN THE BACK!
(Pajarito speaks but no one is listening)
Tanguy: I'm in complete agreement on this subject.[163]

The sojourn at Chémilieu had been transformative for Onslow Ford, Matta, Francés, and Jacqueline, and later was expressed in their painting. "We all made very interesting paintings," recalled Onslow Ford, "all made new things. Esteban probably made the best paintings of his life, two or three of which he made very slowly, and with great detail and great invention. Matta made a series of really extraordinary paintings and drawings, and I must have made twenty paintings, one of which is now in the Tate, London."[164]

Matta recalled: "I had never made a painting, only drawings, it was too complicated, and one year, I found this house ... Jacqueline was very young, very pretty, like a ballerina; like a medium, [she] began to take interest in these things I called 'morphologies,' in a certain way a form of surrealism."[165] But Matta's "morphologies," shaped by angst, projected a destruction and sexual violence that were dissonant to Jacqueline. She was drawn to the idea of transforming disquiet into balance. During the day, they painted, and in the evenings they talked art. Matta continued: "Everyone worked on their painting, and every few days we would take out our paintings and line them up against a whitewashed house, because it was easier to look at them against the white. Then everyone would discuss the paintings, and criticize them, and we could all see each other's mistakes or what was good in relation to the others. It was very beneficial. At night, after dinner, we played poker, wrote, painted, and spent the summer together."[166]

Rather than telling the group, Jacqueline wrote to Maar about the difficulty she was having painting at Chémilieu. Maar replied:

*In regard to painting, I am not in a better place than you, and
I see that the whole world goes the same way, including those who
have the most talent, like the black Chinaman [Wifredo Lam]
about whom I have spoken to you and who has said to console me
that the painter's life is a martyrdom, and that mine just began.
So be happy. Over all, after having left it so long ago, you have to
consider that you will go through hard times, but must continue
at all costs, otherwise you will have to begin at zero. For me, it's
a bit like when you wear laces after exercising.*

*In regard to the Midi, what I want most is that you come. I am
trying to see whether I can get to organize something, but as always
I know nothing, and nothing is certain. In about a week, I will know
better whether in the end, it will be yes or no. In Paris, abominable
weather and quiet life. I am sorry for not having written you before,
but you should see how much effort it takes me to write a letter.*

So, with this one you can judge how much I love you.
Many kisses for you, and regards to Aube.
Dora[167]

For Jacqueline, it was a new way of working at Chémilieu. Historically, she
tended to work quietly and alone, opposed to showing unfinished work. She
believed that one did not discuss one's work until it was finished, and sometimes
not even then, a rule she followed strictly until the end of her life. Onslow Ford
recalled: "Jacqueline made an important discovery when she began to get into
the inner world, where there are many colors. She had a powerful inner life,
which she kept to herself, and her painting was her way of expressing it. Her
world was original."[168]

When they left, Onslow Ford took with him some of his works and
some by Francés; most works were left behind and lost. Nothing produced by
Jacqueline survived, although discussions about morphologies were not lost on
her. After immigrating to New York in 1941, under their influence, she broke
ground and began painting her most daring work.

Onslow Ford recalled this period as a time of "great creative activity
and exchange of ideas. Breton often read poetry and talked to us in the evening.
Breton was a man who has really given a direction which will go on for centuries,
in the sense that he realized that automatism was at the root of creation, that
you have to create in the moment, something has to happen naturally and
spontaneously out of yourself."[169] Sometimes, they took day trips—to Le Palais
Idéal, the palace of stones built over thirty-three years by mail carrier Ferdinand

"Facteur" Cheval, inscribed with his poetry, inspired by a dream he recalled after tripping on a rock; or to the parish in Fareins, where, in the previous century, a parishioner of revolutionary priest François Bonjour volunteered to be crucified.

On August 21, 1939, Jacqueline wrote Frida:

> I have not had a <u>free</u> moment to write to you until this evening. The first moment when I am alone (with Aube who sleeps). It is half past eleven. I am in my bed happy to speak with you—I have spoken to you often since the boat, you know? And sometimes I feel you so near that it is even more painful <u>not to see you</u>. Also, I light for you some cigarettes around the end of the trip. You went far away. Aube came—she is not at all like in the photo, but there is something very beautiful about the way she is, her way of speaking, that hurts and intimidates me. She does not wish to leave my side for a second.
>
> And now I miss you terribly. Paris is not the same without the same activities that I expected, not yet. There is no one that I see more than Dora.
>
> I have not been to see Pierre [Colle], forgive me, I spend all my time running after a doctor who will want to take away the young child that I have in me (it's true), they are all sons of bitches that love the law.[170] As soon as I am done, I will do as you told me.
>
> Will you write to me, Frida, or don't you love me enough for that? ... I have forgotten your voice, except when you call me from far away. I don't have copies of the songs that you sang—that the gardenia leaves do not take more than half of the glass heart. That your self-portrait is always marvelous but that you only appear there from time to time, but most of the time it's a memory of you that I saw one evening and a Paris of <u>your own reality</u>—you have no idea of that evening.
>
> That I find you absolutely beautiful, that you are absolutely beautiful, that you should find yourself all done, near and far, and be one I LOVE YOU this evening, at ten minutes.
>
> I still hold onto your life always.

War

Less than two weeks before the outbreak of World War II, the group split up, each going their own way. Breton and Aube left Chémilieu to visit his parents in Lorient, and shortly thereafter he was called up to join the army and serve as a medical assistant. The next time Onslow Ford saw André was in military uniform at Les Deux Magots café in Paris—the last thing he would have imagined.

Since leaving for Jersey to stay with Cahun, Jacqueline had done what she could to avoid direct contact with André. At Chémilieu, if the group sensed the couple were having problems, nothing was said. After the stay, when André and Aube left, Jacqueline, alone again, wanted to die. She sought refuge with Maar and Picasso. But when she arrived in Paris, Maar's mother told her that they had left for the Midi, and gave her their address. Days later, again she called Maar's mother, who, realizing the gravity of Jacqueline's state, wrote to Dora on September 7: "Jacqueline has called twice to ask me for your address. She sent her daughter away from Paris and now is back." Had Jacqueline only wanted Maar's address, one call would have been enough. But Jacqueline did not call Julie Maar a second time to get Dora's address. She called because, unable to soothe herself, she felt suicidal. There was nothing in life that she felt she could hold on to that would provide a need to go on—not Aube, not her marriage, nothing within her Self. It was one of those times when she needed her mother's support, when Jane's early death came back to haunt her. Throughout her life, Jacqueline felt proud that she had survived being orphaned at seventeen. But surviving had not been enough. Jane died too soon, and Jacqueline needed her now. So, as before, when she had felt empty and visited Marianne Clouzot's mother, she was calling on Julie Maar.

In August, back in equilibrium, Jacqueline escaped the outbreak of war by retreating to the beach at the Midi with Maar and Picasso. During that stay, Picasso painted them together for the last time in *Night Fishing at Antibes*, standing on the jetty, Jacqueline sporting green hair and Maar licking an ice-cream cone. In the foreground, under a *fasquie* lamp, a man wearing a sailor's striped shirt fishes with a trident.

The Surrealist exile began before André was drafted in early September. Dalí and Matta were safe in New York; Tanguy and Sage followed them there, as would poet Nicolas Calas and painter Kurt Seligmann; Wolfgang Paalen and poet Alice Rahon were in California, with plans to settle in Mexico. Until André decided what to do next, Jacqueline and Aube shifted about with Picasso and Maar, who took them under their wing at Shady Rock, the home of patron Marie Cuttoli in

Antibes. In February 1940, before Jacqueline returned to rue Fontaine to meet André (who was briefly on leave), Picasso gave the Bretons a painting, a distorted portrait of Maar, to ease their desperate financial situation. Had they sold it, they could have lived like wealthy people for a very long time. Instead, Breton hung it at rue Fontaine, where it remained on the wall long after he died. Julie wrote to Dora: "The lack of money is a calamity—for the B[retons]. It's tough to receive alms, as well as giving them, afterward, one feels uncomfortable, bothered, and that harms even the best friendship, nothing resists that."[171]

By mid-March, Jacqueline and Aube were in Royan with Picasso and Maar, staying as the former's guests at the Hôtel du Tigre (its name an homage to Prime Minister Georges Clemenceau, known as "Le Tigre") near Boulevard Albert 1er, where Marie-Thérèse Walter and Picasso's daughter Maya lived. Maar stayed in the room painting while the mothers chatted, and Maya and Aube, the same age, played on the beach; they remained friendly into adulthood. Picasso got a kick out of people confusing the two blonde girls and their two blonde mothers on the street. Aube recalled Picasso, who liked children, being playful with her. When she passed below his window, he would drop candy for her to catch. His affection for her never waned.[172]

On October 18, 1939, Jacqueline wrote again to Frida:

> *Chula darling, I see that I have not written to you in about 4 months, since I was in Jersey. Then I went to the mountains to meet André for a month in a great house full of friends among which was Esteban Francés whom you met. Then, I left for Antibes (Côte d'Azur) to rejoin Dora and Picasso. Then, I returned to Paris until the mobilization, which forced me to stay in Paris* <u>*because of Aube,*</u> *[then] returned to Antibes with her, to the home of a lady, and in a house that bores me to death, where I have been for a month and a half and who, thanks to the devil, cannot last the whole war. We are going to go back in 3 days, and I will try to find work because there is no other way to survive. André is mobilized but really not in any military post that I know. He will give me his military allocation that I don't [yet] know, that will give me 17 francs a day for Aube and me—it will be difficult to find work in a household with Aube [but] I am forced. The good ladies that can take her momentarily and care for her while I establish a possible life will be difficult (too heavy a responsibility in time of war, etc. etc.)[,] in this case, Madame Ratton, who only knows how to complain all day with her "husband" in the house, naturally. But enough of that. I want to inform you of the general situation.*

André made me understand your telegram rather than the one of Paalen's—it is pointless to say that I would love to be at their place, that speaks for itself—you see that I write you always without knowing if you will understand again, if you will be happy to receive a letter from me. I write you much so you don't forget me through all your life changes. Today, Esteban sailed for South America to arrive to you—I don't know when and neither does he. Perhaps only in two months or three. I would like him to arrive quickly so he will know to speak to you about me, perhaps to avoid you forgetting about me absolutely. There are days when I would like so much to know what you're doing, and then I am disgusted, and I detest you because you have never written me and that you will never write me again; beyond that, I love you always tenderly, and I would like to see you. It seems to me I have changed, Frida, I have changed after your departure. I believe that it was you who made me understand a little better REAL life. I do not want to explain more here. It seems in any case that when we meet again, there will no longer be arguments, nor angers, nor sorrows. There are thousands of things that were not serious in me that are partly abolished and that you will not find in me. I do not say that specially to please you or to feel interesting. I say them because it's real and you are partly responsible for the change.

Aube has not forgotten you. I told her to write something for you, and she made a scribble and said she will show you a blue necklace and also to "Rivera." Tanguy leaves for New York in a few days and will certainly go see you, he said he'll be able.

Frida darling, will you receive this letter? I would like to be in a market with you under the full sun. I have started to work again, you know, small paintings and some watercolors here, soon, I will send you something from me. I have not sent you the telegram I said I would, in Jersey. This telegram had to be sent from Paris. Nevertheless, I did not send it because everything I had written in a state of excitement in a letter, passed (state where I thought everything possible). I no longer believe anymore in your reply and I have a terrible fear, nevertheless to wait to suffer too much from receiving nothing back—and now it's over. I don't expect anything from you. I love you as you are, and I write you when it gives me pleasure. I am in your arms. Embrace Diego and greet everyone whom you love, for me.

Jacqueline

The letter was sealed with a pink lipstick kiss, inscribed "Don't forget me." Ten days later, on Saturday, October 28, Jacqueline wrote to Maar describing conflicts within her marriage, motherhood, her affair with Francés, her "exaggerated attachment" to Frida, and work:

> *For you*
>
> *Dora, it has been a while since I wrote. Many things have happened ... and I never knew on what day I would go to Antibes. We were waiting for the return of Marie Cuttoli to leave, and she took her time. Before she came back, I spent two and a half days with Francés in Lyon ... It was quite pleasant, but beautiful and sad. He has left, who knows where to, some place in South America. Forced by his situation and, it appears also by my exaggerated attachment to something else that is not him* [i.e. Frida]. *He still loves me terribly (I feel more affection than I thought) ... He* [André] *never is what I expect from a man, mostly, after what took place in Lyon* [they spent the weekend having sex] *... Things are once again very bad with André. It would have been better staying in Antibes ...*
>
> *Here, he has me as maid, nanny. I'm in charge of the housework. I do the shopping, cook, clean. And the rest, in the afternoons, if I take Aube to daycare, which I'm going to do regardless of what André says.*
>
> *In the afternoons I could work for myself. That is, if they don't bomb Paris, because if they do, I'll have to part to another place and work for others. Well, write me soon, you must be very angry with me. Paris is horrible without you ... I think you have to work without resting a moment. Huguette in Biarritz is teaching children, at least two months.*
>
> *It's horribly cold ... With much love, Jacqueline*[173]

When Frida Kahlo returned to New York, she could not have imagined a new chapter in her life was being written. Before leaving for Paris, she had encouraged Muray to meet other "wenches," but on discovering he was doing just that, she could not face it and, on an impulse, left in April. What was the right choice for him to make? He was left in a predicament, for there was no way to win. He could no longer deny the truth about his relationship with Frida.[174] She had led him on, never intending to leave Diego, meaning to go only so far with him. As intense as their affair had been, she never lost sight of the fact that it was a passing fancy.

What did Frida really want? Only everything. She wanted Diego. She wanted Nick. Nick had been his usual self—clear, direct, upfront—but also reserved, holding back from saying what he had been observing. Perhaps he questioned what good it would do to bring it up; if there was a chance, he might lose it, so he stayed on, quietly hoping. But devotion, without questioning her motives, backfired. He finally could no longer avoid seeing that she did not care about him. What mattered to Frida was the effect she had on others, how her life revolved around the impression she made, how everything else followed. Her life was an act, and the rest—her painting, her relationships—spun out of it. Finally, Muray decided to confront her without holding back, telling her that much of her demeanor was an act: "I understand well that, on the whole, the attraction of the majority of your friends, sweethearts, lovers, husbands, revolves mostly about (you know what I mean) the sweet little number—everything else comes after, if you have energy, money, and work—if all this is convenient."[175]

Frida had been gone from Mexico nearly five months. Contrary to what she expected upon her return, Diego's welcome was divorce papers. Through the gossip Rosa Rolanda, the wife of painter Miguel Covarrubias, he learned of the affair with Muray. Frida maintained that she wouldn't have taken Muray as a lover because he was in the process of remarrying, but that did not convince Diego. Shortly thereafter she began looking for a divorce lawyer. The news reached Jacqueline through Paalen, who, having befriended Frida during her sojourn in Paris, had settled in Mexico. But, as Jacqueline explained in a letter to Frida, she could not offer condolences for she lacked the capacity to empathize with others' pain or to applaud their good fortune:

> *Tuesday 28 November 1939*
>
> *Frida Darling,*
>
> *It is difficult to tell you anything that will make sense that can help you. I can imagine the state you are in, but not enough to tell you anything worthwhile. I have always been terribly poor at finding what to say to console and also to congratulate people no matter how much I love them. My pretty one, my heart, despite distances and silences, I am always near you, never doubt one second because I search to read your thoughts and your sorrows. I see you cry and seek ways to distract you by telling you stories. I don't think about myself for a second, you must believe, [that] for you, I am no longer selfish, as when you were in Paris, I cared more about your sorrows, about your pleasure. I would like so much that you be happy <u>always</u>. If I had the money, I would come immediately to see you. You know that, don't you?*

I don't know how that story arrived. Paalen did not have any comment, therefore, perhaps it didn't matter to him to know the reasons for all that, because the least detail of that which touches you matters to me, and maybe I will see more clearly to tell you anything. Yet, I know you will not write me. And as always I am left to tell myself stories ... do not think for a second that I wanted that, I didn't want to write. You are that way: that is all.

I would like to tell you also that I believe you [are] STRONG, that I have an immense trust in your strength. As you are, do not allow yourself to be <u>deeply</u> torn down by anything, you're the one to care about the most. And I know that it was that way for you with Diego. Frida darling, you have all my friendship, all my tenderness, all my trust, beyond life, that does not allow you to be beaten for a second. You have a very great number of friends who love you and admire you, and your smile is also as precious as the sun, the air can't take it. You are young and you are STRENGTH ITSELF.

I embrace you tenderly
Yo te quiero
Jacqueline

Air-Bel

On June 14, 1940, as Hitler took France and the Germans marched into Paris, the French government collapsed and the country split. The Nazis occupied the northern territory, and in the Unoccupied Zone to the south, the new French State established its seat in Vichy. Jacqueline recalled:

As the phony war was drawing to a close, the whole army had been thanked for its excellent service, which had not lasted that long. M. [Philippe] Pétain was making arrangements with Hitler. I was actually with Aube and Picasso and Dora in Royan. I received a telegram [from André] telling me to join him because he wanted at that point to go to America, and that he found this committee and wanted to sign up for departure as soon as possible, so I left the others, to my great regret, otherwise I would have stayed.[176]

Days later, André, Jacqueline, and Aube met at the home of Pierre Mabille, the Surrealists' physician, in Martigues, Salon-de-Provence, on the Mediterranean, near Marseilles—the only seaport in the Unoccupied Zone. Jacqueline recalled: "There were peasants who lent us things, a well for water. I did the cooking in the garden, in a wood-burning fireplace. There, we waited for the [American Rescue] Committee to decide whether to accept André."[177]

Thanks to Victor Serge—Russian Trotskyite, historian, poet, and refugee—André and Jacqueline were added to the Committee's list of artists, writers, and political dissenters saved by Varian Fry, the head of the Committee. It was Serge's way of thanking Breton. While Serge spent two years imprisoned in the Soviet Union for speaking out against Stalin, André had loudly defended him and challenged French Stalinists on his behalf.

Between October 1940 and March 1941, the Bretons lived in the Villa Bel-Air, a three-story nineteenth-century farmhouse half an hour from Marseilles, rechristened "Air-Bel" by the group. Serge was there with his companion Laurette Séjourné and his son Vlady. Villa Air-Bel, furnished with bourgeois accoutrements—gilt furniture and mirrors and landscape paintings—was detested by the Surrealists, who referred to it as "the château." "The two drawing rooms and the dining room on the first floor," wrote militant socialist Daniel Bénédite, "which are too gloomy during the day, are occupied only in the evenings and when one is about to sit down for dinner around the huge table, and seated with a certain solemnity on high-back chairs ... surmounted by lions holding coats of arms in their claws ... [Vlady] has taken pleasure in affixing to the massive tarnished frames golden tablets on which he has handwritten 'Nicolas Poussin,' 'Hubert Robert,' 'Attributed to Claude Lorrain,' 'The Ingres School.'"[178] Air-Bel was enclosed like a fortress, the walks and garden were overrun by weeds, and the hedges had not been trimmed in years. The Mediterranean, however, could be seen across the valley.[179]

With nostalgia, Jacqueline recalled the group's camaraderie, the solidarity: "It was marvelous, and I regret to say it was during a particular period ... André was pessimistic, but I have never spent such a happy time in my life as there. It's being very egotistical, but I was surrounded by a whole host of people, groups arriving from Paris ... the most civilized people I have ever met."[180] Many who had been making contributions were attempting to obtain immigration visas.

Five years earlier, in 1935, Fry had visited Berlin as correspondent for the American journal *The Living Age*. There, he watched in helpless horror a Nazi stabbing the hand of a Jew sipping his beer, pinning it to the table. Impelled by the trauma of that memory and by other horrors he had witnessed, Fry created the American Rescue Committee on August 14, 1940, in Marseilles. With a group of ardently anti-Nazi friends and the support of US First Lady Eleanor Roosevelt, he helped some 4,000 "undesirable persons" to escape death at the hands of the Nazi regime—writers, scientists, artists (including a number of Surrealists), refugees from the Spanish Civil War, Jews, and stateless persons. Jacqueline remembered Fry as a spiritual person: "I have never met such a being. He gleamed, really like a priest. It could be seen in his face, in his eyes. He was a warm person."[181]

Fry's collaborators were Bénédite, Bénédite's wife, Theo, and anti-fascist Jean Gemähling, militant in the Resistance. To the last named, "the villa's unconventional inhabitants and weekend guests were totally bizarre. Jacqueline, stiletto-tongued and sexy, went shopping adorned with bracelets around her ankle and a fake bird pinned in her hair. Tall and beautiful, eccentrically dressed, she must have looked like a conqueror to the local villagers at the market," Gemähling recalled.[182] Jacqueline remembered admiringly Mary Jayne Gold, an American heiress who gave up her lavish life in Paris when World War II broke out. Joining Fry and other volunteers, she helped to subsidize an operation that eventually saved two thousand lives.

Laurette and Jacqueline accompanied Madame Nouget, the cook, to the market. Sweeping the terrace and firewood duties were shared between Victor, Vlady, and André, and no one tried to shirk their job. André did not show the least outburst of temper when his literary activity was interrupted: "Oh, that's right, I was about to forget. I will go right away." Far from being distant, he often showed unexpected kindness. One night, when Rose—a cleaning woman and a drinker who helped Madame Nouget from time to time—fell down the stairs and was lying in a pool of vomit, howling with pain, André was the first to rush to the scene. He picked her up carefully, carried her to the third-floor room he shared with Jacqueline and Aube, and came down to say that the poor woman had not broken a bone, and to let her sleep off her wine before leaving.[183]

Fry recalled: "Jacqueline Breton, André's Surrealist wife, was blonde and beautiful and savage, with painted toenails, necklaces of tiger's teeth, and bits of mirror glass in her hair. Aube, their four-year-old daughter, was already hailed by the Surrealists as a promising artist. Laurette Séjourné, Victor Serge's friend, was a woman as unlike Jacqueline as Jacqueline was unlike everybody else. She was dark and quiet and reserved."[184] Vlady Serge, seventeen years old and a budding artist himself, was awestruck by Jacqueline, and followed her with his eyes from a distance, too shy to approach, watching her exercise daily on her trapeze, imagining her a circus performer. He never heard her utter a word or even knew she was a painter; to him, she was a presence. Finally, unable to divert his gaze, he drew her portrait in bright colors.[185] Jacqueline recalled: "Serge's son was a marvelous sweet boy," but she also never spoke to him.[186]

As usual, André's ability to bring artists together in a creative frenzy took over at various times at Air-Bel, especially on Sundays, when they were joined by other Surrealists: Victor Brauner, René Char, Max Ernst, Óscar Domínguez, Marcel Duchamp, Jacques Hérold, Wifredo Lam and his partner Helena Holzer, Peggy Guggenheim, André Masson, Benjamin Péret, Tristan Tzara, and Remedios Varo. Photographs of the group and their activities were taken by André Gomès, husband of art dealer Henriette Gomès (pl. 24).

André's invented games encouraged the group's expression of its collective experience. One was a new form of exquisite corpse designed to include several participants. A theme was chosen, and each member drew or made a collage; when placed side by side on a large sheet of paper, these became a visual narrative (pl. 26). Jacqueline noticed that, free of pressure, her art veered away from orthodox Surrealist iconography. At Air-Bel, she reported, "I was really taken with painting, because in painting one has a chance"—by which she meant she was free to do as she pleased.[187] But even away from the governing principles of Surrealist imagery, she did not waver from "light" and "freedom," her obsessions. In one drawing, she explored a dark street corner lit by a lamppost; in another, a bird soaring toward the sun.

"Playing was serious," Jacqueline asserted.[188] It was André's way of doing creative work with tension in the air, drawn from within the group. Their historic collaboration was "*Le Jeu de Marseille*," a deck of cards exhibited the following year at the MoMA in New York, and subsequently printed. It followed the traditional playing deck format but used instead Surrealist themes and subjects. The deck was drawn by Brauner, Breton, Domínguez, Ernst, Hérold, Lam, Lamba, and Masson, and Frédéric Delanglade drew the verso.[189] The four suits were Love (a flame); Dream (a black star); Knowledge (a lock); and Revolution (a bleeding paddle-wheel). Jacqueline drew the last of these, basing her imagery on the notion that revolutions cause cycles of bloodshed (pl. 28).

The American Rescue Committee not only helped people to leave Europe legally, but also smuggled money and falsified papers for those who could only escape illegally, and at some point each person at the château contributed. One evening, shortly before one of the Committee members was expected with 40,000 francs in stolen postal orders, a commissaire arrived to inquire about a small suitcase that arrived for Huguette Lamba, who was visiting Marseilles to say goodbye. When he began asking questions, Jacqueline asked Holzer: "What kind of trouble has that simple girl gotten into now?"[190] From Huguette, they learned that she had become pregnant after a brief liaison with a Spanish Republican, a prisoner of war in a camp near Biarritz. She found out only after she returned to Paris.[191] Jacqueline, impatient yet worried, tried convincing her to depart with them to the United States. But Huguette did not wish to travel pregnant; and, not speaking English, she could not imagine what life she could have there. After three months at Air-Bel, she went home. The small suitcase that had caused so much trouble contained only sheet music.

In searching the château, the commissaire came upon one of the collaborative collages on which Breton had written "*Ce terrible crétin de Pétain*," (that terrible moron Pétain), confirming the officer's suspicion that the occupants of Air-Bel were infiltrating Marseilles with Communist propaganda. As Breton attempted to explain that the word should have been *putain* (whore), the "smuggler" arrived. According to Gold's recollection:

> *My eyes fell on Jacqueline's lithe body, tense with controlled anger as she watched André's interrogation. Her weight was on one foot, and with the other she was gently tapping the floor. She could certainly take a man's mind off his duties.*
>
> *"Jacqueline," I whispered, coming up behind her, "go flirt with that policeman over there by the door."*
>
> *"Me flirt with a policeman! What do you take me for?"*
>
> *"We have to cause a distraction. Buy some time, please. Please."*
>
> *"Ah, bon."*
>
> *She turned straight around and made for her man, her hips swaying a little more than usual. With what must have been one of the most enchanting smiles in France, I heard her say, "Ah, monsieur l'Officier, why do you give us such hard time?"*
>
> *The fellow was quite overcome with pleasure and stammered something about doing his duty. On the contrary, he would only like to please her. André who caught the scene out of the corner of one eye, turned toward them and muttered "Stupefiant [amazing]."*
>
> *That short moment was long enough to hide the smuggled postal orders behind a painting, at the foot of the stairs.*[192]

On August 20, 1940, Leon Trotsky was assassinated in Mexico when "Jacques Mornard" (Ramón Mercader) struck him from behind with a pickax whose point cracked his skull and entered his brain. The Bretons and the Riveras managed to speak on the telephone. Afterward, Frida wrote to Jacqueline and copied the letter into her diary: "The death of the old man hurt us so much that on that day we spoke and we cried together."[193]

Aube took in her parents' reaction to the murder and, duly impressed, informed Gold next morning: "Papa cried a lot last night." At school she caused a commotion by describing the event to the other children, who, mesmerized, listened to details of the assassination. This upset the parents, and a commissaire told André:

> *I am very embarrassed, sir, but your daughter is perhaps—oh, but so unknowingly—partly responsible for the incident. She is tall, blonde, very alert, and speaks to the point. She is a little queen in the midst of this group of smallish, swarthy kids with their hardly polished language, and who are subject to her—yes—I think that's the word. What brings me here today is that I overheard a curious conversation. Aube was saying, "My papa was very sad when he learned about the old man," or something like that. Her infant court was asking her—and the questions led one to believe that it was not the first time that Aube had spoken about this old person. Who is this old man that you speak about all the time, was it your grandfather? "Of course not," your daughter replied with a superior voice, "It's Trotsky, for goodness sake!" The parents of pupils are not on our level, you know.[194]*

In November, Jacqueline did not want to celebrate her birthday. She confided to Holzer her fear of aging: "In turning thirty, my life has come to an end."[195] Despite Jacqueline's obvious femininity, Holzer noticed an androgynous quality in her looks and behavior, which gave her an alluring presence: "Jacqueline looked like a young boy. Her features were very strong, masculine, and her voice was raspy and deep like a young boy's. She was aggressive like a man. Even in dealings with men, she always wanted to be the dominant partner in any relationship. With me, no, we were good friends. I guess she realized I could be as harsh as she was. Breton had to do what she told him, which he often camouflaged, making it appear that he was the one who decided things."[196]

In the quiet of the day, Breton, still very much in love with Jacqueline, wrote "Fata Morgana" for her, a sorrowful 500-line poem about individuals in a landscape where reality and fantasy overlap. The title—one of his affectionate names for his wife—is a reference to Morgan le Fay, the fairy sorceress of Arthurian legend, and alludes to Jacqueline's illusion-creating abilities in water. He writes:

> *... Because you hold*
> *Within me the place of the diamond set in a pane of glass*
> *That would point out to me in minute detail the rigging of*
> *the stars*

Two hands seeking each other suffice for tomorrow's roof
Two transparent hands yours the murex from which the
ancients drew my blood ...[197]

Jacqueline thrived on the attention, and in the company of the group she momentarily forgot her troubles, including her conflict with André, leading him to believe (mistakenly) that their problems were over. Jacqueline recalled: "I was happy, in other words, selfish. Those were the Surrealists. What did you expect us to do? One had to hold on. One wasn't at any rate to go sobbing into a synagogue. It would have been stupid to do that. We did what we had done before, we just continued."[198]

While preparing illustrations for "Fata Morgana," Lam drew an intuitive portrait of the Bretons, revealing the role each played in the family (pl. 25). Jacqueline, knife in hand, looks straight ahead, disregarding André and Aube. Using André as a stool, she sits on his back, while Aube, arms open for a hug, seeks Jacqueline's attention by holding a mirror to her mother's face.

For Helena's birthday in January, Breton gathered in a small notebook drawings made for her by friends, including Aube, Brauner, Domínguez, Hérold, Huguette, Jacqueline, and himself. Jacqueline worked a long time on her contribution. Carefully, she constructed a detailed collage out of fragments of black-and-white illustrations she clipped from an old book and illuminated lightly with watercolor. A woman in a landscape stands alone on a steep, narrow rocky formation facing the empty flatland and distant sea. On the horizon line, a flowered disk and a treetop are partially submerged in the ocean. A white moon, haloed in black, glows in a gray sky.

It was a cold winter in Marseilles, made worse by the scarcity of food at the château and people having to sleep in their coats.

The Christmas Tree of the World

On March 25, 1941, thanks to Peggy Guggenheim's patronage, Jacqueline, André, and five-year-old Aube sailed to New York via Martinique and Santo Domingo on the SS *Capitaine Paul-Lemerle*. Among the travelers were Victor and Vlady Serge, with Séjourné; Hebraic scholar Oscar Goldberg; anthropologist Claude Lévi-Strauss; and Holzer and Lam. During the trip, Lévi-Strauss developed a friendship with Breton but, "except that she was strikingly beautiful, my recollections of Jacqueline Lamba are few. During our sea travel to Martinique, I was not yet aware she was a painter. To me, she was only Breton's wife."[199] Jacqueline and Holzer had met in the fall of 1939 but grew closer in Marseilles. Holzer told the present author: "We enjoyed being together. Jacqueline was courteous and discreet. At least, she and I had a very good relationship, cordial with lively dialogues; no gossip or intimate details were ever discussed, not with Jacqueline or with other females. We all had a lot more serious problems on our mind."[200]

The Bretons arrived in New York at the end of May on the Dominican cargo ship SS *Presidente Trujillo*, from Fort-de-France, Martinique. Their first home, a fifth-floor walk-up in Greenwich Village at 265 West 11th Street, was found and furnished for them by Kay Sage. She had two rooms with red floors, small but bright, the access to which was via a metal stairway. Guggenheim not only paid for the voyage, but also gave them a 200-dollar monthly stipend until André could find work in New York. Upon their arrival, Jacqueline wrote to Frida:

> *Good morning Cherished Frida. Perhaps you have forgotten me.*
> *I want to greet you arriving here where everything is so amazing.*
> > *We had a terrible and magnificent trip.*
> > *Embrace Diego.*
> > *I send you all my tenderness.*
> > *Jacqueline*

(She sealed it with two lipstick kisses, one by herself and one by Aube.)

When Jacqueline wrote to Fry on June 24, she apologized for not writing sooner and described her experience:

> *Everything is different from what it was like for Christopher*
> *Columbus;* [but] *no less marvelous. The trip a bit similar to his,*

I don't remember how long [his] *was, but ours, pretty disgusting and beautiful, was two and a half months. Your wife, whom I especially liked very much, received us marvelously; I found her very lucid and particularly sweet—(I think sweetness is lacking in women around here) ... I still don't know if I like New York, everything is much too new to pretend to like it at such cost. What is for sure is that America is the Christmas tree of the world.*[201]

Being able to eat what she wanted and when she wanted in New York, Jacqueline could not help but recall the frugal meals at the château and recognize her good fortune. In September, she wrote to Dora Maar in red ink:

We are living in an apartment in the artist's [sic] *quarter with a very pretty studio (skylight!), a room for me and another for André ... There are more antique shops than in a whole neighborhood in Paris. But I don't want to buy anything, even if I could, because it would be a bad omen for the duration here. To be seen, the only bearable people are Nicolas* [Calas], *Gordon* [Onslow Ford] *(who is leaving) and Yves* [Tanguy] *who is unfortunately handsome and married to the "princess," the worst ever emmerdeuse* [pain in the ass] [Sage]. *Yves does not speak, you can see that from here. Marie Cuttoli is here. We speak tenderly about P*[icasso]. *There is a wonderful complete show on him at the Barr Museum* [MoMA], *ranging from the Moulin de la Galette to Guernica. You appeared so often* [in the paintings], *I shed several bitter tears ... Mme Gugg*[enheim] *is helping us* [with expenses]. *She's going to create a museum for her collection. She is angry because she has nothing from the father of the Demoiselles d'Avignon, which I finally saw at Barr's and which I adore. She's running everywhere to have some, but everything is too expensive despite André's protestations ... André is bored to death ... we are thinking about going to Frida's place whence "S"* [Esteban Francés] *is writing me romantic letters. Convey all my affection as well as André's to the one you love best. There is a primitive painter aged 67 years here, absolutely sensational. Something of a medium* [Morris Hirshfield].[202]

Unable to hold back, Jacqueline bought a large plant, which she placed in the living room. She followed it with another, and another, and another, until the earthenware pots overflowed with Douanier Rousseau-like vegetation; the smaller pots crowded the balcony, and morning glories mingled their petals with green moss suspended in space. Poet Charles Duits remembered Jacqueline sitting surrounded by plants like a nude Jadwiga in Henri Rousseau's jungle painting *The Dream* (1910).[203]

Most significantly, the move to New York had an overall positive effect on Jacqueline. As her chronic irritation toward André toned down, a sense of wonder awakened by New York emerged in her painting. Once settled, she described to Maar her studio, where she painted under a skylight: "Now I am working in a completely serious way, to such an extent that I cannot possibly understand how I could have managed to avoid it before."[204] Although André was gradually adapting, he missed his treasures at rue Fontaine. But he felt immediately better once Dolorès Vanetti, now living in New York, took him to meet Julius Carlebach at his gallery of antiquities—which became a haven for the Surrealists—where Breton acquired a Teotihuacán funerary mask.

Back in 1936, Vanetti, then a rising actress at the Théâtre Montparnasse, had been working in Paris under the direction of playwright Gaston Baty when she met Theodore Ehrenreich, an American medical student at the Sorbonne.[205] An exquisite beauty with perfect olive skin and doe eyes, Vanetti was intelligent, unpretentious, and universally liked. By the time she left France, she had met and become friends with everyone who became someone—from Albert Camus to Picasso, from Lévi-Strauss to Jacques Prévert and Marcel Duchamp. In 1940, after Vanetti moved to the United States to marry Teddy Ehrenreich, she worked as a broadcast journalist for the Office of War Information as "Nancy Smith" on the Voice of Free France.[206] She wrote for *Vogue* and later authored *The Querulous Cook* (1963); she smuggled a slow loris from Thailand in her handbag and kept it as a pet. Over the next fourteen years, even after Jacqueline returned to France, Vanetti was Jacqueline's friend and confidante. In 1945, when Jean-Paul Sartre visited New York, he fell in love with Dolorès; he spent several months with her and he was back the following year. Smitten, he returned to Paris and paid for her divorce. His mother was certain they would marry, but she was mistaken.[207]

As a couple, Jacqueline and André were making an indelible impression in public. "Together they looked wonderful, very unique people, something about them escaped definition, utterly fascinating. They seemed very well matched," recalled Ethel Baziotes, wife of artist William Baziotes, who first met them at one of Guggenheim's parties.[208] Poet and artist Mina Loy recalled "André having the expression of an outrageous man and Jacqueline resembling a reanimated mummy of an Egyptian sorceress." Unaware that the source of Surrealism was the unconscious, Loy wrote: "People who get mixed up with black magic do suddenly look like death's heads."[209]

But the Bretons' reality was more prosaic, and Jacqueline's dormant discontent would soon come to the boil in New York. Conflict began as their roles in the art community were reversed, proving difficult for André. In France, he lived in the limelight; when he spoke, everyone, including Jacqueline, listened. Now, his refusal to speak English—fearful of making a mistake—forced him into the background. In France, his admirers were everywhere. In the United States, he had no special status and was considered just another Surrealist. He felt neglected. While Jacqueline, fluent in English, translated and drew attention with her knowledge and openness, Breton, unable to adapt, became like a "caged lion."[210] As positive acknowledgment fed into Jacqueline's sense of security, she became more sure of herself. Word got around that their marriage was teetering.

André, who had known Anaïs Nin in Paris, met again with her in New York. During one evening, they "talked about hypnosis and all the writers we believed clairvoyant or prophetic." That night, she dreamed:

> *that he and his wife embarked on my houseboat, and that a huge transatlantic ocean liner brushed by and set it heaving and rearing like a wild horse, breaking its mooring. Then my houseboat started to whirl, eddying vertiginously among icebergs. Mme. Breton was very angry with me. I felt we would soon be shattered to bits. We collided with an iceberg. On this iceberg stood two masons quietly mixing cement. I asked them to help us. They suggested a coat of cement at the bottom of the houseboat, to give it stability. I watched its operation with sadness. It seemed to me that the cement would make it heavy and that it would never float again.[211]*

Before André and Jacqueline arrived in New York, Joseph Cornell, influenced by Max Ernst's collages, had exhibited his work in a group show at Julien Levy's Gallery of Surrealism in 1932, and his *Soap Bubble Set* in MoMA's *Fantastic Art, Dada and Surrealism* in 1936. Mesmerized by the allure of women, Cornell created a number of poetic portraits in various mediums. Some were exhibited in December 1946 at the Hugo Gallery in a show titled *Portraits of Women: Constructions and Arrangements by Joseph Cornell*. He renamed the gallery "The Romantic Museum" for the show, and the invitation reproduced his *Penny Arcade for Lauren Bacall*. Among other women whose portraits were in the show were Fanny Cerrito, Eleonora Duse, Greta Garbo, Hedy Lamarr, and Jennifer Jones. In Cornell's journal, where he described ideas for turning moments of intuition into projects, was a reference to Jacqueline's arrival: "Jacqueline Breton, walls lined with 'flotsam and jetsam' material. Analogy to virtuosity of fashioning all manner of gadgets, imprisoning strips in bottles, scrimshaw, whale's teeth. Museums in old whaling centers. New Bedford [Whaling Museum]."[212]

After Jacqueline and André returned to France, their visions of the experience were diametrically different. André spoke as if he'd been living in a wasteland, where there was nothing to do, where he did not make a friend, even with one American. That, of course, was inaccurate. Everyone in the art world knew who he was, and he'd made good friends with Arshile Gorky and his wife, Mougouch. But his alienation made him feel an outsider. In turn, Jacqueline could not get enough attention. "She adored the United States," recalled friend Dominique Noailles. "I believe it marked her life completely. She adored everything she had done with David Hare, the trips with him, the Indians. She always wore Indian bracelets. She had Indian artifacts at home. Indian things were part of her soul. She had a lot of respect and admiration for them."[213]

VVV Almanac

Jacqueline and André's excitement did not rub off on Aube, who at five had become accustomed to being dragged around by grown-ups. In New York, she was disregarded and left to entertain herself for long periods while her parents distracted themselves with new projects: Jacqueline immersed in painting, and André in assembling the magazine *VVV Almanac*.[214] Jacqueline walked her daughter in the mornings to the Little Red Schoolhouse at 196 Bleecker Street, where the education was more experiential than intellectual, and she walked her back home in the afternoons. Aube was unable to speak English, so the other children bullied her and she felt out of place. In the morning, should she complain when Jacqueline pulled hard to remove the tangles from her long hair, her mother would slap her until she learned to keep quiet.[215]

That was the beginning of Aube's resentment of her mother's painting. She saw how the minimal interest Jacqueline had once placed in her waned steadily: "I had the feeling she was putting me aside for her painting, that her painting was far more important for her than I was." Aube recalled less the apartment where they lived than the experience she was having:

> *The first apartment, I don't see it anymore. Lots of sadness and boredom and loneliness. I don't know why. Just that I couldn't find a place for myself and an occupation for myself. Probably because they had just arrived, and they were unorganized, they had me,*

*which was very unusual. And outside these periods, they left me with
friends. There were children there. I have the memory of playing
with bottle caps of Coca-Cola on top of the table for hours and
being bored for hours. In David's apartment, he had a kinkajou
in a cage. David made a huge cage, as big as possible, because
the kinkajou was a nocturnal creature, which they didn't know.
He bought it for Jacqueline. She loved animals, to a certain point.
I don't know who loved them best, David or Jacqueline. In the
daytime, sometimes he [the kinkajou] got out, hanging up, they
have long tails, and he'd hang on Jacqueline's trapeze by his long
tail, and sleep with his head down. I was fascinated by him, and
I would play with him.*"[216]

Steady income from Kay Sage and Peggy Guggenheim brought financial security
to the Breton marriage, but it also drove a wedge between husband and wife.
Jacqueline became a different person: focused on painting, she showed little
interest in what went on around her or in others. Leonora Carrington, who
had escaped Europe in 1941 and joined her friends in New York, babysat. One
day she witnessed André's arrival, asking what was for dinner; Jacqueline, busy
painting, told him to look in the refrigerator. When he opened the door, he
spotted a sardine on the bottom and became livid. Raising his voice had no
effect: "What is a sardine doing on the bottom of the refrigerator?"[217] Without
looking, Jacqueline replied that she didn't know. What André feared most was
happening before his eyes. She was painting—she was not about to stop and
find out. He had lost control of her; immersed in painting, she was slipping away.

In later years, she recalled that "André did not approve" of her new
work, but it was unlikely her painting was the root of the problem. Rather,
he experienced her freedom as a form of neglect, like the time, seven years
previously, when he realized he had lost control of Giacometti. Carrington
surmised: "He didn't approve of Jacqueline's painting because it pulled her [away]
from the stove. He was a real *cabron* [bastard]; the *macho* would come out."[218] In
1946, when the writer André Thirion asked, without naming Jacqueline, "what
the war, exile, and time had done to the woman who had inspired *L'Amour Fou*,"
André confessed that their marriage had not endured, that absurd details had
destroyed everything: "She was incapable of turning off a faucet," he added, "Can
you imagine how irritated a man can get in a hotel room or a tiny apartment if
the other person never turns off the faucets?"[219] Breton also had not referred
to Jacqueline by name. If for no other reason, this would explain why she left
him. In his mind, she was a non-person, a woman without identity. Yet, after
divorcing, they remained friends on her terms.

David Hare

In June 1942, the first issue of *VVV Almanac* came off the press in New York. André Breton intended to produce a journal that would attract work by exiled artists and members of other disciplines—plastic arts, poetry, anthropology, psychology, and sociology—as well as disseminate the ideas of Surrealism. The title, *VVV Almanac*, alluded to Victory over the forces of regression and death, double Victory over all that is opposed to emancipation of the spirit, and triple Victory, taking into account what occurs beneath appearances. With the war raging, though, the name of a foreign editor on the masthead would be unacceptable. André needed an American editor with experience. As an artist and writer, Robert Motherwell was the ideal choice, but the decision came down to money, so photographer David Hare (Kay Sage's first cousin) got the job. André wrote to Benjamin Péret: "*VVV* appeared under the direction of David Hare, ... extremely friendly, dedicated, and positive. But he speaks only English, that should give you an idea of the difficulties in which I find myself being so knowledgeable in this language."[220] (The conclusion of this sentence was ironic; André's English was poor, and he knew it.) Hare had no experience of editorial work. Learning difficulties—he was dyslexic and could never spell— had prevented him from mastering the school curriculum. In 1929, his mother founded Fountain Valley School, a progressive boarding school for boys, where he could learn at his own pace without worrying about passing exams.[221]

David Meredith Hare was born in New York City on March 10, 1917, the only child of Elizabeth Manning Sage Goodwin and her second husband, Meredith "Bunny" Hare. David was a scrawny boy who had difficulty learning to read and write but "had a feel for the land."[222] His mother had studied painting, had been a backer of the Armory Show in 1913, was friends with Constantin Brâncuși, Marcel Duchamp, and Walter Kuhn, and a lifelong supporter of the arts. David was not quite ten when his father, to whom he was very attached, contracted tuberculosis and the family moved to the American West seeking a climate cure. While living in Colorado Springs, David received a chemistry set as a gift and caused an explosion in the basement—not bad enough to do serious damage, but good enough to arouse serious curiosity; he decided to study chemistry. After receiving as a Christmas gift a one-shot Jos-Pe Tri-Color Camera that held three glass plates and filters to capture faithful flesh tones, he developed an interest in the chemistry of photography.[223]

Charles Duits, a friend, recalled that David "belonged to one of those rich and broken families in which the children have a different mother or father and who, growing up amongst savage love and divorces, learn quickly to depend on themselves. David had an unusual childhood. Undisciplined, he had been expelled from many schools and had spent a relatively long time in the desert areas of Arizona among the American Indians. He was more at ease naked than wearing clothes, and being out in the sun than indoors ... He always had a tool in his hand and, when one was lacking, he crafted it."[224]

For the purposes of *VVV Almanac*, David would be used as a "front," so his lack of experience did not matter. Breton, Duchamp, and Ernst would be doing the editorial work. Fortunately, David was gifted. His dyslexia turned out to be an asset; it made him talented in design, a natural Surrealist. His vast knowledge of photography—informed by Belgian photographer Raoul Ubac, who produced ghostlike imagery by heating negatives before printing them—was extraordinary. But, since David did not speak French and neither Breton nor Ernst spoke English, Jacqueline was brought in to translate: "The minute David saw her, he fell head over heels."[225] As their affair developed, for the first issue of *VVV Almanac* Jacqueline contributed a photo collage of a night scene, with a couple gazing into the heavens, a puzzle integrated by various skies, some starry, some cloudy. The woman is shaped out of a fishing net, through which one can see the ocean. David contributed a photograph, *The Retroactive Wish as a Reality*, one of several nude portraits of Jacqueline printed from a heated negative.[226] Before their affair was exposed, Carrington watched over Aube, covering for Jacqueline during their secret trysts. Carrington recalled Aube, starved of attention, using an admixture of endearing and tyrannical traits to get it. But mostly, they had fun together playing the candle game or hide-and-seek, or acting out invented stories with character dolls that Carrington fashioned out of sanitary napkins she painted with glow-in-the-dark colors.[227]

Sensing something was off, Breton wrote to Péret on August 27: "Silence—considerable depression. Quite unhappy. I can hardly give you a sign of life, I am sorry. You know I think of you. Everything in life is very dark; as far as Jacqueline, incomprehensible, moving further away."[228] He had been looking at photos taken in Marseilles that he had not seen before, in which they are together, seemingly happy. He almost regretted those days. A week later, on September 3, Péret replied: "I am sorry to know you are depressed, and I hope, especially for Jacqueline, that it is like one of those episodes she went through before."[229] On October 22, Breton wrote back that he and Jacqueline had separated. "Ooh la la! So that is why we haven't been writing. Ooh la la! We're 'working,' we're 'making a living,' we're speaking English as brilliantly as ever, and we're even living all alone."[230] On November 1, Péret wrote: "Jacqueline's parting hit me more than I expected, given the tone of your last letter. It's truly irritating! Although I was expecting it a little."[231]

On leaving, Jacqueline gifted André a life-affirming drawing in soft, hazy pastel colors using paper ground as a source for light, with translucent hills and valleys, populated with the archetypal objects that she and David had made together and reproduced in *VVV*. The phallic shape, evidently representing David, would become a recurrent motif in her work. She inscribed it *Pour André Breton dessin pour la vie* (For André Breton Design for Life, 1942). "If you leave me," he warned, "I will destroy you."[232] At that moment, André's threat meant nothing—Jacqueline just wanted out. Moving in with David offered no guarantees, but she had had enough of being "the wife of André Breton." Jacqueline was anxious for a change, ready to leave the marriage regardless of the consequences.

Back in 1935, when Hare met Susanna Wilson, her mother, Frances Perkins, was Secretary of Labor under President Franklin D. Roosevelt. Their mothers were friends, and the adolescents liked each other. Suzy was bright, pretty, personable, and working toward her art history degree at Bryn Mawr, with an interest in archeology—co-authoring with Edith Porada (archaeologist from Columbia University) a study of Assyria's tyrannical king Sennacherib. David was a handsome, bright young man who had entered Bard College to study chemistry but left after one semester. When Suzy confided in him that she "wanted to get out from under the heel of [her] mother," and he confessed that he "wanted out of the control of [his] mother," they agreed to marry.[233] But their mothers would not allow it until both turned twenty-one. On December 3, 1938, the couple celebrated their wedding in New York's Church of the Resurrection.[234]

When Sage returned to the United States from France and worked to help artists escape France, she was instrumental in rescuing the Bretons by contacting Perkins directly and having Suzy sign affidavits for the Breton family. Sixty years later, Suzy recalled signing Jacqueline's affidavit to help her immigrate, because she was married to a poet: "I regretted it," she said, adding, "that bitch was a very unpleasant person, not a roughneck, except in her morals. Jacqueline had not been among those worth saving."[235]

Suzy's appendix had recently been removed, and she was convalescing at home in Roxbury, Connecticut, when David arrived in 1942 with Jacqueline and Aube. Friendly since their arrival in New York, the three of them had recently worked together at the Reid Law Mansion with Duchamp installing white twine to envelop the ceiling, the partitions, and the works themselves for the forthcoming show *First Papers of Surrealism*, opening on October 14.

Jacqueline and Aube's stay at the house did not go well. Aube, hungry for affection, immediately took to Suzy; later, when Jacqueline would yell at her, Aube would react, "Why can't you be more like Suzy?" Initially, Suzy—unaware of what was going on—assumed they were visiting for a few days. But as time passed and they did not leave, she asked David, who replied that they were staying and it was she who was leaving. Suzy and David had been married four years when he informed her, short of throwing her out of the house, that he was divorcing her for Jacqueline. Suzy recalled vividly the night she left, going directly to her mother-in-law's home.[236] Later, David claimed the marriage was annulled because he had "been misled about Suzy's mental illness,"[237] despite the *New York Times* publishing the facts of their divorce.[238]

Jacqueline's star began rising steadily once her work was included in the inaugural show of Guggenheim's gallery Art of This Century in October 1942, with three collaborative drawings in which she had participated at Air-Bel with André, Victor Brauner, Óscar Domínguez, and Jacques Hérold. Guggenheim also included her work in three other shows: *31 Women* (*Non, Il ne fait qu'en chercher, me replique-je*/No, He's Looking for Them, I Told Myself, 1942; lost); *Spring Salon for Young Artists* (*Circus*, 1944; lost), and *The Women* (unknown, 1945). Ethel Baziotes, who met the Bretons at one of Guggenheim's parties, described Jacqueline as mesmerizing:

> She was utterly enchanting, a most magical subject, a work of
> art herself; she did not have to do anything. She herself was out
> of a fairy tale; she took great interest in how she appeared in the
> world, her choice of clothing, make-up, her whole state of being
> was highly rarefied. At parties, she'd wear 18th-century clothing
> bought at theatrical establishments, always long with narrow
> waists and full around the hips. Her presence was extraordinarily
> beautiful and she had a forceful personality.[239]

The double issue of *VVV Almanac* for March 1943 reproduced in color all the images from *Le Jeu de Marseille*. And Jacqueline and David's collaboration on *VVV* continued uninterrupted. Their collaborative artwork *Animal Vegetable Mineral—Two Movements Each* (1942) comprised two companion sculptures of wire, plaster, rocks, and feathers. In them, André would later recognize the archetypal personage from the farewell drawing that Jacqueline had made for him. Observing that he was good with his hands, Jacqueline innocently asked David whether he made sculpture. Recognizing his natural talent in the playful way in which he made small objects with plaster and surplus materials, including wire and string, she pressured him to do it seriously and seek technical advice from friend Alexander Calder, who was creating "drawings" with wire.[240] With her knowledge of art, Jacqueline became instrumental in shaping David into one of the leading sculptors of his generation. No one suspected that her influence, paired with his trust in her knowledge of art, was the fuel for his meteoric career, although proudly he would have been the first to admit it. Without experience, David started exhibiting with Guggenheim.

Reverting to her maiden name, Jacqueline contributed to the 1943 issue of *VVV Almanac* the fractal landscape she had lent in January to the *31 Women* exhibition, *Non, Il ne fait qu'en chercher ...*. A fluted pillar rises from a cavernous opening, giving off a crystalline luminescence through a frosty mist. Opposite a wall of fractured rock, a horizonless landscape populated by dark cones rises from pools of light. The title, a line from Rimbaud's *A Season in Hell*, draws from a scene in *The Infernal Husband* where a wife describes her spouse:

> *I saw the entire setting with which he surrounded himself in his mind; clothes, sheets, furniture: I lent him weapons, and another face, I saw everything that affected him as if he would like to have created it for himself. When his mind seemed inactive to me, I followed him in strange, complicated actions, very far, good or bad. I was sure that I would never enter his world. How many night hours have I stayed awake beside his dear sleeping body, wondering why he wanted so much to escape from reality. Never did a man have such a wish. I recognized—without fearing for him—that he could be a serious danger for society. Does he have perhaps secrets for changing life? No, he is only looking for them, I told myself. In a word his charity is bewitched, and I am its prisoner.*[241]

Jacqueline was getting back at André, who still loved her, by humiliating him publicly. Timidly, he still referred to her as "my wife."[242] His pain was evident to others. He became irritable and clinically depressed, lost 50 lbs (22.6 kg), and began lashing out at people around him. He wrote of her distance from him:

> *Interior*
> *A table set with utmost luxury*
> *Inordinately long*
> *Separates me from the woman of my life*
> *Whom I dimly see*
> *In the starburst of variously shaped glasses that keeps her*
>   *tilted backwards*
> *Her neckline plunging in a flash*[243]

That summer, David rented a house in Long Island: "Summer for him[,] like for Jacqueline, was the season for nudity."[244] Both walked nude in front of their guests, including André, who joined them on weekends, and sixteen-year-old Duits, who had become infatuated with Breton. Breton and Duits, too inhibited to change into their bathing suits, remained clothed.[245] Intimidated, Duits recalled:

> *The close proximity of these two bodies, so different, so superb in comparison to mine, had a chilling effect. They were both excessively slim. Chaste like animals or statues. He was the color of wheat; as for her, the features of an adolescent through which Egyptians represented a hidden God. My modesty amused them, I refused not only to remove my swim trunks but wrapped myself in my beach towel; I exposed only my legs to the sun. Nudity scared him [Breton] as much as it did me. "Why?" he would say, with charming insincerity, "we are quite comfortable here." Then we would go out ... One day as I was walking with him, we came to an abrupt halt in front of some flowers that I did not know ... "It's Nerval's flower," whispered Breton.[246] "The hollyhock! Do you recall?" Visibly moved, he began to recite ... He seemed to be reading from a book that was more ancient than man, this book composed of words that only lightning knows how to write, that only prophets and the thunder know how to pronounce. At that time, I was madly in love with him.*
>
> *To Jacqueline, who was complaining about my inefficiency, he [Breton] explained with false sweetness that poets don't know how to wash dishes. "But," said Jacqueline, furious, "I cannot do everything in this house! I no longer have the time to paint." Breton held his tongue: his smile was less compassionate than cunning. The spiteful nature of his look expressed far better than words the feelings he held regarding Jacqueline's artistic ambition.[247]*

Julien Levy recalled being "under a cloud with Breton because of my close relationship with David Hare, the cause of André's divorce from Jacqueline."[248] When the Bretons split, Jacqueline, Aube, and David lived a comfortable life in David's apartment at 42 Bleecker Street, free to live and make art as they wished.[249] They subsequently moved to Hare's house in the Hamptons and eventually to Roxbury, each move making it harder for André to see Aube regularly. Each visit was a reminder of his losses; he missed Jacqueline and watching Aube grow each day.

By chance, at a *bouquiniste*, a second-hand bookseller, André had come across a horticulture catalogue, *Jeunes Cerisier garantis contre les Lièvres*, the title of which amused him in French but took on a painful meaning when translated into English.[250] Pouring his helplessness into the anthology he was preparing, he gave the title as *Young Cherry Trees Secured against Hares*.

> ### From the Eyes of the Gods
> *A brazier was already yielding*
> *In her bosom to a lovely romance of cloaks*
> *And daggers ...*
> *But while she speaks there remains but a wall*
> *Beating in her tomb like a dark-brown veil.*
> *Eternity is looking for a wrist-watch*
> *Shortly before midnight, near the landing-stage.*

> ### From Freedom of Love
> *My wife with the hair of a woodfire*
> *With the thoughts of a heat lightning*
> *With the waist of an hourglass*
> *With the waist of an otter in the teeth of a tiger*
> *My wife with the lips of a cockade and a bunch of stars of the*
>   *last magnitude*
> *With the teeth of tracks of white on white earth*
> *With the tongue of rubbed amber and glass.*
> *My wife with the tongue of a stabbed host ...*[251]

Meanwhile, David, under the tutelage of Jacqueline's educated eye, was mastering the sculptural medium and attracting the attention of critic Clement Greenberg, who wrote that Hare stood "second to no sculptor of his generation, unless it be David Smith."[252]

The American West

In May 1946, Jacqueline and David decided to leave Roxbury and drive through the American West to California, where they were exhibiting at the San Francisco Museum of Art. They drove through New Mexico, Arizona, Montana, and Wyoming, visited Native American museums as well as Hopi and Navajo reservations, saw Indian dancers in Taos, camped beside streams, and fished for their meals. Jacqueline wrote to her sister on May 26:

> *My little Huguette,*
>
> *We are seeing only admirable things since Sioux City. In order to get there (look up where it is on the map) we were doing 500 miles a day (800 km), but since then we are now taking all the time possible, we are stopping to camp or to fish, we are visiting Indian museums. Yesterday, we were at an elevation of more than 3,000 meters [nearly 10,000 ft] as we crossed a small section of the Rocky Mountains; afterwards, we crossed the sea where the earth and the mountains were entirely rosy red. I have never in fact seen anything so beautiful in the way of landscape since I was born. I am not writing well because of being in the car on a bad road. We are going to stop soon to fish and breakfast on fish. I await with impatience news from Paris. Write to me at Santa Fe. I will tell you when we intend to leave there. I will send you photos*
>
> *Love, Jacqueline*[253]

Nearly two months later, on July 18, Jacqueline wrote again to Huguette:

> *It's been a long time since I wrote to you. We went to see the dances and festivals in Arizona, to see the Hopis and Navajos. These dances are such great beauty. I will never forget, and the Indians are delicious, although distant especially the Hopi, and secret about everything concerning their ceremonies but they are marvelously hospitable and generous ... they have never mingled with the Whites as opposed to the majority of the Indians in Mexico. We are leaving in two weeks for San Francisco.*[254]

Invariably open to new experiences, Jacqueline was profoundly impressed. "I have never seen anything more beautiful," again she wrote to Huguette after visiting the Painted Desert and the Petrified Forest in Arizona, as well as Yellowstone National Park in Wyoming. One of her postcards described "multicolored sands, rock and petrified wood interspersed with fantastic erosion, rolling hills of soft yellows and greens, their crests blackened, seemingly charred."[255]

As planned, they arrived in San Francisco to attend the opening of their show, *Painting by Jacqueline Lamba and Sculpture by David Hare*, August 13 to September 8, 1946. Martica Sawin recalled that David's sculptures had to be restored: "He was still learning his craft, and they were falling apart."[256] For its collection, the Museum acquired Jacqueline's *Galère* (Vessel, n.d.; lost).[257] It was inspired by Rimbaud's poem "The Drunken Boat," written from the point of view of a vessel adrift at sea, assaulted by storms, representing the erratic journey of the poet's tormented soul:

> *Now I, a boat lost in the foliage of caves,*
> *Thrown by the storm into the birdless air*
> *I whose water-drunk carcass would not have been rescued*
> *By the monitors and the Hanseatic sailboats.*[258]

Jacqueline and David subsequently made Roxbury their home (pls. 32, 33). The landscapes she produced following their trip through the American West portrayed what she saw, as well as what she experienced, emphasizing a Native American's reverence for the land and closeness with nature. *Indian Teepees* (1951), roofs open to the sky, portrays a place where vegetation and human life converge harmoniously along man-made habitats. In *Le Puits* (The Well, 1946), the evening sky, cleared by a full moon, shines above a well ringed by plants, where water draws life from the numinous deep. Jacqueline's wonderment is seen in *Roxbury Astres* (Roxbury Stars, 1946), where twinkling objects in the night sky invite celestial interpretations.

For *VVV*'s final issue (February 1944), Jacqueline illustrated the section on *Affinities* by juxtaposing the heads of men from two different cultures: a Central European, the main personage from Seurat's *Bathers at Asnières* (1884); and the photograph of a descendant of pre-Columbian people from Ecuador. The publication also reproduces a full-page portrait of Jacqueline in the Bleecker Street apartment, sitting on the floor below her trapeze, among potted plants and three scintillating nightscapes, a preview of her forthcoming one-woman show.

An Exhibition

By this stage in her career, Jacqueline was producing art that was radically different from her early work: it was now large, non-objective, monochromatic. Her output during this period is often likened to that of Roberto Matta, but the emotional content of the two artists' work was worlds apart. Jacqueline's was about creation; Matta's about destruction—a cover he had recently done for *VVV* was a vagina dentata.[259] In the same year, the book *Abstract & Surrealist Art in America* was published in conjunction with the traveling exhibition *Abstract and Surrealist Art in the United States*. Jacqueline's loan, *In Spite of Everything, Spring* (pl. 27), and Matta's *The Disasters of Mysticism* (both 1942) were reproduced side by side in the "Artists in Exile" section, among works by Breton, Marc Chagall, Dalí, Duchamp, Ernst, Fernand Léger, Masson, Piet Mondrian, Amédée Ozenfant, Seligmann, and Tanguy. In Jacqueline's painting, life transcends death; in Matta's, higher powers bring destruction. The show opened in Cincinnati, traveled to Denver, Seattle, and Santa Barbara, and closed in San Francisco. In the catalogue essay, art collector Sidney Janis compared and contrasted Jacqueline and Matta: "Light is her forte. Contrary to Matta, who dissolves form through light, in her paintings form is crystallized by light, which is then mirrored back from a thousand facets. Line and color are subservient to the magic of the shimmering and sparkling iridescence, which she visualized as genesis."[260]

In Spite of Everything, Spring is a nightscape from which light, born from darkness, bursts into prismatic living forms that reflect off one another. The statement that accompanied the painting in the catalogue was drawn from the text Jacqueline wrote for the brochure of her forthcoming exhibition at the Norlyst Gallery in New York. The painting, she explained, refers to their escape from war-ravaged Europe and safe arrival in New York. Life, despite destruction.[261]

Behind the Sun (1944), the other known painting extant from Jacqueline's first one-woman exhibition, celebrates her once-concealed relationship with David. Stained with flat, translucent earth tones, the richly painted canvas resembles a fabric in which cut-outs reveal a blue on the other side. Symbolic sources were Native American fabrics and artifacts David collected while he lived among the Hopi. The viewer's eye is drawn toward a familiar phallic shape standing by an opening.

Mougouch Gorky recalled Jacqueline at the vernissage of her show, holding court coiffed like Ophelia, with exotic flowers woven into her auburn hair.[262] Swiss sculptor Isabelle Waldberg wrote: "The whole world was there."[263]

Mougouch also noticed that Jacqueline's friends were present—except André, who explained his absence as having to work.[264] His excuse confirmed Jacqueline's belief that even in the face of reality he would not support her need to paint. Three paintings and a pastel drawing sold before the show came down. One painting went to David's mother, two to Rudi Blesh.

The exhibit showcased the following paintings: *La Place de vivre*, *The Town of My Friends*, and *Malgré tout, le printemps* (all 1942); *Momie d'ibis*,[265] *We Won't See Her Anymore*, *L'Homme, Egypt*, and *Behind the Sun* (1943); and *The Hollow Tree*, *Le Sang, le cuivre*, and *L'Entrevue* (1944); and *Drawing 1* (1942); Drawings 2, 3, *L'Amour fou* (Mad Love), *Tournesol* (Sunflower; all 1943); Drawing (1944); Pastels 5 and 6 (1943).

Before her show, which opened on April 10, 1944, Jacqueline confessed to Dolorès Vanetti that she'd had difficulty writing; it did not come as naturally as painting.[266] But she told Isabelle Waldberg that, regardless, she was "determined to speak with her voice even if women do not have a chance in life." Rather than having someone else write about her work, Jacqueline herself described the sources of her creativity in the exhibition brochure:

> *Art, poetry, is the precipitate of beauty in emotion. Man has only two motor-emotions: love and liberty. Any expression in art not stemming from liberty and love is false*

> *Method*
> *While the creative state is impermanent, and the thing that confers meaning, emotion, outstrips in time every technique of expression, a key to communication does in fact exist: automatism, proposed by André Breton in 1924. This key, cast to all, remains today the ultimate treasure of avant-garde artists and poets; but many can only play with it, they have the key and they are content. The problem is to open the door as wide as possible, not to do so would only lead to confusion. This key, in liberating the unconscious, must yield the most coherent message of emotion. It is necessary to eliminate with increasing severity everything which does not aim at the direct realization of this emotion and at its objectification.*

> *Form*
> *Insight into form develops historically, like science: any expression not coinciding at least intuitively with the limits last reached in this process of development is reactionary.*

Moreover, any mind tending to push form to the last verge of
dryness, for example, rejecting space, that double door between
life and death, can be called abstract, although caution is required
in using this word, which in art seems to have no more living
significance than the word prison

Light
Light is the most free expression in space, light destroys space
giving birth to forms, colors[,] textures. The line does not exist

Space
Space is filled by light with full and empty forms. The full forms
constitute objects, parts of space which light has just captured.
Empty forms are new objects coming into being

Object
The object is thus only part of space created by light.
Color is its only non-arbitrary choice in transfiguration.
Texture is the crystallization of this choice.
The line does not exist, it is already form.
Shadow does not exist, it is already light.
The secret would be to capture on canvas each form in its special
light, that is to say at the precise moment in which the light becomes
form. This would be like seeing a rainbow in the fullness of night.

Jacqueline Lamba, 18 February 1944[267]

The *New York Times* reviewer confessed that he did not know what to make of the exhibition. Other press critics were moved by the power of the show; two could not help mentioning that Jacqueline was André's wife.

The *Art Digest* critic wrote: "She thinks of space as something destroyed by light when light makes full forms and objects in it. One would expect this theory to be illustrated by just such cobwebby plasms, sparkling jewels and abysmal blues as we do find in her paintings; but I was unprepared to see these things laid down on canvas in so direct, clean and unfussed a manner. We would say she has indeed taken light's measure, she creates an intoxicating dream world at the Norlyst Galleries this month."[268]

Howard Devree of the *New York Times* wrote a tongue-in-cheek review: "Jacqueline Lamba, whose paintings at the Norlyst reveal an obviously decorative taste, but the forms seem to me quite arbitrary, and for me, at least, they fall off any communication. *L'homme*, it would seem might be called Cherchez l'homme, and *La place de vivre* is certainly not La Place de la Concorde. And to *We Won't See Her Anymore*, one is tempted to retort: 'We don't now.' The artist's foreword to the catalogue moreover leaves me feeling as if I had been trying to read a harangue in old Swahili."[269]

The *New York Herald Tribune* from Sunday, April 23, wrote: "At the Norlyst Gallery, large freely flowing, softly colorful designs by Jacqueline Lamba (wife of André Breton, the French poet) adhere to the new lyrical direction in abstract painting. They are not only fluent but imaginative and show technical cultivation."

CUE, the weekly magazine, of April 22, 1944, noted: "[She is] One who paints on the evasive subject of light and how it makes forms in space; yet does so with such clarity of understanding that not one brushstroke is seen to correct another. This exhibition of eleven luminous paintings is the most extraordinary debut you'll ever see. Her husband is André Breton, the godfather of automatism. His wife is a remarkable painter."

For those who had wondered about Jacqueline's capacity to create, her first solo exhibition left no doubt that she was a fine painter with an individual style. The work showed creative richness, demonstrating what it meant at that moment to be a painter, a woman artist, a member of the Surrealist Movement, *and* the wife of André Breton. The show had taken Jacqueline years of emotional turmoil to shape, but when the time came, pure poetry flowed out of her, confirming that she was the artist she believed herself to be. And to André, she proved that his far-reaching power was not far-reaching enough to impede her from being her own person or making her own art.

These issues were discussed in the epistolary dialogue between Isabelle Waldberg and her husband, Patrick, an art historian and critic. On May 24, 1944, Isabelle wrote:

> *My dear Patrick,*
> *… In what concerns Jacqueline, in your letter of May 12, I am charmed and surprised to see you become unexpectedly indulgent with women artists. Perhaps that preface had a better effect after some traveling. I could not help myself finding her in the New York climate naïve and a bit ridiculous, and I am not the only one, for example Georges* [Duthuit]. *This enormous effort of Jacqueline's, because indisputably there is an effort, will it be incontestable and rather commendable? In any case, it is certain that after Jacqueline's words, she herself wants to become someone independent, that she would like to affirm her personality apart*

from André, and that she has had every opportunity from the patronage and light that comes from him. Her desire to shine on her own is evident, although it won't help if she continues to repeat what André is saying, maybe without realizing, a bit twisted, if evil tongues, of which we have plenty around here, are to be believed.

I have to tell you that your acts of indulgence, so little like you, leave me a bit perplexed. I often feel that we exaggerate "in our environment" the malicious side and in talking to you about Jacqueline I have perhaps come under others' influence. Robert [Motherwell] *has already spoken with you, I believe, of this question that worries him enough, the tendency here to systematically denigrate what is happening to others. Your attitude with regard to Jacqueline, could it be a sign of possible change?*[270]

On June 3, following a lengthy critique of the fourth issue of *VVV*, Patrick replied, although less about Jacqueline than about the effect Isabelle's comments had on him:

My dear Zab,
Here very briefly and superficially, how the New York publications strike me. You are surprised at my "indulgence" for Jacqueline's preface, and I persist in not understanding how one could find this preface "ridiculous." Jacqueline uses a simple language, sincere and young. Understandably, it is not new, as we know it, but it is said with undeniable fervor and a seriousness that strikes me ... Jacqueline believes in what she is saying and certainly does everything that is in her power to be in accordance with what she is expressing. It is infinitely more than the majority of great minds of modern art can say. I find that Jacqueline's activity is all that there is of the most valuable and merits as much encouragement as possible. Unless one does not share [Roger] *Caillois' taste for polished "beautiful language," and as for symmetry, ready like the former Mr Achras*[271] *to slap the icosahedron on each and every face when the latter has the audacity to revolt. I really have a lot of difficulty putting myself in your place, and even then, I fail to understand your ill will. Severity should be reserved only for dishonest people, fakers, adulterers, even idiots, the senile or cowards. But if you demolish systematically each sincere demonstration which is directed in the direction that we all like, I don't know what else to do. How can you be so unjust? I speak also for Georges* [Duthuit] *whose judgment*

matters for me. You are both of incredible indulgence for whatever I send you, letters or poems, whereas my letter is very naïve for the VVV reader, full of affirmations and not further discussable, and sometimes ridiculous (for he who has easy sarcasm and who refuses to understand what it is about), and at the same time, you reject out loud Jacqueline's excellent text, which I conceive may not inspire anything other than great sympathy, even if it is through the sincerity in her accent, by the fact that it is appealing in a moving and just way, liberty and love, that it affirms a wish for a constancy and consequence, that it is written by a woman, fighting in a man's world of bad faith, and that this woman has an additional handicap, in her case, that being Breton's wife, etc. You, yourself, have pointed out in the moving case of Jacqueline; how can you not recognize the value of her efforts? In short, Jacqueline has tried to express who she is and what she wants, using a text accompanying some works: an enterprise which presents certain dangers (for example, that of being unfavorably judged by you) and requires a certain audacity. May I respectfully draw your attention, my dear female-sculptress, to your not having done as much? Perhaps if you attempted to demonstrate as did Jacqueline, you would find censors also as severe and unjust, and you would understand your pain, as my friend [René] Bricard put it.[272] You can always reply that you prefer to write nothing rather than to risk feeling badly or misunderstood than to express badly or clumsily your thinking, weak reply, weak argument, because then what would we read? In any case, I do not share your reservations![273]

In the fourth issue of *VVV*, Patrick noticed that Jacqueline, in the photograph taken by David in the Bleecker Street studio, was unrecognizable. While working on the exhibition, her external appearance had undergone a radical change. She stopped dyeing her hair blonde, allowing it to grow long and regain its natural auburn. She wore regular clothes and avoided her usual fashion statements. In the photograph, the paintings drew the attention first. It whetted Patrick's appetite to see more.

Jacqueline and Aube in Mexico

In the spring of 1944, Jacqueline, frustrated by Frida's lack of response to her voluminous correspondence, wrote one more time. Determined to see Frida again, she asked for help with the visas she had applied for to travel to Mexico once Aube was out of school:

145 Bleecker St

Frida—it is me Jacqueline

> *You know, for two years I wanted to go to Mexico. Now I am ready for it after my first show which is on April 10—and when Aube is free from school* [in June] *we could both of us go. About the papers, everything is done here at the consulate, and they must have sent already my demand* [visa application] *to Mexico—but they told* [me] *it would be better* [quicker] *if you could do something about it directly in Mexico. The papers I send you, they have them already at the immigration service. Having them it will be easier for you to get "through my case" if you ever want to bother about it! If they let me go, we will stay all summer with Aube. Maybe a little longer if I find a school for Aube (English-Spanish-French school!).*

> *Very strange, I write to you as if I left you yesterday. You never wrote to me, and I don't like very much to speak alone into space. Many things happened since we saw each other. Not many good things—anyway, since I am here I started to paint "seriously" at last, and I won't stop—I will send you the catalogue of my exhibition in two weeks. It is the most sad thing, André can't come ... he is entirely unhappy and has to work very much. Maybe I will hear from you before I leave.*

> [In French] *I embrace you tenderly with Diego.*
> *Jacqueline*

As she requested, Frida contacted immigration services supporting Jacqueline's temporary visa application for her and Aube, and paid 1,500 pesos to expedite the process. On April 12, Dr. Héctor Pérez Martínez signed off the permit. Jacqueline's predicament in New York and imminent visit to Mexico triggered in Frida the need to paint two works.

Since Frida's departure from Paris, Jacqueline had kept her informed about life, their escape from Europe, settling down in New York, her painting, difficulties with André, and her affair with David. So this visit would be more than a social call. In Mexico, Jacqueline would have a respite from the clinging needs of both men and momentarily feel free. She would also have the opportunity to discuss with Frida her situation with André, hoping to arrive at an objective sense of what it might mean to leave the security of her marriage to the most powerful figure in Surrealism. Frida could empathize, having suffered her own uneasiness during two years outside the safety of her marriage to Diego, although she was not one to offer advice. Frida, like Jacqueline, was living as a wife doll, afraid of embracing her autonomy.

Frida represented Jacqueline's predicament in a still life arranged on a bright yellow table that Frida's mother had given her as a wedding present. Diego explained that this particular yellow, *amarillo congo*, was used in the homes of poor people to scare away pests, such as cockroaches and lice. Jacqueline is the blonde doll dressed as a bride who peeks over an arrangement of fruit from the upper left. There is a photograph of her coiffed and dressed as the doll in the painting.[274] Until she met David, Jacqueline had taken on the identity of ornament in Surrealism. Portraying her as a bride doll blended Jacqueline's conflict about the marriage to Breton with the memory of the bride doll that she and Frida had bought together five years earlier at a flea market in Paris. In a letter to Jacqueline, transcribed in her diary, Frida revealed the doll's identity: "The bride doll is yours also—that is, it is you."

In *The Bride Who Becomes Frightened When She Sees Life Open* (1943), conflict in Jacqueline's triangular relationship with Breton and Hare gives the painting its emotional hold and title, inscribed along the table's lower edge.[275] A cluster of fruits serves as a protective barrier from which Jacqueline, as doll, peers out past the halved watermelon cut with jagged edges to witness the event on the other side. In the foreground, a green katydid, standing for David, and a mottled owl, standing for Breton, have their backs turned to each other, as the doll observes, fearful of what might happen should the owl turn and discover the insect. Katydids or bush crickets are pests known for causing events of catastrophic proportions, destroying crops and bringing famine. When these large green insects with leaflike wings that press tightly against their sides mature sexually, the males spend nights singing in hopes of warding off competitors and attracting a female. Katydids do not sting and are nutritious food for many species—including owls. In Mexican mythology, the nocturnal owl, considered a messenger from the underworld, is associated with bad omens and premonitions of death, and a companion to Tezcatlipoca, the most sadistic and dreaded of the gods.

Jacqueline's fear of trading the security of marriage to André for the uncertainty of a life without him gave Frida the idea for the painting, but it left many questions unanswered. What guarantee did she have with Hare? What about Breton's threat to destroy her? What could he do to her? What would the divorce do to Aube, who was deeply attached to her father? Despite her fear of uncertainty, Jacqueline chose freedom over the security of a gilded cage and returned to New York ready to divorce André.

From Mexico, Jacqueline had kept in touch with her friend the ceramist Jeanne Reynal, and with Mougouch Gorky, leaving gossip to brew in New York.[276] On September 24, Isabelle Waldberg, an indefatigable gossip, wrote to her husband:

> *Jacqueline does not give a sign of life from Mexico. It's expected that she is not returning due to André's new relationship, which has a very serious air, and, according to theory, it's real love and appears to have affected Jacqueline, despite the separation. Without a doubt, she expected being able to maintain certain ties with him while still keeping an independent life; but André is now entirely detached from her, and she is tolerating that very badly. Insofar as Hare goes, he does not play a great role in this because he did not accompany her to Mexico.[277]*

Juicy gossip, but not the whole truth. David did not accompany Jacqueline to Mexico, but he visited while she stayed with Frida, and he again met her in Nuevo Laredo on her return. An uncomfortable event preceded his early departure from Coyoacán when he, Jacqueline, and Frida were sitting in her living area and Frida asked him to pour her some juice from the pitcher on the table. He did, but did not stop, spilling juice on the floor. Frida did not find funny his explanation that she had not said when to stop.[278]

Jacqueline and Aube's arrival at Frida's Blue House was like walking into a paradise populated by monkeys, idols, dogs, birds, ducks, rare flowers, a magnolia tree in bloom, and Frida, the Great Goddess, all waiting for them. For Frida, Jacqueline brought from her show *Mad Love*, a drawing of three personages in pinks and blues. On the right are a male and a female; he points an erection toward his companion as he turns back to look at the female behind. *Sunflower*, also from her show, is a drawing of three personages—one, the recurrent phallic shape in her painting—in grays and yellows, which she brought for Alice Rahon.

In Mexico, Jacqueline was reunited with old friends, other Surrealist émigrés who also had escaped: Leonora Carrington, Gordon Onslow Ford,

Esteban Francés, Wolfgang Paalen, Alice Rahon, Benjamin Péret, and Remedios Varo. Frida had met or befriended each at different times.

Sometimes, Jacqueline would leave Aube with Frida for days and stay in the center of the city at the homes of Carrington, Varo, and Péret; or in the south, with Rahon and Paalen. In Mexico, Francés and Jacqueline reinitiated their on-off affair. He still wanted something serious, but again she was not interested. They traveled to Erongarícuaro, staying with Onslow Ford and his wife, Jacqueline Johnson, who had rented a house there.

Lamba tried painting at Péret's house in a "patio where there were sunflowers and giant butterflies."[279] But she gave up; the light of Mexico was too intense, she wrote to Reynal.[280] Some days, she sunbathed nude and walked naked around the house, recalled Arturo García Bustos, one of Frida's students.[281] Meanwhile, Aube made two playmates—the gardener's son and Frida's nephew Antonio, who, infatuated, wrote her little love notes.[282] But mostly, Aube enjoyed time with Frida, whose health was deteriorating rapidly. In 1944, Frida painted *The Broken Column*, referring mainly to her physical infirmities but also to her emotional stability. Bedridden much of the time, she was suffering from evening fevers, dizziness, and chronic pain.[283] In Paris, Carrington had heard Leonor Fini refer to Frida, but she met her only through Jacqueline, and recalled her as "very ill and bedridden."[284] Aube remembered Frida as

> ... *Mysterious. Jacqueline and Frida were so different, but on the love plane, on the intellectual plane, they went very well together. But that is my impression, with the passage of time, because I was too little when they were together in 1938, especially. And then in 1944, I returned to Mexico with Jacqueline. I suppose it is based on this time, because we were living with Frida. As for me, I was not aware of the relationship between Frida and Jacqueline. I don't know if it was continuing at that time on a level of love. I know that I was totally fascinated by Frida. So this absorbed all my time when I was in Mexico. And Jacqueline was mixed up with it too; she was free. She went walking, I don't know where or with whom, visiting places. And since Frida could not move about as much because she was ill, I spent whole afternoons with Frida in her studio, surrounded by all the marvelous things, ancient dolls, in wax, lace, wild animals, parrots that would fly in the garden, which was huge. There were monkeys, some wild. For a little girl, it was paradise.*
>
> *When I arrived there with Jacqueline, at the age of nine, I saw Frida, a type of extraordinary queen, with Mexican clothes,*

with skirts, one overlaying others, wearing pre-Columbian jewelry, ribbons in her hair. As for me, I circled around her like a little child who was not timid, as if I was looking at a fairy queen, out of a fairy story. She had rings on all her fingers, jewelry everywhere. I was looking at all her skirts. And since she adored children but didn't have any, and since she had so many servants, she had some of the same dresses made for me. For a young girl like me, it was something quite unimaginable ... total paradise. I don't have those dresses anymore. She was very powerful for me, being a little girl. She did that sort of thing with her magic wand, and I had a beautiful dress. It was like Cinderella.

She had this extraordinary four-poster bed, that we have seen in the photos with the mirror above. As a child, I didn't understand the reason for the mirror; but at the same time, it was used for painting, often lying down because she looked at her paintings as well when there was no one in bed. And I recall every morning that I used to jump into her bed and we recited limericks, nonsense rhymes by Edward Lear. And we laughed, both of us. It was total joy. And she had two dogs. They were on her bed. I used to play with the dogs. And I had permission to sleep with them on my bed. And so these were extraordinary things that I had never seen before.

The monkeys made me a little afraid. They lived on the grounds. There was one that was chained because he was a little bit dangerous. I recall one day there was panic because one or two monkeys had escaped. And so all the servants from all directions had gone back into the house, and someone was able to catch them. And with her, it was always miracles. I recall one day some people from the area put a squirrel in this small cage. He had some sort of illness that caused watering of the eyes and so he was half-blind, which was horrible. Frida was horrified too, as we saw this. She said, "We will give him back his sight and bring him back to life. We must now find a larger case. He is ill and we must take care of him." She had him put in an immense cage, gave him fruit, and we took care of him. It was some form of miracle to have a living being that we had rescued from death. And the day he was in good shape, we opened the door of the cage, he was cured, and let him go ...

When I was alone with her, I asked her why she didn't have any children. She said that she wanted to have children but could not. So we were in her studio and she opened her desk: "Here are the children I had." And she took out for me two bottles of formaldehyde in which there were the fetuses that she had lost. Well, some years later, much later, I said to myself "Oh la la!" It was done in such a natural way that it didn't shock me at all. I don't know why. It seemed to be part of her. At nine years old, I wasn't affected at all. I accepted it as altogether natural. I was a little surprised, but that was all.

In *The Bride Who Becomes Frightened When She Sees Life Open*, Frida visualized Jacqueline's conflict in her relationship with Breton and Hare. But Aube's imminent arrival brought to mind Frida's barrenness, triggering *The Flower of Life*.[285] Although Frida had not seen Aube since 1939, she had learned about her through Jacqueline's letters that included Aube's lipstick kisses. So when she and Jacqueline finally arrived in Mexico, Frida and Aube instantly took to each other. In the painting, Frida represents her sense of personal damage, exploring procreation and its vicissitudes, specifically her sense of inadequacy and inferiority as a female, her difficulty conceiving, even her lack of sexual interest in a male partner. When she exhibited the work in the *Primer Salón de la Flor* in Mexico City, immediately Justino Fernández, critic and friend, picked up on its emotional content and described it in his review: "Frida Kahlo de Rivera has a small painting, 'The Flower of Life,' in this exhibition, in which she has expressed with a great simplicity and delicacy an idea that is hard to express, and she has achieved it ingeniously."[286]

Reference to *The Flower of Life* came to Frida from the mandrake root, the oldest magical plant in botanical history mentioned as a cure for infertility. In the Old Testament, as far back as the Book of Genesis (30:14–16), Rachel uses it to cure her sterility. Mandrake roots tend to grow in the shape of human limbs. Frida personalized the plant, giving it the identity of a female to convey the complexity of her predicament by flipping it upside down, changing its color from ivory to red, and making the leaves spread out like a billowing skirt. She shaped its body to resemble her internal organs, adding arteries to feed the vaginal walls, and turned the arms into fallopian tubes from which ovaries are missing. Above the vagina, where the uterus would be, is an opening through which a penis's ejaculation is shaped as the flower's sexual organs, the pistil and stamen. The lightning on the left and the sun on the right emphasize the male orgasm. The flower is Frida's self-portrait as an incomplete woman, deficient, mechanical, and sterile, available to gratify a man's desire but unable to conceive nor experience sexual pleasure.

Aube recalled:

One day, when she [Frida] was resting in her lounge chair in the garden, I was always turning and turning around her. I was so fascinated. On her hand were many rings, so I was playing with her fingers and all that. "Choose a ring, take whichever you want!" I chose a ring with an orange-colored stone. I don't know exactly what it was. I have long lost it. It's a pity.

On the grounds, there were some bandstands made of metal in which one could climb that held pre-Columbian statues. And there were many in the garden. And I played often with the gardener's son. As we were running, we knocked over a pre-Columbian statue. Horror! It broke in two. And I said, "Ay, ay, ay." Diego came out and didn't say anything. That was very generous. I was perhaps less afraid than the gardener's son because I would simply be scolded. But as for him ... But Frida was very nice to the servants.[287]

Frida began painting *Magnolias* in December, following Jacqueline's departure, as the magnolia tree in the garden was beginning to wither and drop its flowers. Magnolias have long been associated with dignity, splendid beauty, and womanly charms. In a photograph of Jacqueline taken in Frida's garden, she is looking into a magnolia blossom as if contemplating the value of her beauty while gazing into a mirror, without considering that it is transient and will soon fade. The quiet, reflective mood of Frida's still life provides its silent dignity and belies the melancholy behind its creation. The ivory-white flowers are made to look like a simple bouquet, but the work is more complex. Frida knew that once Jacqueline was back in New York, she would hold her own as long as her beauty, as ephemeral as a magnolia blossom, held up. But afterward? The answer would come as she aged.

Frida painted *The Chick* after learning of Jacqueline's ordeal attempting to cross the Mexican border to the United States. Journalist Mario Monteforte Toledo described the emotional content of the work without knowing what had triggered the disquieting still life: "Next to a web of thorny branches and lime-greens, where spiders and all those dry insects from the fauna of the high plain dwell, a small dove or chick appears to have freed itself from torment thanks to its innocence, simply for being harmless and unarmed."[288] In a letter to Frida dated December 27, 1944, Jacqueline describes what happened when she was stopped at the border:

My darling, first you have to know how mighty proud I felt when I opened your surprise. I wear the stone around my neck; and on each arm the two obsidians. I won't have them separated because I believe it is you and me—David will fix them together in a way I can wear them too. I showed your beautiful postcard to David, and he smiled and said he likes you because you understand him and because you are beautiful.

I sent you a telegram, maybe you didn't receive it, to tell you what happened here. I think if David was not there, I would really become mad with anger and boreness [boredom] ...

How can I explain to you why we have been here for 7 days—they had an order from Philadelphia to all borders in the state not to let me through. I have been reported by somebody in the States as a very bad sort of a sadist, they told me. Three men were interrogating me with Aube outside for the decency,[289] *asking me about my private life and everything—at the end, they were smiling with me because it was so stupidly funny—but they can't let me pass without a "bright order" [permission] from Philadelphia—they told me they didn't know <u>who</u> reported me—with David, we have some idea about it. We will see— naturally—a lawyer, so many people and André are going to help—but it is not very certain that the cross-over will be even so on the other side. If they don't let me through [to] the States, I can't come back immediately to Mexico because my tourist card is no good anymore—it was only for six months—and it is over now—so you see I am hardly tolerated here just because I wait to leave, only I think the real idea from each side is that I wait in the middle of the river till I hear of my fate ... and what a town, a rotten one, full of garbage from both countries—it is raining without stopping and filthy cold. David stays on the other side, is tolerated here by the day—we pass our time eating, walking, there is more garbage and holes—but we are together and he is such a marvelous creature you do not know. Can you imagine me and Aube alone in that mess???? My Darling, I hope you are better and out of bed and can go to a movie and enjoy the life a little bit more. I think of Diego if he heard of all that and the remarks he could make about it! Kiss him for me and Aube.*

I keep you in my heart.
Jacqueline

The duties of David's mother-in-law as Secretary of Labor included overseeing the Immigration and Naturalization Service (INS) in charge of the US entry ports, and she had given orders not to allow Jacqueline to re-enter the US, hoping that keeping her away would help Suzy and David's marriage. When Jacqueline and Aube arrived at the border, and she was questioned about their stay in Mexico, Jacqueline replied that they had been guests of Frida Kahlo and Diego Rivera for six months, confident that their names would make border officials look upon them favorably. In response, the customs officer explained that Frida and Diego were Communist sympathizers, and, this being wartime, she and Aube could not be allowed to re-enter the States until they had been cleared, for security reasons, as not posing a threat. Jacqueline and Aube checked in to Hotel Rudon in Nuevo Laredo and returned each day in hopes of being cleared to pass. Word got around New York, and the Surrealist community, walking on eggshells, wondered how the situation could end, considering Jacqueline's boldness—fully aware of her precarious immigration status. In her letter to Frida, Jacqueline alludes to David's mother-in-law being behind the stalling. André asked his friend Pierre Matisse, the most influential of their art dealer friends, to intervene. In a carefully composed letter in English of December 29, Matisse counsels patience; his uneasiness over saying anything about the government's involvement is evident:

> Dear Jacqueline,
>
> I am awfully sorry to hear of your interrupted trip. I know how disappointing and unpleasant it must be but I have no doubt that all will be straightened out very rapidly and you will soon be with us. Of course the most difficult thing is to wait patiently and it is necessary to be patient in such case as it is for the best. It is of course so unfortunate that you and Aube should not have been with us for the holidays which we are spending in the country at the farm although Paul is now in Arizona, at school, on account of his asthma ...
>
> Both Teeny and myself and the children send our very best wishes to you and Aube and until then ...
>
> Sincerely,
> Pierre Matisse[290]

Each day, they went back, and each day Jacqueline was informed that the situation was being reappraised. Some days, she was subjected to embarrassing questioning; other days, they sat waiting for a reply. David, who had long ago returned to New York from Mexico, traveled to Nuevo Laredo to be supportive while they waited in customs for the green light. One day Aube complained of hunger, and Jacqueline explained to the officer that she had to leave briefly to feed her child. Day after day, he had seen them waiting patiently, believing their situation was being appraised. He knew he would get in trouble, but, pointing to the door that opened into the United States, he said, "Go on."[291] Fifty years later, Suzy explained, "Jacqueline had been allowed to go through because she used Aube to make herself appear respectable."[292]

In *The Chick*, Frida created a visual narrative of Jacqueline's customs ordeal. In the center of this small still life, a bunch of indigo hyacinths in a blue Puebla pressed-glass vase has been invaded by insects, caterpillars, and a katydid, and engulfed in a web by two venomous spiders.[293] Only the chick, standing in the foreground to one side, is spared the suffocating experience. Monteforte Toledo's intuition was accurate, although he had no way of knowing the facts—unless Frida told him—about the situation that gave rise to the painting.

As in *The Bride Who Becomes Frightened When She Sees Life Open*, in *The Chick*, the katydid stands for David. Here, the two venomous spiders are Suzy, his wife, and Frances Perkins, his mother-in-law, while the insects populating the web are the Surrealists gossiping about Jacqueline's fearless involvement with Madame Secretary's son-in-law. Aube is the chick that stands apart, untouched by web or weavers, despite being part of the situation. In early December 1944, when Jacqueline and Aube were expected back, but were stuck in Laredo, Mougouch wrote to Reynal about the Surrealists: "You know, they are so merciless these surrealists, you fall from grace so suddenly, it is rather frightening. I am more glad than I can say that we shall be at a distance, not only from them, from everyone. The backbiting and opportunism couldn't be worse in Mexico."[294] Typical of Jacqueline, she did what she wanted—and, regardless of the consequences, was ready to accept responsibility. No one was going to stop her, not even the US government.

Jacqueline and Frida met for the last time in New York in the summer of 1946, when Frida was in the city to have a spinal fusion performed by Dr. Philip Wilson. She and Cristina, her sister, were staying at 399 Park Avenue in the apartment of Sonja Sekula, Jacqueline's lover at the time.[295] Before returning to Mexico, Frida gave Jacqueline a blouse woven with brightly colored ribbons, which she wore in hospital after Merlin was born.

Although Sekula was a Swiss-born painter associated with the Abstract Expressionist movement, she considered herself an "Abstract Naturalist."[296] When the Surrealists arrived in New York, she befriended André and Jacqueline, and later David Hare, Matta, Ernst, Guggenheim, Carrington, and Motherwell. In 1945, she traveled to Mexico, where she met again with Alice Rahon-Paalen, with whom she'd fallen in love when Alice was in New York for Guggenheim's

31 Women show. A dedication to Sonja in a book of poetry by Alice shows that the feeling was mutual: "… our meeting was that of two waves coming from opposite directions which rose and broke at the peak of their surge—to you who runs along the same slope as I/Sonja, who I awaited for—Alice Paalen."[297]

Sekula told Cicely Aikman: "Alice Paalen was a medium through which I could see. She taught me how light can be transformed to inventive creation, to look and observe always."[298] After returning from Mexico, Sekula held her first one-person exhibition at Guggenheim's gallery Art of this Century, which got her a contract with Betty Parsons Gallery. Hare recalled: "The Surrealists liked her, the way she talked and the poetic ideas she had. She liked them because they thought the way she did and they appreciated the way she thought. They didn't ask her to be practical."[299] They accepted and liked her as she was. But generally making outstanding art and being personable were not enough for many. Sekula was often shunned for her schizophrenic episodes, for which she was hospitalized off and on during her lifetime; and for her openness about her bisexuality. Of the former, she wrote in her journal: "I do not feel part of any country or race. I was well when they called me sick and often sick when they thought I am well."[300] About her sexuality, she wrote: "To feel guilty about having loved a being of your own kind body and soul is hopeless—let us hope there were many moments in each of these attractions and loves—into which the realm of sphere and eternity and silence entered as well."[301]

Jacqueline was living in France when Aube learned about her mother's homosexuality and her affair with Frida, and it bothered her because they couldn't talk about it. Had Aube been "more daring," she thought, she would have pressed the question, saying, "I have just read this. Is it true that you were in love with Frida and Frida with you?" But at the time it didn't matter whether Aube brought the subject up or not. Either way, Jacqueline would not speak about it; she would skirt around any inquiry, never answering her daughter directly:

> She would only say tender things about Frida, that Frida was
> a marvelous woman whom she adored, that she was a very "free"
> woman who did what she wanted and couldn't care less about
> conventions, which Jacqueline also admired and was surprising for
> the era. At the same time, perhaps it was easier for Frida because there
> was money. Diego Rivera was Mexico's official painter, and Frida
> was treated very much like a queen. So it was much simpler to do
> exactly what she wanted with her life, without [considering] social
> conventions. But I believe that Jacqueline admired her extraordinary
> strength, intellectual force, and the fact that she resembled no
> other person.[302]

Home

By all accounts, the Lamba–Hare relationship was initially a happy one (pl. 29). Jacqueline loved being loved by David, who could not get enough of her. She, too, was in love with him and in awe of his prodigious talent. It seemed there was nothing he could not do with his hands; he could build or fix anything, and his creative strength in turn encouraged hers. His knowledge of Native American cultures and their art and artifacts made its presence felt throughout her painting and their Connecticut home.

Jacqueline went from being adored as an ornamental wife to being adored as she was—blunt, outspoken, often to the point of cruelty. Ethel Baziotes found her open contempt for "the bourgeoisie" fascinating, as well as her readiness "to tell others they were not original. She was full of likes and dislikes. She was very strong with her opinions, very forceful, especially about people. She was very instinctual and expressed it in practically every way. When Jacqueline and David came for lunch once, in the 1940s, she noticed how I loved my domesticity," Ethel recalled, "and she said how much she hated it. She was a very beautiful animal."[303] A friend, Ernestine Lassaw, wife of sculptor Ibram Lassaw, recalled: "Jacqueline was not an easy person, and people did not like her a lot; she was very contentious, demanding, hard on others, expecting them to live up to her expectations."[304]

After the experience with Matta, when she destroyed all the unsold paintings from her show—which she would later regret—Jacqueline's demeanor toughened, as did her painting. Building on her training in fabric design and Maurice Denis's use of planes of color tending toward abstraction, she blended painting and quilting techniques, evoking a sense of the puzzle-like outlined by sinuous lines of intertwining rhythms drawn from Cloisonnism. Picasso's influence is most apparent in her handling of flat fragments filled with color, with outlined edges and integrated with soft color lines to suggest boundaries. Although Abstract Expressionism was the current American idiom, Ernestine recalled: "Jacqueline did not care much about American artists. Picasso was the love of her life. She had very close ties with him [and] wanted to paint like him. She thought Picasso was the last word in art. She idolized him."[305]

On July 4, 1945, Patrick Waldberg wrote to the Belgian Surrealist E.L.T. Mesens: "Jacqueline is getting in trouble trying to become a great painter. She lives with David Hare, whom she will undoubtedly marry since formalities are completed. Hare himself has, after three years, made very beautiful sculptures surprisingly original and exquisite."[306]

120

On September 6, David and Jacqueline took out their marriage license. He was twenty-eight, she thirty-four. The *New York Times* reported that David sued Suzy for "desertion" before filing for divorce, and she countersued for "mental cruelty."[307] Their divorce was granted on March 2, 1945, in Reno, Nevada. Jacqueline divorced André on July 30, 1945, also in Reno.

On September 8, Jacqueline and David were married by the Justice of the Peace in Sag Harbor, New York. Witnesses were Michel Lukacs and Dolorès (Vanetti) Ehrenreich. It had not occurred to David to get a wedding ring, so Dolorès lent them hers. The couple had not considered a honeymoon, so following the ceremony, they went swimming at Haven's Beach.[308]

Back in Roxbury, David wrote Suzy a chatty letter, catching up on recent events:

Summer 1945

Darling, I got a letter from you while I was at the Hampton Bays, but I dident anser it because I thought that I would see you in New York however I missed you there. I just got your note from N.Y. this morning. What have you done with your two dogs? The fox hound sounds wonderful. They are marvelous dogs.

I never got around to making the sculpture from the drawing you sent me but I expect to sometime. I was so busey making things this summer that I really had no time for the sun and water but at least I really got some work finished. Twelve things all small, and I shall make eight more large ones here before my show.

Jacqueline and I got married a couple of weeks ago in Long Island.

It was really becoming necessary because of school for Aube, because of hotels because of traveling and all kinds of practical things like that.

I found this tray that you wanted when I got up here. It is the painted one as you know I also found a pair of sandals and those apothecary jars and a few other small things. Miss Wagners card table is here. The Gorkys dident send it. Also that brown bookcase, if you want it And I have made some lamps so if you want I shall send you the square glass lamp and some other one Let me know where to send all of those things and someday soon I will get them expressed but maybe not until after you leave.

How wonderful to be going to Europe now [to work with Brâncuşi on a monograph for which she already had a publisher] *I wish that I had the chance to hear all about it. Perhaps if I can I will come sometime the end of the week but if*

I don't make it the best of luck and everything to you. I shall look
forward to seeing you when you return full of news and things
happening in other parts of the world.

I sent you that tax refund and I thought that it would help
pay the dentist with it but I got another bill from him which was
only minus twenty-five. Maby sometime I will be able to pay him
but certainly not for a long time. I hope that they the teeth, dont
hurt you anymore. I will try my best to see you befir you go.

Lots of love and a good trip, David I don't know what first
name their Roosevelt ____ so I have to send it to a Roosvelt, made
but they forgot it tell me the first name. My <u>dearest</u>, take some
[care] of yourself and keep well if I don't get a chance to see you
before you leave.[309]

Jacqueline and David settled in the wooden house in Roxbury, where previously he had lived with Suzy, and let the backyard grow wild. His photography studio became his sculpture studio; Jacqueline, too, had a studio apart. They entertained friends, and each painted or sculpted as they wished. When Wifredo Lam and Helena Holzer visited, they were admiring of David's talent. "His creative reach was often prodigious," Holzer recalled. "It seemed he could make anything, which held practical as well as aesthetic value."[310]

Recalling a visit to Roxbury, Holzer mentioned Jacqueline being very happy with David: "With David Hare, I was under the impression that she loved him very much, and I always felt the only time she had economic stability was with him—maybe emotional stability too, because he was very much in love with her. I remember one time Jacqueline very proudly showed me the bed David had made for them and told me in French, *C'est mon homme qui l'a fait,* 'It was my man who made it.'"[311]

Despite admiring David's talent, Holzer was put off by his table manners: "He burped at the table, never excusing himself. He had a lot of white skin imperfections on the face; he would pick at his sebaceous glands and eat them in front of everybody. It was repulsive, and Jacqueline who was so clean and proper ... it must have been hell in front of all the people."[312]

"The house was beautiful," Aube remembered. "David made everything, the beds, the chairs, the tables. He took down the old fence surrounding the house, good bleached wood, and used it to make furniture. If Jacqueline wanted anything, he'd make it for her. He'd do everything she wanted in the beginning."[313] Aube could see that Jacqueline initially was very much in love with him but became disappointed over time. Jacqueline would say to Aube: "You know, I never really loved your father, only for six months and that was all. And we stayed together nine years." She would also say: "I didn't love David, it was just convenient because I could do what I wanted. I could paint, I had the materials." "But that was not true," Aube explained. "That was at the end of her life, when she was bitter about everything."[314]

Aube, in any case, loved life in Roxbury. The house was surrounded by nature, and when not in school she was left to explore and play for hours on end, making discoveries on her own. There were brooks where she could watch otters groom and swim. In cold weather, she also had a sleigh that she used on the road in front of the house.

The family often saw the Tanguys and the Calders. Aube being friends with Sandra, the Calders' daughter, made it convenient since there were not many children around. Both Sandra and Aube recalled one unforgettable morning when Aube was waiting for the bus to school and planning to stay overnight with a woman in the nearest town, where she usually stayed when Jacqueline and David were away. Jacqueline had prepared her lunch box the previous evening, and Aube was waiting by the mailbox across the street when suddenly the door flew open and Jacqueline, stark naked, stormed out, screaming, "Your pajamas, you're going to need them!"[315] She threw them at Aube from across the road as the bus was arriving. Aube was accustomed to that sort of behavior, but everyone on the bus looked uncomfortable.

André took the train to visit Aube in Roxbury, sometimes by himself, sometimes with friends if they happened to be visiting. If David was in a good mood, he would come along to the station with Jacqueline to pick him up. However, it was usually uncomfortable for everyone; Jacqueline translated for both, since neither made any effort to communicate. David's interest typically lasted half an hour or so, then he would get up and disappear without excusing himself. "He was impatient," Aube recalled, "a rude person, which made things difficult. In France you say, 'I have an appointment,' even if it's not true, or 'Excuse me, I'm tired,' but you just don't do things like that. André would ask, 'Did I say something wrong to make him upset?' Jacqueline would reply, 'No he's just bored of hearing French.'"[316] David never learned French, and although André had learned English, he refused to speak it. Jacqueline, obviously uneasy, explained to André that David didn't say "excuse me" because he didn't speak French.

Jacqueline and David often traveled to New York and left Aube with various people. There was Granny Hare, whom Aube adored as a kind of fairy godmother. At times, Aube was left with her in a huge house by a lake. When André and Jacqueline were busy, they always found someone to leave her with. Aube liked that, because then someone paid attention to her, "and at those moments, I thought the world was opening for me." Knowing that David tended to be tough on Aube, Granny Hare would go out of her way to show affection. At night, after dinner, she'd teach Aube to play chess. When asked about her, Aube said: "I remember her well, she treated me like a human being, as if I existed. I was not used to it."[317]

Aube recalled one Christmas when Granny Hare took her into a room full of presents for the family, friends, cousins, grandsons, and granddaughters. Aube had never seen anything like that in her life: "'I have something for you,' she said. 'This is for you.' And in a box was a heart pendant made of quartz, an antique, with 'Aube' engraved on it. And that was one of the most beautiful things anybody ever gave me. And of course, I lost it. I am always looking, all over the world, for the same size heart in quartz. Today, I don't feel comfortable wearing something with my name on it because I think it's childish. This lady knew I existed, and she was telling me I existed, and that was something. I saw her more often when they wanted to get me out of the way."[318] After Granny Hare died, when Aube was thirteen, Jacqueline, David, and Aube traveled to New York to see David's older half-brother, John Goodwin, and he said to Aube: "'Granny loved you very much,' then added 'I want to give you a souvenir of her,' and he gave me an absolutely beautiful Indian bracelet with stones all around. I wore it for a long time. And one day, it broke. It was old and fragile. And I showed it to Jacqueline. At that time, Merlin went back and forth to see David, and Jacqueline said, 'You should give it to Merlin. He will fix it for you, because you can find turquoise in America.'" For months they never heard back. When Jacqueline asked about it, Merlin said he had been unable to find the turquoise. He returned it with a small stone, all that was left. "But I wear it all the time," Aube added.[319]

1947

Simone de Beauvoir, following in Sartre's footsteps, made Roxbury one of the stops on her tour of the United States. Hiding from the press, Sartre and Dolorès Vanetti would stay at the Hares'. Naturally, de Beauvoir had to visit to judge David and Jacqueline for herself and write about them. In her recollection, she described elaborately David's art and his studio, barely mentioning Jacqueline or her painting, her resentment concealed as indifference. Marveling at David's well-heated and well-equipped studio, she observed that "no American artist" could work in a studio such as Giacometti's, where poverty is obvious. De Beauvoir forgot that, to speak like that, she would need to know every American artist, which she did not. No doubt most struggled, but Giacometti was not poor: he could afford any studio; he just loved the one in which he worked, even without running water. De Beauvoir's hidden disdain for Jacqueline and her painting surfaced slowly five months later:

> *A day in the country will not do me any harm. I'm happy to have been invited by the Hs* [Jacqueline and David Hare]. *I take the train that gets me to M.* [Dolorès] *at 11 in the morning; there I'm told that the bus for Roxbury doesn't leave until two. It's a beautiful day, and I'm delighted to spend three hours in a little American village for no special reason ... My presence seems all the more gratuitous because no one is expecting me at any particular time. Besides, I don't know the Hs. (I met them briefly three months ago), and they have no more reason to invite me than I to see them.*
>
> *S.H.* [*sic*; Jacqueline Hare] *is French; she paints (she is also André Breton's ex-wife). Her husband has long been interested in the Indian's civilization, and his house would be the envy of the residents of Santa Fe's Canyon's Road. In the studio, where a wood fire is burning, there are Indian masks, dolls, beaded necklaces, jewelry, feathered headdresses, rugs, blankets, and pottery among flowers and branches. Nothing is excessive; everything is beautiful. On light wood shelves, there are old books—a vast library that H. inherited from his parents and which anchors the new house in the old past. There are the complete works of Hawthorne, George Meredith, Henry James, and Thackeray—old American culture with its English roots. The beautiful New Mexican objects amid the New England flora, the weighty tradition of books between freshly painted walls—it's an apt synthesis of various charming aspects of America. And it's even more complete when the voice of Billie Holiday rises from the corner of the large rustic fireplace.*
>
> *H. is a sculptor—I saw a fine exhibition of his in New York. I take a quick look at his studio. I remember G.'s* [Giacometti's] *studio in Paris, in an overgrown garden: bits of plaster and other debris, stained walls, rain trickling through the ceiling, and G. shivering in the winter. I don't think any American artist could work in such extreme poverty. In this vast, well-heated space, which is carefully lit, the contingency of the seasons and the caprices of the outside world have no place; everything is clean,*

*scoured; everything has been anticipated and has its own place.
There are minute tools and precision instruments, as if it were
a clockmaker's studio. One expects the plans conceived by the
brain to be executed with a strict exactitude, so it seems shocking
when they are embodied in the crude form of something palpable.
It would be ideal if the emptiness could be left to speak for itself.
But H. manipulates matter—it resists; he struggles, winning or
losing. Despite the striking difference in equipment, I suppose
that the same problems arise* [for sculptors] *here and in France.
And undoubtedly the same problems confront men in general,
whether they are using America's great new machinery or our
old tools back home.*[320]

In June, Jacqueline and David traveled to France to attend *Le Surréalisme en 1947*
at the Galerie Maeght, the first Surrealist exhibition since the war. Having left
behind painting traditional Surrealism, Jacqueline participated with *La Promenade,
les jeux* (The Walk, the Games, 1945; lost), a work from the fractal series. *Clair
de forêt* (Forest Clearing, 1947), a black-and-white lithograph of a jungle scene
lit by a crescent moon, in her current style, was included in the portfolio of
graphics published to accompany the show. Also included were works by Jean
Arp, Victor Brauner, Alexander Calder, Enrico Donati, Marcel Duchamp, Max
Ernst, David Hare, Roberto Matta, Kay Sage, Dorothea Tanning, and Toyen.
André hung the show according to correspondences, coupling Jacqueline's
painting and Frederick Kiesler's sculpture, although in the catalogue, titles
of children's games provided the equivalence Breton was looking for and her
painting was reproduced together with Leonora Carrington's *In the Garden,
He Played Peacefully on the Bagpipes* (1944). The startling cover of a rubber breast,
designed by Duchamp, was inscribed "Prier de toucher" (Please touch).

      Donati—whose first wife, Claire, had been a childhood friend of
Jacqueline's at the Lycée—forwarded a letter from Aube to which she replied:
"Thank you very much for sending me the letter from Aube, which touched
me very much. I received it at the same time as a little notebook [from her]
filled with glued flowers. Paris is wonderful despite all the material difficulties."
Jacqueline informed Donati that Péret was trying to return to Paris but had no
way to raise the money to do so. On Tuesday, June 19, triggered by the show,
André organized a sale with paintings donated from the exhibition, to open on
June 29, and Jacqueline took charge of asking artists to donate works. The sale
would be important, since the sale of Antonin Artaud's work, which included
his manuscripts and paintings, would help to finance Péret's care and return
to Paris after his release from the psychiatric hospital. "Would you give one of

your paintings from the exhibition, if not, urgently, would you send another by airplane as soon as possible?" Jacqueline asked Donati. "Please reply about this chez André."[321]

Jacqueline went with Dolorès to Picasso's to ask that he donate a work for the Péret sale. Picasso refused. "He makes fun of me and of my painting," he said of Péret. "He is a friend," Jacqueline insisted. "He needs help, and friends help friends."[322] She did not leave until he gave her an "important work."[323] Thanks to Jacqueline's perseverance, Péret was able to finance his return to France from Mexico, and his care afterward.

On August 14, Jacqueline, David, Aube, and Huguette stayed at Dora Maar's summer house in Ménerbes, which Picasso still felt entitled to since he had bought it for her as a "separation gift" by trading a painting.[324] Jacqueline and Dora had much to catch up on. In common with most of Picasso's relationships with women, his relationship with Maar ended badly. He had discarded her for the younger Françoise Gilot, whom he shamelessly brought to meet Dora at her apartment on rue de Savoie, after the break-up.

Eleven-year-old Aube recalled the awkward visit and her observation of the discomfort among the grown-ups, as if she were invisible. Dora and David disliked each other instantly, and neither made an effort to be sociable, rendering the stay unpleasant for everyone. David took many photographs of Jacqueline but only one with Huguette and Dora, who would not look at him. He could not wait to leave.

"One night"—Aube recalled an indelible event—"there was a visit of [Jacques] Lacan and his wife Sylvia Bataille.[325] There was also Marguerite Matisse [elder daughter of painter Henri Matisse]. She [had] just come back from the concentration camps. She had been arrested and tortured by the Nazis, being part of the Resistance. It was a very hot night. I remember the windows were open, and we were having soup. Insects, attracted by the light above the table, some fell in the soup. As Marguerite Matisse was telling us about the camps and what she endured, Sylvia Bataille rushed to the window to vomit." Aube had no way of knowing that during the war, Bataille's Jewish identity had placed her at risk of deportation, forcing her to hide in unoccupied territories, while Lacan sought to destroy documents detailing her family origins. For a long time, Aube wondered which of these events unsettled Sylvia more, but eventually she decided that in the moment they were both equally shocking.[326]

David did not like writing letters, but, needing a distraction from the uncomfortable situation at Ménerbes, he wrote to Donati with his opinion of the Surrealist show and its aftermath:

Well, I suppose that now is so late I might just as well not written and then I could tell you about it when I got back to New York that I wanted to wait until the show was on before writing so that I should have some news for you and then after it opened I thought to myself everybody must have written you about things so what was the use of adding my two cents. The long and short is that I hate writing letters and so I put off as far as possible. Before I go any further I had better tell you in case you don't already know, that I can't spell a word. All this mistaken calligraphy is unintentional and not done to be funney. However any amusement which arises from it is given gratis.

Kiestler [Kiesler] as you know is here beating his branes out and getting some of the success which he has missed these last 14 years in ny. it will take the French sometime that he is a fake and so he has some while to enjoy himself yet. The show finely opened after all the various disagreements that you can so well imagin since you remember VVV. However the public dident know all that and so they are labering under the impression the surrealists are one happy family. It is strange how Surrealism has become changed here. I emagin that before the war it was looked on as a rather revolutionary movement. The attitude now is quite different. The general publick accepts it, not as anything new but as past history which they never clearly understood but which they have come to accept not because they have understood it but partly because they have become accustomed to it as perhaps mostly because they say to themselves (After all, it is French, it developed in France and now it has come back again. We are pleased to have it back because it belongs to us but how could one expect us after what we have been through in the war, to take it seriously.) this general attitude and as a consuquence the gallery is at all times crowded but not with people really interested or even with those realy against. It is simply crowded with humanity, nothing better to do on an afternoon. There are no discussions, no fights, no real interest and yet in spite of this it is a suces as a publicity stunt for the gallery. It is strange but one would almost say that it was popular suces but an intellectual failure.

All of this i[s], of corese, the way it is accepted from the point of view of the public. Amoung all the surreasists themselves there is the same old excitement. However hear it seems to be a meaningless excitement, a small group of people amusing themselves with ideas which they invented in 1930 and sadly forgetting to keep ahead

of their times. I know all this sound depressing and as far as the
particular works in the show go of corse there are a lot of good
ones, but I do Not speak of the aesthetic side of the exhibition,
I only speak of the general attitude to surrealism amoung the
other intelectualss here in Paris. I should rather see them against
it than find this of-hand attitude. So much for the general state
of affairs. Your pictures look well and are nicely hung. The green
hand with the eye in the window stares malignantly out at the
passers by. The piece of mine which belongs to you arrived in the
best condition and I am going to see the repacking of it myself so
that it will return in the same condition. We are returning on the
begining of Oct. so it will be nice to see you then.

> *Best of luck to you,*
> *David[327]*

Jacqueline was also in France to open her one-woman exhibition at the Galerie Pierre, October 7–21, 1947, her first show in Paris. Pierre Loeb's gallery, historically among the most reputable, had shown work by Artaud, Balthus, Lam, Miró, Picasso, and others. Jacqueline's small but comprehensive retrospective brought together paintings she produced between 1942 and 1947, the years she lived in America. Critics were uniformly complimentary; one mentioned that she had been André's wife.

> *SPECTATEUR*
> *Jacqueline Lamba, returning from America, has brought back some*
> *twenty canvases of an unquestionable ornamental value. She goes*
> *from abstract to decorative stylizations most often treated with the*
> *tender colors of the fruit of the West Indies.*

> *FRANCE SOIR*
> *Jacqueline Lamba escapes the last constraints and frames the most*
> *diverse landscapes of the world. She undertakes explorations of*
> *the unknown of a universe yet to be created ... Jacqueline Lamba,*
> *painter worthy of the name, keeps moving forward without rest or*
> *contentment ... her work shows that painting is her constant concern*
> *... her canvases belong to a melancholic world where ancient works,*
> *like Malgré tout, le printemps, contain the beginning of darkness.*
>
> *The former wife of André Breton presents at Pierre some*
> *poetic ex-votos. Is it possible to call these great images anything*
> *else? Yet poetry and painting come together at their source ...*

Again, Simone de Beauvoir, suddenly an art expert, could not pass up the opportunity to let her opinion be known. She and Jacqueline had met ten years earlier, after Jacqueline married André, and occasionally ran into each other at one of the cafés frequented by the Surrealists. They shared similar opinions on feminism and the difficulties women faced in a world of men. They were not friends, but were friendly enough to say hello. In *The Prime of Life* (1960), in which de Beauvoir wrote about her early years, she described Jacqueline neutrally. Her resentment toward Jacqueline might not have developed, however, had not the Dolorès–Sartre affair made their paths cross in an unsavory way; she was, after all, Dolorès's friend. De Beauvoir's visit to Connecticut had been intentionally planned, her conflict ever present in her mind. Since de Beauvoir and Sartre, like two old fishwives, fed off each other's gossip about their respective and shared affairs, she had learned through him that he and Dolorès spent long periods in Roxbury with Jacqueline and David.[328]

Sartre's attachment to Dolorès was a threat to de Beauvoir, who met Dolorès in New York as the latter was heading for France to stay there until de Beauvoir's return. Simone wrote about her as "M" in the first volume of *The Force of Circumstance* (1963): "She was as charming as Sartre had described her, and she had the prettiest smile in the world."[329] But to Sartre, de Beauvoir described Dolorès as hostile. De Beauvoir had known about Dolorès much earlier, long before she immigrated to the United States, when she "had often admired [her] at the Dôme where her stunning entrances never went unremarked," but now she pretended that she was not threatened, that she had just met Dolorès, was not jealous, and was open-minded—trying to blanket over the experience with a pseudo-blasé attitude.[330] She also had to reframe the relationship as just another episode of the ongoing Sartre–de Beauvoir saga, about their eternal competition, always under their control, purportedly evolving in the area of freedom. So, like Sartre, de Beauvoir, too, came to America to present lectures; like Sartre, de Beauvoir, too, took an American lover (Nelson Algren); she purportedly also fell madly in love but would not marry him, just as Sartre decided against marrying Dolorès. But to outdo Sartre, de Beauvoir referred to Algren as her husband, even though she felt no sorrow when he died, she told her sister—yet she was buried wearing the wedding ring he had given her. Her anger overflowed and she made a target of Jacqueline, administering the *coup de grâce* to her art while condescendingly referring to her as a friend, even though earlier she claimed to have just met her months earlier. Disregarding the favorable reviews of the show, de Beauvoir wrote to Algren the evening after Jacqueline's vernissage:

Wednesday

Yesterday evening, coming back from a little nightclub, I found your letter; I just read it and fell asleep. I love you. A friend of mine had an exhibition of paintings. She is a nice and even a beautiful woman but a very poor painter. So it was sad, everybody knowing it was so poor, and looking at the paintings without saying anything, and she knew too that it was not good. So on the evening, we tried to comfort her and went to eat couscous and then to drink whisky with her and her husband who is an American sculptor. The man looked very poetical for me because he takes his airplane for New York this morning. It was his last night in Paris.[331]

A Lover

From France, thirty-seven-year-old Jacqueline returned pregnant. She described her pregnancy to Huguette, and, like her parents before she was born, expressed the same preference for a son:

> *Don't be upset with me if I write you seldom, but there was my show as you can see, and I am less and less available for communicating. I am fine but uncomfortable in my body. The child is taking all that I have in the way of energy, and I am as if sleeping or trying to in order not to feel my body that I feel does not belong to me anymore. The spirit follows the rhythm. It's nice weather. We are back in Roxbury. I cannot paint, and I don't feel like drawing. The gallery where I had the show was not large enough for all the works I wanted to show, but it was not too bad. Next year, there will be a much larger one. The house has been invaded by a baby scale, special blankets and layette furniture. If it's a girl, the name will be Eriff. A boy, surely rather a boy, it will be Nemo or perhaps Merlin.[332]*

Aube later recalled Jacqueline's pregnancy as difficult, but also as a time of heartwarming moments:

David did something very nice with me, when I was a child.
I remember that was in Roxbury, Jacqueline was about eight months
pregnant, and the three of us were having dinner. She was serving
soup, and I asked for more and she burst out, "I'm sick of it! You're
tiring me! I'm fed up with all that! Leave me alone!" She was a bear,
exhausted from her pregnancy, and she probably didn't accept it, in
a narcissistic way. And it came out towards me. I went to my room
and cried. And David came and calmed me. I was sobbing in my
bed, and he held my head and said, "Don't think that she does not
love you. She's just tired because she's expecting a baby. I'm sorry
she talked to you that way. Don't be upset, she loves you anyway."[333]

As happy as David was about Jacqueline's pregnancy, and as eager to have a
child of his own, he had no patience with the fatigue and withdrawal that came
with it. He, too, craved attention, needing her to be available as before, but it
was not in her. He loved her, he said, but clearly had lost interest. One friend,
recalling David's many girlfriends, explained: "He wasn't a very good husband
to any of his wives. He was too egocentric. I don't know if he loved anybody.
He liked people, but he was a very mixed-up person. He enjoyed his life, he had
lots of money, and did whatever he wanted. He was unique, fascinating. He had
a great sense of humor and laughed a great deal. He was fun to be with, he sang
and played the ukulele. Women were crazy about him. He didn't have to work
very hard."[334] Martica Sawin recalled being at a gallery when David walked in,
and the reaction of those present: "Everyone turned to look at him. He was
incredibly beautiful. It was like Apollo descending ... It was rumored that he was
the illegitimate son of John Barrymore."[335] Aube recalled the strong impression
he made on her as a child: "I would describe David as a very important person,
a personality. He was someone who, if you met on the street, you would turn
around and ask, 'Who is he?' A big presence, a very handsome person, looking
very different from anybody else, and not pleasant, a very interesting personality,
but oh, what a selfish person. Narcissistic, too."[336]

 While Jacqueline was pregnant, David began an affair with Mary
Abbott, an exquisite beauty eleven years his junior. Abbott was a member of
the School of Abstract Expressionism and, despite being a good painter, was
best known for her looks. As Debutante of the Year, she graced the covers of
Charm, Glamour, Vogue, and *Harper's Bazaar.* Her *Mayflower* ancestry included
two presidents—John Adams and John Quincy Adams.

 Abbott, a neighbor of David's studio on 79 East 10th Street, befriended
Jacqueline: "I wanted to be like her," Abbott recalled.[337] One thing she and
Jacqueline had in common, before meeting David, was their affinity for nature. At

a time when artists were exploring non-objective painting, Jacqueline consciously made art influenced by nature. Unlike artists who liked talking about art with other artists, she preferred to focus on painting. At thirty-seven, Jacqueline remained striking. Abbott recalled her as worldly, educated, and opinionated, although she could be intimidating when she spoke. Sure of herself as a person and as a painter, she questioned traditional values intelligently. Even conventional fashion was of no interest to her, Abbott recalled. She wore Native American or Mexican clothing and exotic jewelry. After Jacqueline had given hand-me-downs to Jeanne Reynal, Reynal would pass on to Abbott those that she did not want, and Abbott would wear them eagerly: "I admired her tremendously from afar, of course. She was jealous of me—David did play around a lot—she thought of me as the worst kind of American, a blonde American slut."[338]

Before becoming one of the three women who belonged to the Artists' Club on 8th Street—Joan Mitchell and Perle Fine were the other two—Abbott met David's artist friends, and particularly liked Barnett Newman and Willem de Kooning. "Generally speaking," she recalled, "the women at the Club weren't treated differently than anyone else—an artist was an artist. Sometimes, you might get treated like a girl because you were pretty. I was chosen to collect the dues and go buy the booze because I was pretty, and the guys would pay up if I asked them to. Other times, you had to be tough to be taken seriously."[339] The affair with David ended when Abbott became involved with de Kooning, who had an open marriage.

Jacqueline told Dolorès she knew her marriage was over on the evening she arrived at the Cedar Tavern to meet David and saw him "looking at Mary with the special look he once had for me."[340]

Merlin Is Born

Meredith Merlin Hare, Jacqueline's "golden boy," born in New York on June 19, 1948, was given the names of his paternal grandfather and the magus of Arthurian legend (pl. 34). David wanted him to be named after his own father, whom he had lost prematurely. Merlin was Jacqueline's choice. Thereafter, she created for herself a split in her lifeline: "Before Merlin" and "After Merlin." On the backs of photographs, she might identify the sitters, the places where they were taken, and Merlin's age at the time, whether he was in the photo or not.

An uncomfortable pregnancy did not keep Jacqueline from fulfilling a commitment to the Passedoit Gallery in New York, where she exhibited fifteen paintings from April 27 through May 1948. In a note to herself she wrote, "1948 no longer painting surrealism."[341]

Reviewers were impressed. "An individual pure and simple at the Passedoit Gallery admits no classification ... Miss Lamba is daring yet sensitive, fanciful yet credible ... tenderly provocative, elusive as a fragment of music," wrote the *New York Sun* critic. The *New York Telegram*'s reviewer wrote that "The paintings impress one at first ... as being disconcertingly monotonous. And it's true that there is little variety in these abstract landscapes painted primarily in yellow-greens, with strong reliance on faceted stylized shapes, and organized in flat overall designs ... Yet, if you look at each separately ... you cannot help but appreciate its extremely sensitive color harmonies, subtle patterns, [and] delicacy of technique."

Following Jacqueline's exhibition, Aube wrote to André:

May 14, 1948

My Dear Papasito,

I just received one of your letters, which I was eagerly waiting for because I had not received any letters from you for a long time ... I'm surprised that I don't get letters from you anymore; it is usually I who don't write anymore. How sad it is, the news about Aunt Lucy, because I loved her a lot, and I am sure Grandpa was very sad about it. I will write to him tomorrow, and tell me is Grandpa going back to Lorient?

I am reading some Chinese stories from Norman Hinsdale Pitman. They are very interesting because it's almost completely different from other stories. It's the story of a golden beetle or why dogs hate cats. He has good ideas, only a little too short. He is not poetic. I will tell you about the stories that follow if they are better.

This summer break will turn out well, for the month of July I will go to camp in the school where I will be this winter. It is charming, we go horse-back riding, we work in the morning, we swim, we sleep outside, we go to picnics, and many other interesting things. My school isn't bad, I mean it's not too strict, but the teacher is such an idiot, that if it were not for Sandra [Calder] (whom I like a lot and is my great joy), this school would be a boring place.

I am glad to see that you're happy about Péret. I would like so much to see him because I remember in Mexico he was so nice with us. Next time you see him, give him a kiss for me. I have not yet seen Madame Cuttoli. She was supposed to visit us but she hasn't come.

The exhibitions of David and Jacqueline [at the Passedoit Gallery] were really good. Madame [Georgette] Passedoit is very nice, only mom's exhibition had to be closed for a few days because the friend of Madame Passedoit died. I liked David's exhibition.

How is Elisita doing. Is she more rested since the vacation? How I would like to see her.

My dear papasito, I send you a big big kiss and hug in the arms of a cloud, with Uli [the dog] and Elisita [Breton's third wife, Elisa] and with everything in the garden, the apple trees, the almond trees, the pansy, the peach trees, the lilacs, the daffodils, the violets, and the dandelions (my favorite flower), including the ferns, they are all blooming.

XXXX

Aube[342]

Where neglected children develop difficult personalities to seek attention and validation, some became solicitous. While living with Frida in Mexico, Aube learned Mexican terms of endearment and began using them: "I used words of tenderness insistently in Spanish." One day, Jacqueline—forgetting she had used the same tender words with Frida—said to Aube, "Don't call me that way, it's ridiculous."[343]

David was eagerly awaiting the birth of Merlin, his firstborn. He said to Jacqueline, "After the baby is born, I want to be alone with you and the baby." Aube recalled:

I was eleven and Jacqueline spoke to me about it, as if I was a grown-up. "Listen, I'm miserable about it, but I have no choice. The only choice I have is between my child, my daughter, and the man I love. And if I insist on you staying, I will lose the man I love. So you have to go away."

"Where?" I asked.

"I don't know, we will have to figure that out. André can't take you because he does not have any money." At that time André was still in New York, and Granny Hare, as always, was willing to do David's thankless tasks and saved the day. She looked for the best school she could find and paid tuition for the progressive Hickory Ridge School, in Putney, Vermont, near the Canadian border. A year's tuition would pay for a college education. And I left for the

summer. There were as many teachers as there were students. There were boys and girls. When the headmistress, a psychoanalyst, felt we had a problem, she would say, "Well, come and talk." Everything was very friendly. That school was really wonderful. I went there from home, like an unwanted orphan, really miserable, and after two weeks I was so happy there, I didn't even write home anymore. I remember as far as discipline was concerned, we did our own. Everybody respected that, nobody cheated.[344]

The school also encouraged creativity. Hayden Herrera, a schoolmate, remembered that Aube had the kids dancing to music by Stravinsky.[345] Aube's joy turned to misery, though, when André wrote to Jacqueline demanding that Aube return to France. By then, Aube spoke French, English, and Spanish. But when he noticed a misspelling in one of her letters, he could think of nothing else and demanded that she come back. In France, she was placed in the neighborhood communal school, which was "ferocious." She cried every night for weeks, but little by little she got used to it.

Aube was unhappy living with André, having lived away from him for so many years, and was fearful of standing up to his autocratic manner. She made Jacqueline swear to bring her back to the States as soon as possible. Jacqueline kept her promise, and the following year Aube returned. She traveled back on the boat with Sonja Sekula, whom she liked. Sekula liked Aube also and painted her portrait.

Although the problems between Jacqueline and David were intensifying, they had been keeping up a front when, in 1949, they were invited to participate in a pioneering exhibition about nine couples: Jacqueline Lamba and David Hare; Lee Krasner and Jackson Pollock; Jean Arp and Sophie Taeuber-Arp; Elaine and Willem de Kooning; Robert and Sonia Delaunay; Barbara Hepworth and Ben Nicholson; Dorothea Tanning and Max Ernst; Françoise Gilot and Pablo Picasso; and Stanley William Hayter and Helen Phillips. The idea was to present the couples on equal terms, but the show did not turn out as expected. Instead, according to a critic, it reinforced the presumption that women were subordinate to their partners. Anne M. Wagner wrote for *Art News*: "There is a tendency among some of these wives to tidy up their husband's styles."[346]

Although her participation in the show had been more automatic than thoughtful, Jacqueline was not put off by the reviews. She knew her work was strong, that she was painting in a unique personal style, certainly not inferior to David's. But uppermost in her mind was her marriage, keeping it from falling apart and keeping grounded for two-year-old Merlin, who was still getting from both parents the attention he needed. She wrote to Dolorès on January 10, 1951:

It is 12:30 p.m. and I can hear the little one outside returning to eat lunch. He is going to prevent me from speaking to you as I want. Here he is all wrapped up to his nose in red, with (big) boots with fur on the inside/outside. A rush of words flow without stopping from the moment of his waking until night. He has received more gifts for Christmas than you could ever dream about. And here is a very small plastic truck, big as his hand, that he picked up in a heap of frozen sand in Washington Square, that will fill his day with pleasure. He wets in the bathroom; he is wise to keep himself generally dry outside in that it is severely cold. For the other business, he is generally as clean as a cat. Apart, he is the pride of Marie (his nanny) who can answer his questions ... and it is true, no kindergarten will take a child who is 2½ years old, and especially if they wet themselves so abundantly. He is sitting on the carpet pushing his poor truck using the gestures of an amorous truck driver. He does not let you speak, too fascinated in making it go around all the objects on the bench, he likes anything that has wheels, no matter the condition. He has a tricycle that he abandoned immediately for a large tractor toy of a six-year-old child who has had to give it up in that Merlin is in the area so much, according to Marie, the irresistible side of "Sparkle" [her nickname for Merlin] *prevents the mothers from protesting ... when he's not calm, he rolls on the frozen ground screaming as if he's being murdered. He has always great beauty, hair is slightly dark, which allows one to see his eyebrows much better ... He never lends his toys except to a little child his age, whom he treats more or less as an equal. He adores David; one of the reasons is that he can fix his broken toys. He calls him "My David." His key is hardly in the door and he shouts to him from his bath on the first floor and starts a big commotion ... nothing to be done about it; without the truck which follows him to the toilet, which will travel on the toilet seat, and which will follow him to bed and will keep warm near his heart.*[347]

A New Reality

By the end of the 1940s, Jacqueline's painting began reflecting trouble with David, according to Ernestine Lassaw, caused by "his many girlfriends, and experimenting with drugs."[348] Ethel Baziotes witnessed the change in Jacqueline: "Drastically, her whole state of being was different. She was much graver."[349] Her quiet work, previously defined by muted yellows, now transitioned to a harsh, jarring palette, and the puzzle-like compositions no longer fitted together to complete a harmonious whole. The breakdown in the relationship is evident in *Rivière* (River, 1947; pl. 35), where a jagged greenish-blue river meanders from one corner to the other of the square canvas, splitting the space into rough halves. Gradually, perhaps to make sense of what she was experiencing, Jacqueline began shifting back into objective art. In *Soleil ou tournesol* (Sun or Sunflower, 1949), a sunflower covers the canvas with petals and leaves as the sun blends spikes and edges, rounding forms.

One troubling moment was an interlude on a trip the family took to New Mexico. It was unusual for Jacqueline to paint people. But in *USA Taos* (1950), two persons, framed by vegetation, stand in the distance before a brick building, their faceless heads turned toward each other. *Les Papillons noirs* (Black Butterflies, ca. 1950), her largest and most ambitious work from the period, offers a metaphor for Jacqueline's internal agitation. The flat sky is dark gray. Black, whirling butterflies leave shadows of their aimlessness above the field of wild grass and flowers.

Whatever intimacy brought Jacqueline and David together had clearly vanished. Never, in ten years with him, had she thought their life together would come to this. When she met David, he was used to having his life organized, first by his mother, then by Suzy. But Jacqueline, differently aware, had taken over the task, kept his life in balance, planting and nourishing the seed of the sculptor he was becoming, and given him the son he wanted. For as long as he adored her, she was the world to him, but that was over; his interest was now elsewhere. Unsettled by this new reality, she began to lose her way, and it started to show in her painting.

Foreseeing trouble, Jacqueline concluded that the way to deal with this insurmountable problem was by returning to France. On Sunday, December 23, 1951, she summarized for Dolorès her new life:

> *Paris is sad, gray, people the same, too, very few exceptions among them are Jean-Paul* [Sartre], *friendly and interesting as always, given his play* Le Diable et le Bon Dieu [The Devil and the Good Lord] *being the best and outstanding, besides that, the show is finished.*

I am looking for a gallery that will take my paintings for good and sell them. This is what is called "sortir un peintre" [launching a painter]. *It is sordid but I've got to go that way, otherwise, I continue to paint in my studio for myself, so it seems anyway; that is much more important than a show.*

To finish about me, I no longer have any apprehension because I am sure of my work; objectively, so far (?) I remain simply on the plan of searching [for a gallery]—*which is nothing of the assurance that in 2–3 years, perhaps I will be sought out. My painting begins to worry me in another area: I am no longer painting in the current tendency* [abstraction].

Through necessity, we are staying in Cannes two years, at least for me, I'm staying. As for David, I don't know. He will return no doubt to the US from time to time. No apartment in Paris, at least, as you know. It is beautiful in Cannes (where we are calm and relatively warm). I have a tiny garden, two terraces, a room for work, not very big, but wonderful light. The child is going to pre-school just close by. A 14-year-old is taking care of him with a maximum of patience but a minimum of professionalism— Aube is coming on holiday—she has become very nice, even in David's eyes, unless the disagreement which reigns between me and David removes his prejudice—I don't know—with David it has not been nice, at all, for a year, and if we are staying together up until today, it is because of the child—it's been hard to accept for several months, but the happiness that I seek and my working very quickly erases all the rest, including the pleasures—you see, I'm telling you ... it's even for that reason that I have not written you.

All this stuff was too much for me, like in Paris two years ago when we got upset because you did not write—I understand quite well now—anyway, I would like to know when will I see you. Friendship, like work, is until death. I like you enormously and our quarrels do not ruin anything. I would like you to get hold of a job, not simply to pass your time but as a reason for living. You would not need anyone in the sad sense ...

And the little kid, he is more and more hateful because everywhere he goes he is the darling—he reserves his anger for the home, he bites his nanny, he kicks us, and keeps two knives that go with him day and night and talks about cutting up everyone in pieces—that, even before the operation he underwent a week ago, tonsils and adenoids. By the way, from the surgeon and nurses,

139

nothing but flattery, moreover he did not want to leave the hospital.

We are no doubt leaving next Thursday or Friday—
Christmas tree here, the idea of more toys sickens me ...

Love to Teddy,

Write. Your friend Jacqueline[350]

Jacqueline stayed in Cannes until 1952 (pl. 36). To save face, she would not return to the States. The couple's constant fighting had become intolerable, making it easier for David to stay away. She hoped he would follow her after seeing his life unravel and ask her to come back. But David did not operate like that. His mind was drawn to what felt good, not what was right, and he found ways to get what he wanted. Unwittingly, Jacqueline's leaving had provided him with a taste of freedom, and he became even more slippery. In the States he came and went as he pleased. He visited France when he felt like it, got to see Merlin as often as he wished, and had Jacqueline at his beck and call.

Initially, Jacqueline lived at "Le Tamisier," a house that belonged to Dolorès on the Boulevard du Cap, Antibes. During this time, Jacqueline painted three portraits of Merlin, all three—like his golden hair—in bright yellows. In the one Jacqueline gave to Dolorès, hung over the chest of drawers in her bedroom, he wears a boatneck T-shirt like one often worn by Picasso.

Between December 1 and 15, 1951, Jacqueline exhibited in Paris, at the Galerie Henriette Niepce, twenty delicate works reminiscent of Paul Klee's childlike simplicity, likely influenced by Merlin's playfulness. Antonina Vallentin's review of the show—perhaps the most thoughtful and complimentary that Jacqueline had received—must have felt like a godsent balm for her aching soul, appearing in *Les Temps Modernes*, the preeminent intellectual magazine of the era, founded by Sartre and de Beauvoir:

> *Very much of her time, Jacqueline Lamba, with the gift of a colorist of rare quality, has managed to dissolve forms and reach non-figurative art. Her grays are extraordinarily rich, her pale yellows come from brushes of moonlight ... Between the real and the unreal, Jacqueline Lamba seeks a very personal path. In La Nuit, for example, lingers the residue of things seen. She succeeds in transmitting here a sense of the drama through the clearest schematic world being born. The more successful paintings agree with the moonlight, or in the calming pearly harmony of appeasement; her orchestration becomes subtle and alluring. She manages to create her personal universe with her very own shorthand. Yet, if she has been able to free herself from form, she still gets enticed by words, which is one of our struggles*

with abstract artists. She titles her paintings, for example, Grand Jardin au pommier gris [Large Garden with Gray Apple Tree]. She names her most independent landmarks of the universe, forests and rivers, as if imagination needs those deceiving crutches to complete its escape. It is possible that Jacqueline Lamba has not yet reached the peak of her evolution, [but] her love of matter might one day bring her refined art toward a figurative art as personal as her abstract language.[351]

A Visit to Picasso

At seventeen, Aube had grown into a beautiful, golden-haired young woman imbued with the freshness of youth (pl. 37). She had lived extraordinary moments with extraordinary people who cared about her, albeit inconsistently—not enough to implant in her the sense of belonging that one gets from one's mother. Chronic neglect left her feeling unlovable, unworthy, longing for the affection she missed, living with a sense of emptiness. In adolescence, these feelings took over her personality; she became shy and socially awkward, and, feeling unattractive, she sat apart from others. Sometimes, Aube and Jacqueline would visit Picasso at his home or meet him at the beach, where he held court among Spanish musicians, toreadors, and onlookers. It all came down on Aube one day:

> *I was in my little corner, and Maya [Picasso's daughter] was plump, beautiful, with flowers in her golden hair, radiant. Me, I just looked at her, thinking, if only I could be just a little bit like her. How I would be happy. I was in complete admiration of her, sitting in a little spot on the beach, like that. And Picasso came over to me and said: "Aube, what is up with you?"*
> *And I said, "Nothing."*
> *So he said, "What do you want?"*
> *"I want nothing."*
> *He said, "Ask me for anything you want, I will give it to you." He would have insisted, but I was not ambitious, and I still am not, and it would have been nice for me to have someone pay attention to me. That, and only that. It was not because it*

141

was Picasso but the fact that someone would paint my portrait.
He could have well done a portrait of me but he didn't insist. And
I was watching Maya with envious eyes, saying to myself, "Oh how
lucky she is. Oh, how I would like to be like that."[352]

In reality, Aube and Maya did not look much different. As they had when they were children, they played together and people often couldn't tell them apart. What made them different at seventeen was not so much how they looked to others, but how they saw themselves.

A Great Disappointment

When it became clear to Jacqueline that she would be staying in France, she leased a place at 93 Boulevard Eugène Gazagnaire, Cannes, because Picasso lived nearby. She saw him frequently, and, as big brothers do, he watched over her. Things with David had worsened. He cared about Jacqueline, she knew, but he had lost interest in her as a lover, partner, and wife. Perhaps, she hoped, if the right work opportunity came along, he would stay, and who better than Picasso to make him an offer? When Picasso proposed to David that he become his sculpture assistant, adding—as if it were necessary—that "after, every door will automatically open to you," David responded as if he had nothing to learn from Picasso: "He was not interested. He said that what he needed was to concentrate on his work."[353] It was over. The ace Jacqueline kept up her sleeve had been of no help. Single-handedly, she had launched David's meteoric career, soon to plummet. She had provided him with the opportunity of a lifetime in working with Picasso, but he could not see beyond his inflated ego.[354]

After this disappointment, Jacqueline wrote Dolorès on June 20, 1955:

Treasure,

David is returning to the USA by air in two days. Ah, Dolorès, you know I don't have the taste for unhappiness, and that I do not seek [it] anymore since ages ago ... [he] advised me that he is seriously "neurasthenic"—I am in a state of dry despair, and I am gathering my strength. I am fed up with it, but for me, [I have] no strength—

Greetings to you, write—Jacqueline
I GIVE YOU MY WORD THAT I AM DOING WHAT I CAN[355]

On August 1, 1955, Jacqueline wrote again:

> *This morning your letter in homage to friendship—I reply immediately.*
> *Friendship, it's the big revelation for me. All my life, I have benefited*
> *from it without really seeing it—that of Charles Duits, who is so*
> *attentive a few steps away, that of Picasso, tender to the utmost—this*
> *being, reproachful of death, is only a smile and happiness—that,*
> *also of his wife, kindness, kindness, happiness too. We are in a big*
> *garden, maximum charm and space—a big studio for me, even too*
> *beautiful—work, <u>very bad</u>, <u>but very bad</u>. But this will pass, I know.*

In the same letter to Dolorès, Jacqueline wrote about Lila Ferry, a friend from the early years, André's lover before he met Jacqueline.[356] Merlin had a crush on her little daughter:

> *A small girl who has such beauty that the little one no longer*
> *<u>demands</u>. He himself is very happy and strong as possible. The*
> *departure of D[avid] who [he] knows since birth does not worry*
> *him; as far as I am concerned, it is the last time that he troubles*
> *my life. I do not want any more of this being who apparently loves*
> *unhappiness so much. It is not for him to leave (he appears to have*
> *the need of a new being, and young, as it happens so frequently*
> *to men) but he is leaving for nothing—I have shared this error*
> *of believing, because he chose badly and with impatience, it was*
> *me that he always loved. I only wanted too much to believe ... You*
> *tell me that I am alone and ask me when I am coming to America.*
> *I will never return because there is no longer any reason for going*
> *there. I've understood also that one must not trail behind to have*
> *pain and when this is true and no longer sought for, later in time*
> *this pain will be eradicated ... by gathering up all forces that one*
> *has—and no more inventing than subtracting. I am however more*
> *alone as a woman than D. with women, much less unhappy because*
> *I can replace things, and place myself there ... He is prevented by*
> *this taste for suffering, guilty to no end, etc. I pray to the Gods*
> *that he will find himself because I hold a great tenderness for him*
> *and I detest seeing him suffer. Since you know him less well, you*
> *are mistaken about him when you saw him during last winter, as*
> *he was making an error himself. As for the question of nastiness*

linked to the matter of unhappiness, he sets obstinately to work
so that it will not be so.

As for me, I have nearly no more efforts to make in this
direction. I assure you that I do not have the impression at all of
having been spoiled by life, but now, on the contrary, one which is full
that one must place within the work, in love, perhaps, again, or if not,
in daily exchange with others, to pull oneself together with that which
one has acquired and place it in such a manner as to convince. So,
Dolorès, I see you being sad and I would like to show you the garden
here, with all the beauty that it contains—the beaches, all different in
the light, to give you the little one for going fishing for sea urchins in
the rocks—and to see you happy, amusing people and to bring them
life—this life, on the contrary, makes more sense than it ever did.

Possibilities are greater than during one's youth, because
in the final analysis, one no longer invents them—one sees
what they are for oneself. And in the sense when they really are,
it's inexhaustible.

I kiss you as I love you.
Always, as you are precious, you know J

If the separation of Jacqueline and David had a damaging effect on Merlin, that was not evident in his recollections after moving to Paris, which David left for good. On the contrary, Merlin's memories took him back to their apartment on 46 rue Gay-Lussac. He recalled being in the nursery, "listening to Jacqueline paint. The movement of approaching the canvas and retreating could go on for hours. And for me, it had a calming effect. It was life. It was her."[357]

Merlin compared Jacqueline's painting to a form of meditation, a way of emptying her spirit on to the canvas. For a long time, she kept on her work table a piece of paper on which was written "the delivering spirit," which is what Merlin intuited was taking place when she painted. This form of meditation existed outside of conscious awareness. It came from a deeper place within her. Gradually, she learned to let it rise without trying to hold on to it because it rose in a moment and vanished as quickly.

Even as a child, Merlin knew his parents were different from other children's, and that fact was a source of pride for him. The men whom Jacqueline had loved had been artists, and she would have liked Merlin to be one. That did not come to pass, but he still saw the world as artists do: "Jacqueline was passionate about details—observing the moment—she lived in the present more than most. I believe she taught me to observe the instant, especially to feel awe in the face of the incredible beauty of the world—like that, in an instant."[358]

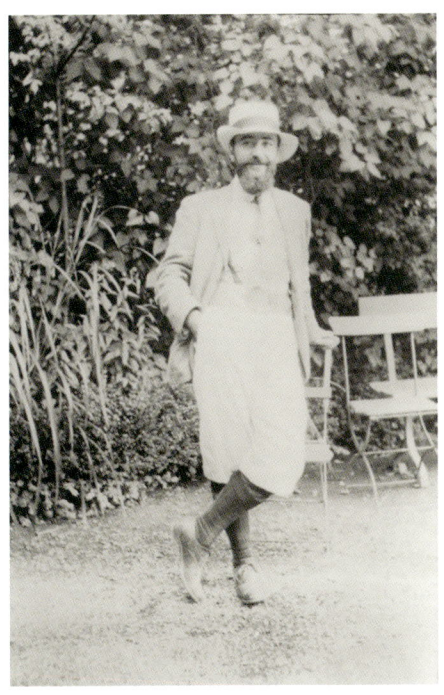

(pl. 1) Portrait of José Lamba, Oberhofen, 1904

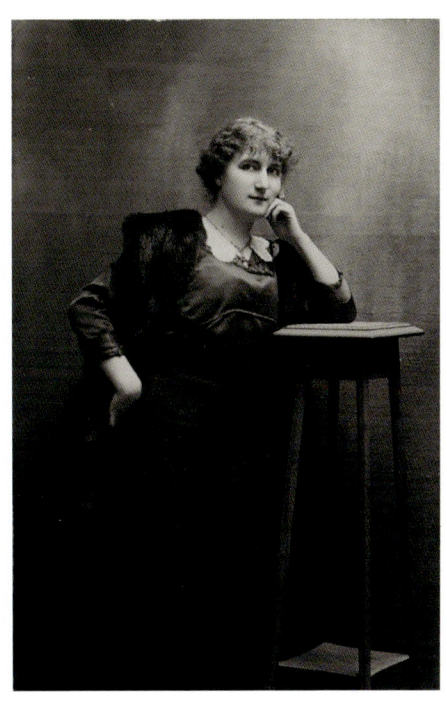

(pl. 2) Portrait of Jane Lamba, Paris, ca. 1908

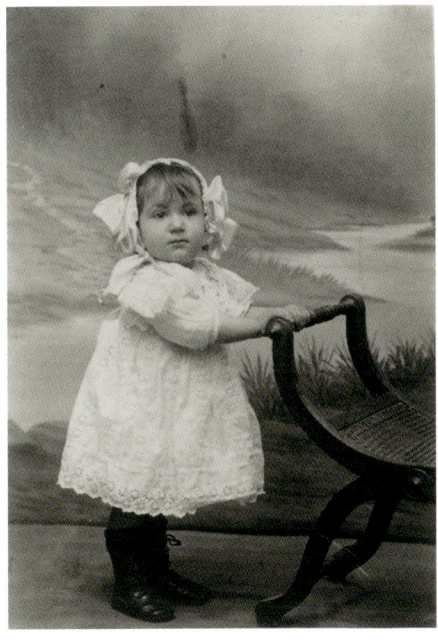

(pl. 3) Jacqueline as a toddler, ca. 1911

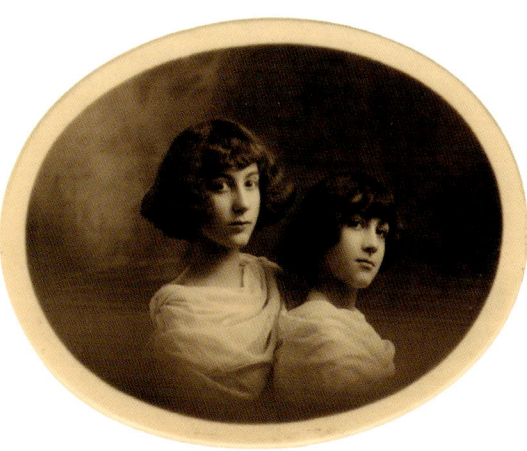

(pl. 4) Huguette and Jacqueline, ages nine and six, 1915

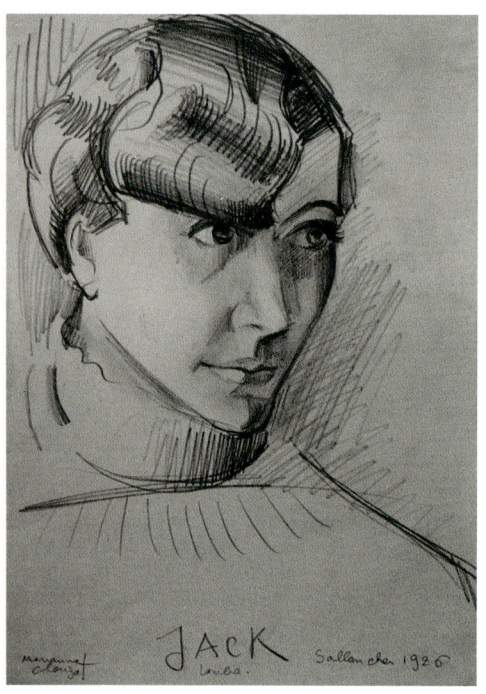

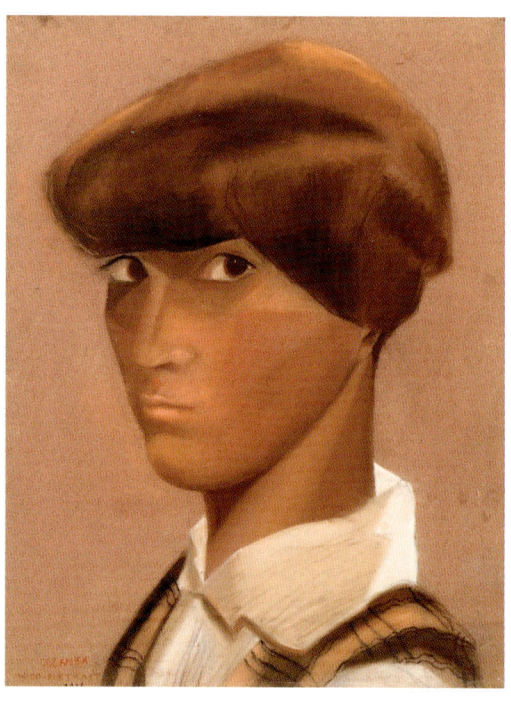

(pl. 5) Marianne Clouzot,
Portrait of Jacqueline as Jack, 1925

(pl. 6) Jacqueline Lamba, *Self-Portrait*, 1926,
pastel on paper

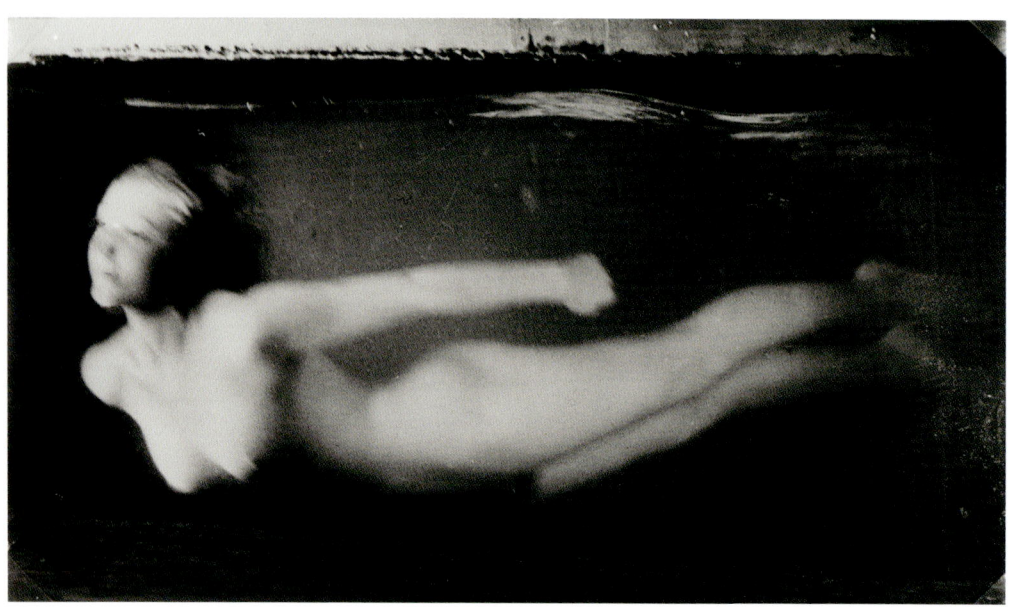

(pl. 7) Jacqueline swimming nude at the Coliséum, 1934. Photo: Rogi André

146

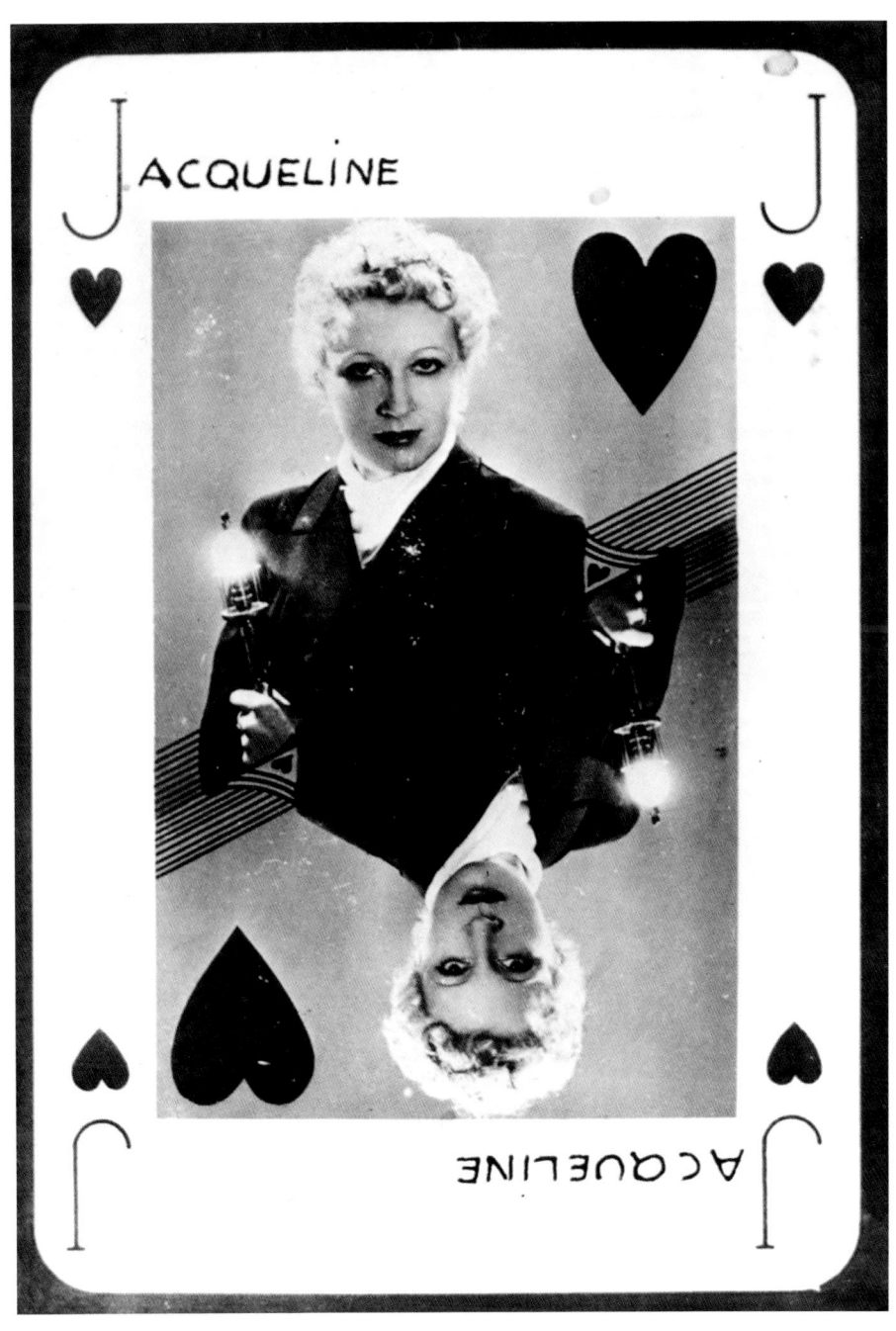

(pl. 8) Jacqueline as Queen of Hearts, 1934. Photo: Man Ray

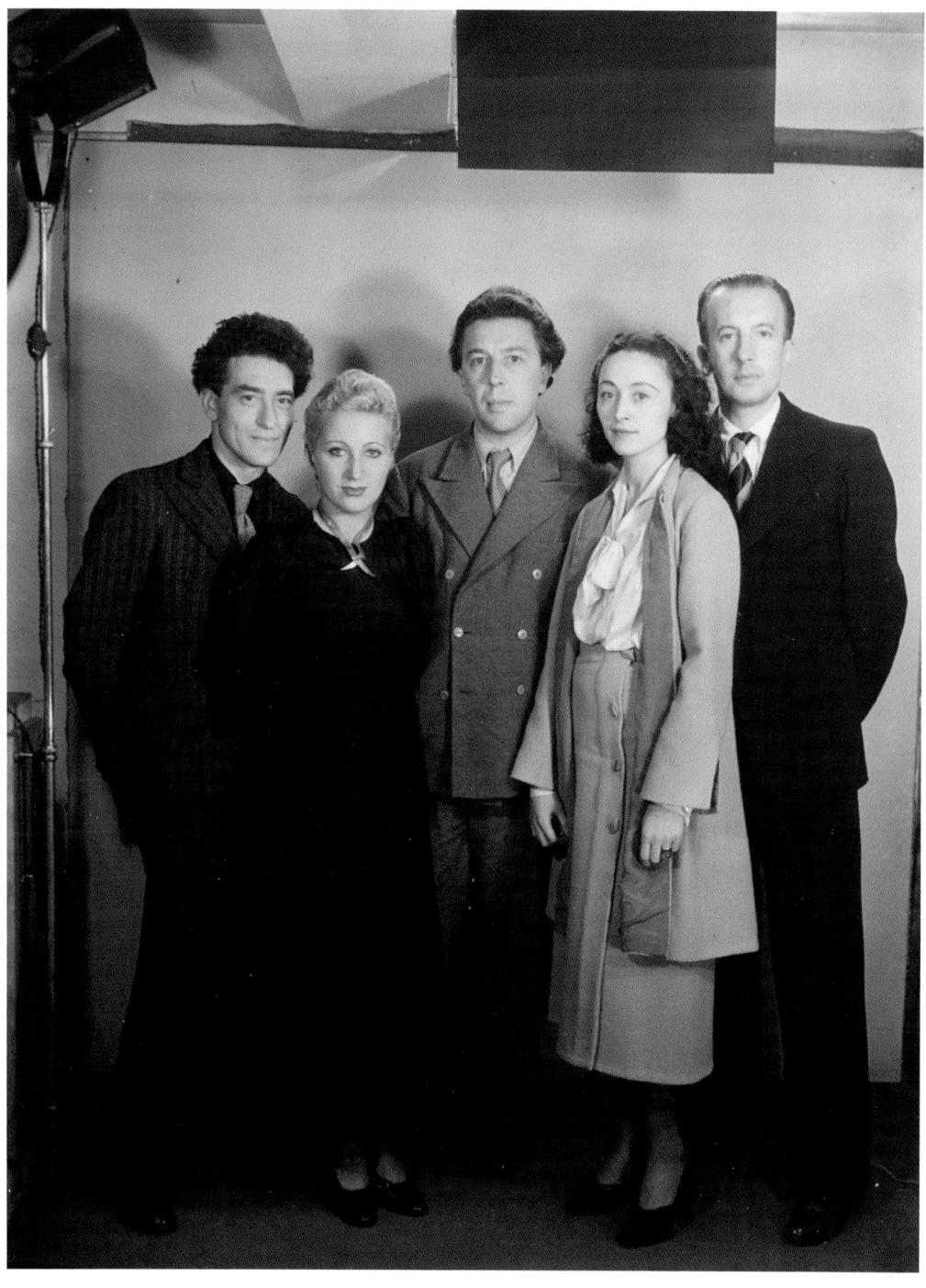

(pl. 9) Wedding portrait at the town hall (*mairie*), 1934. From left to right, Alberto Giacometti, Jacqueline, André Breton, Nusch and Paul Éluard. Photo: Man Ray

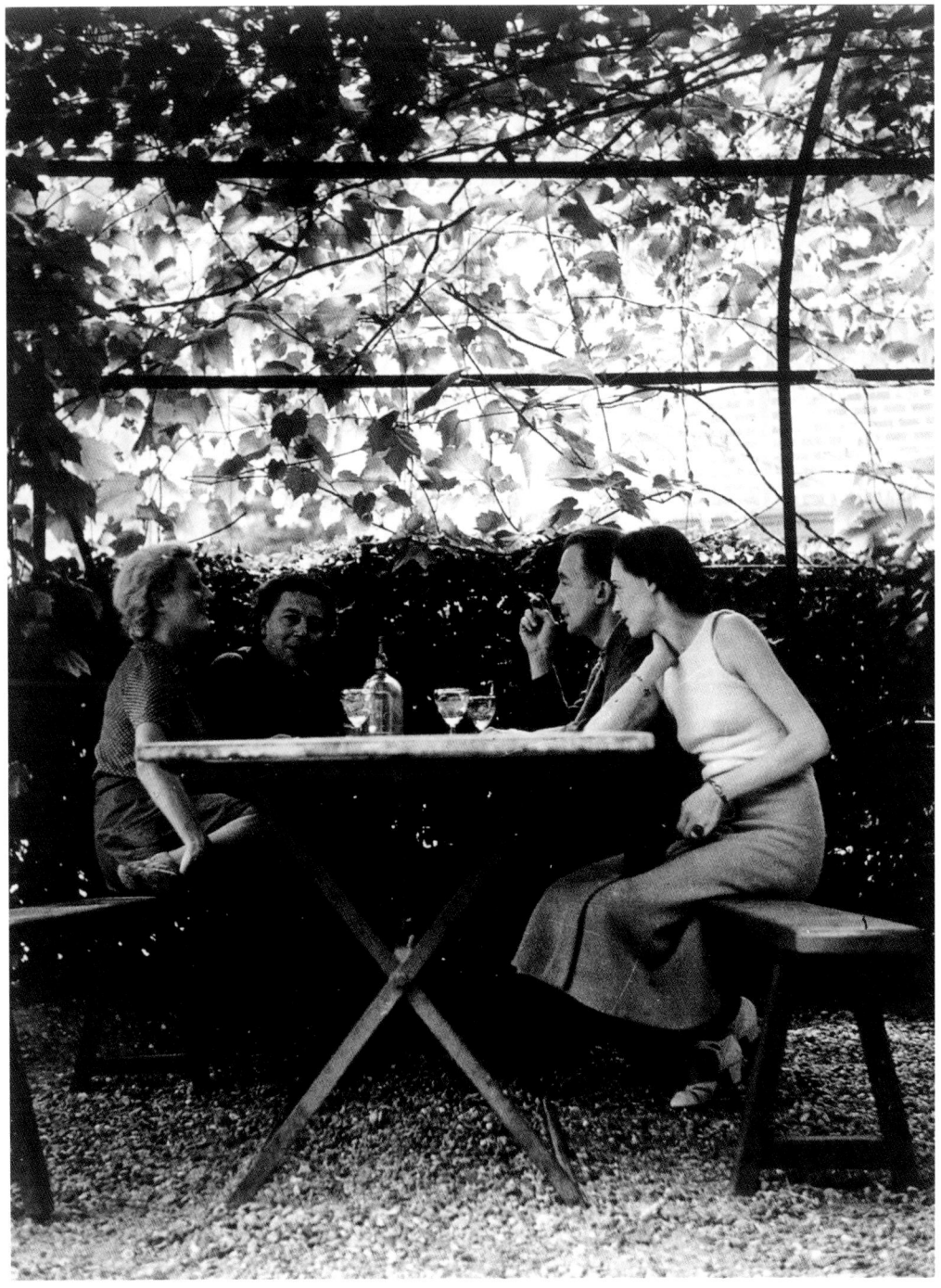

(pl. 10) André Breton and Jacqueline with Nusch and Paul Éluard, ca. 1937. Photo: Dora Maar

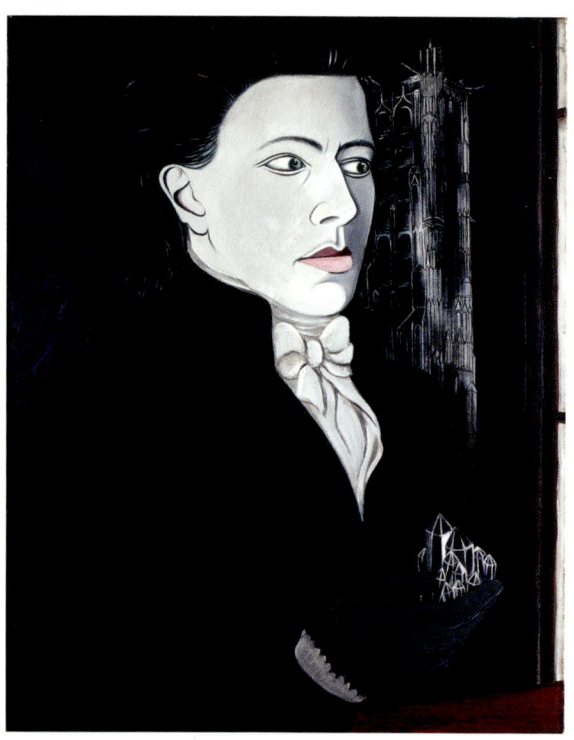

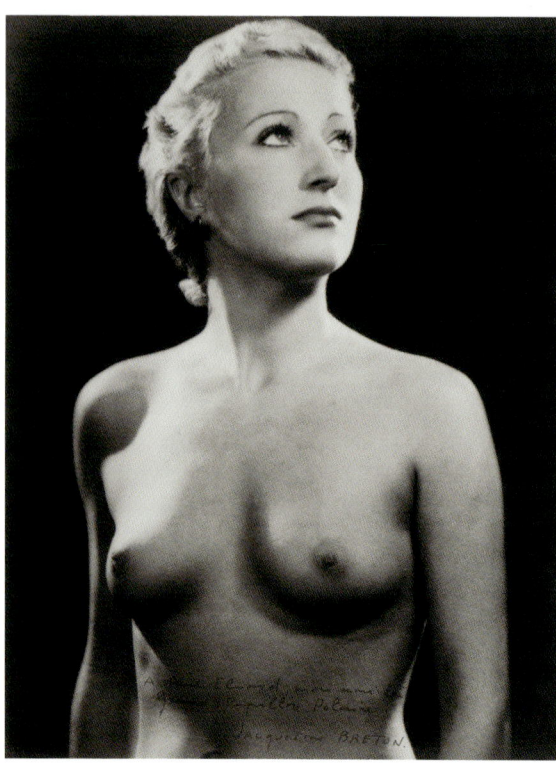

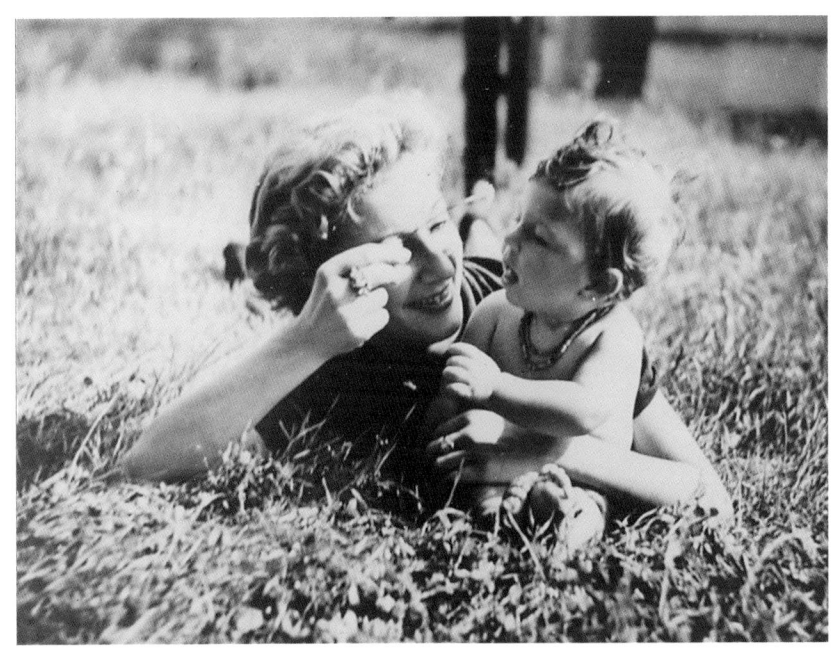

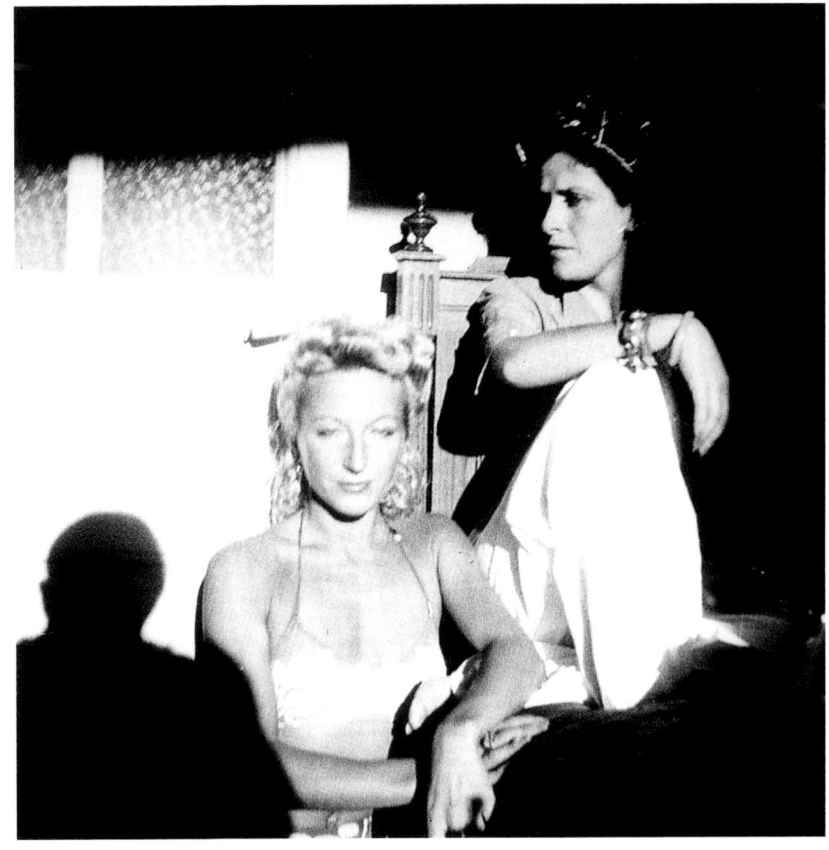

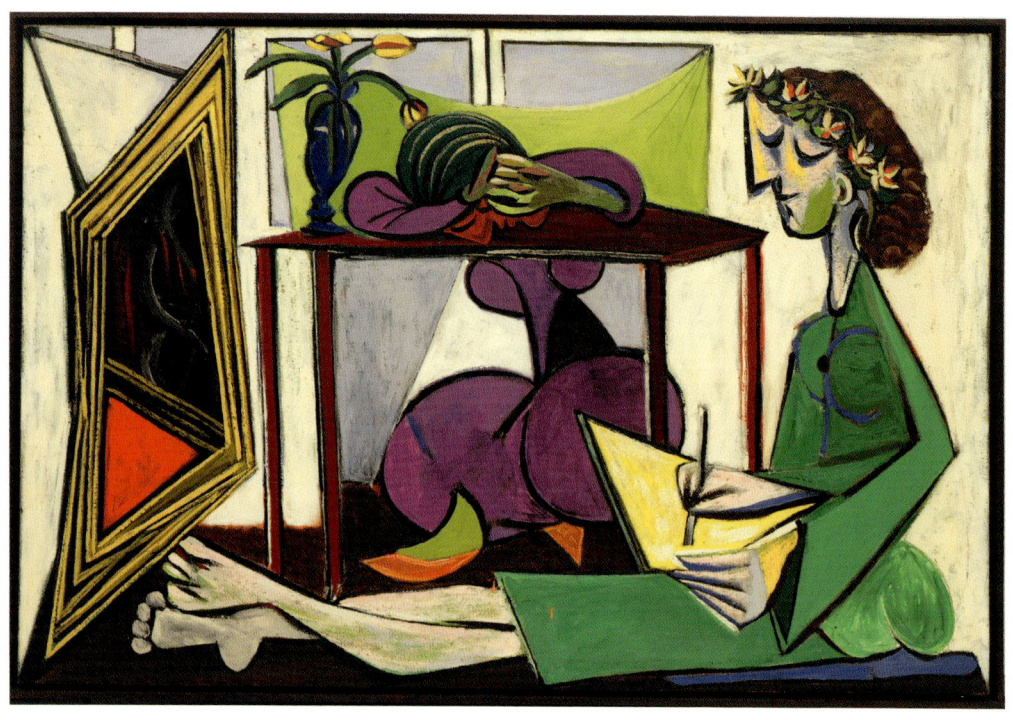

(pl. 15) Pablo Picasso, *Interior with a Girl Drawing*, 1935. Oil on canvas, 51¼ in. x 6 ft 4⅝ in. (130 x 195 cm). Nelson A. Rockefeller Bequest, acc. no. 969.1979, Museum of Modern Art, New York

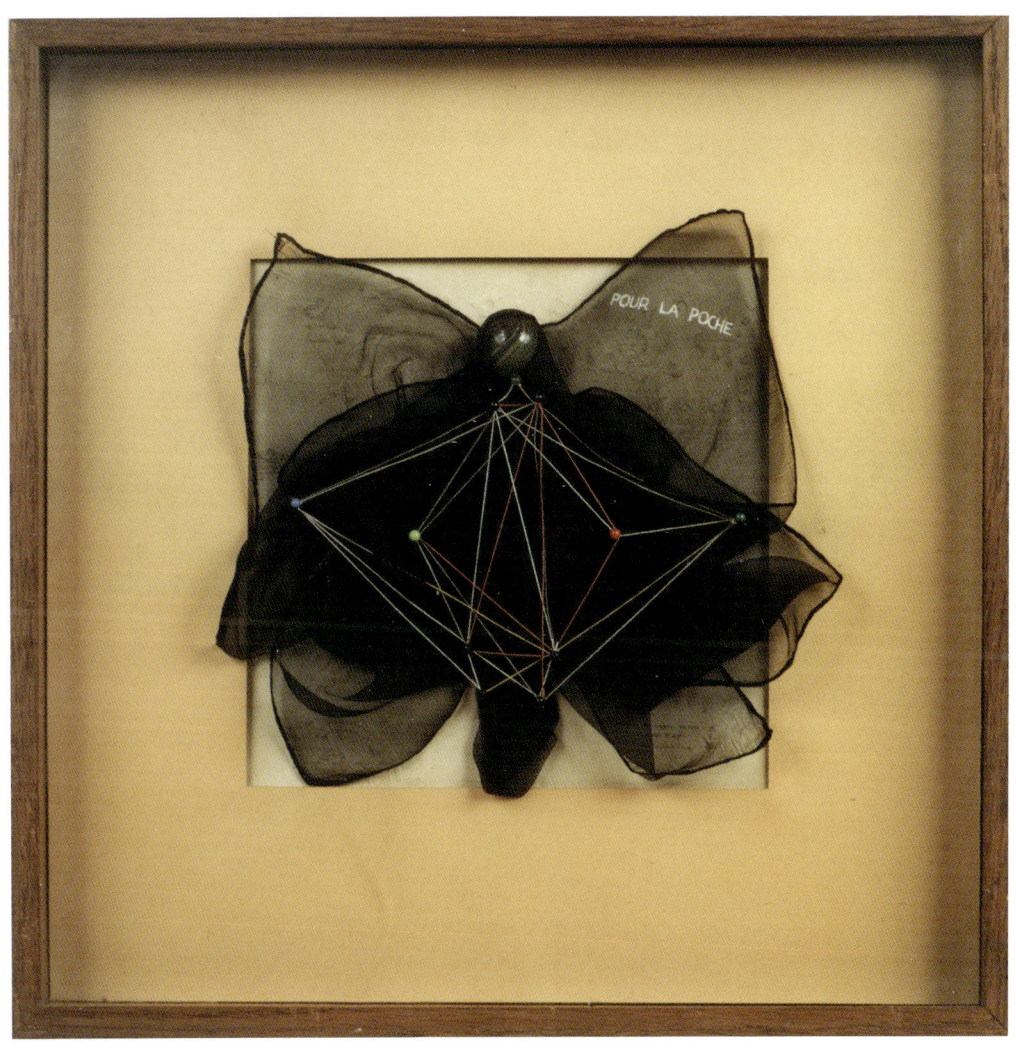

(pl. 16) Jacqueline Lamba, *Pour la Poche*, 1935. Rowland Weinstein, courtesy Weinstein Gallery, Los Angeles

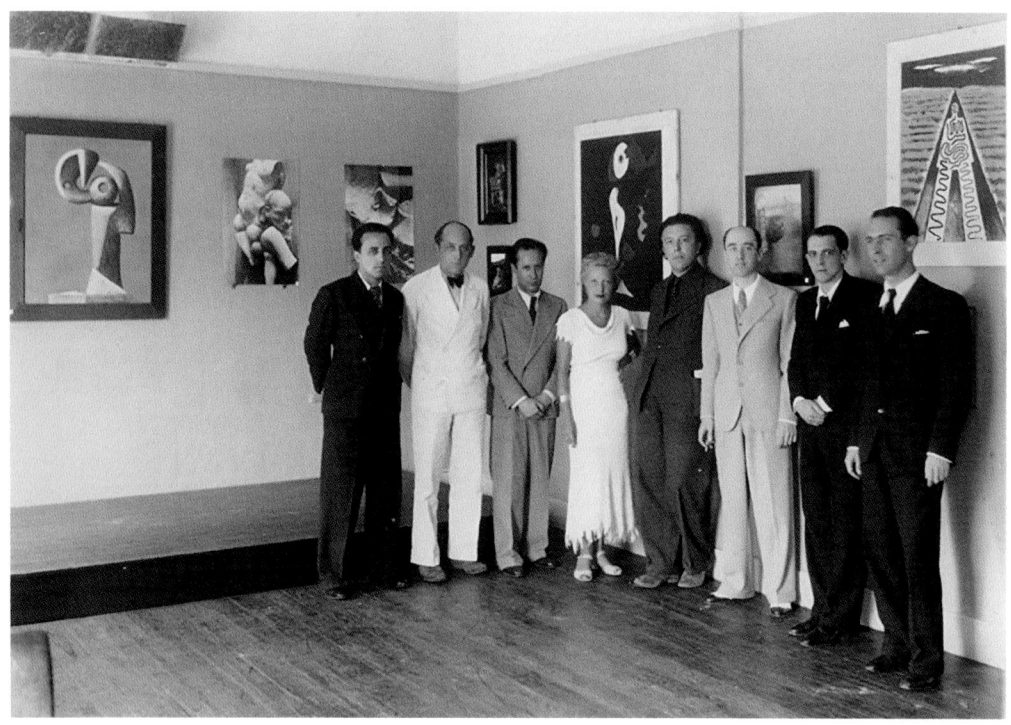

(pl. 17) *International Surrealist Exhibition*, Tenerife, 1935. From left to right, Domingo López Torres, Benjamin Péret, Eduardo Westerdahl, Jacqueline, André Breton, Agustín Espinosa García, José M. de la Rosa, and Domingo Pérez Minik. Picasso's *Metamorphosis* (1929) is seen at far left

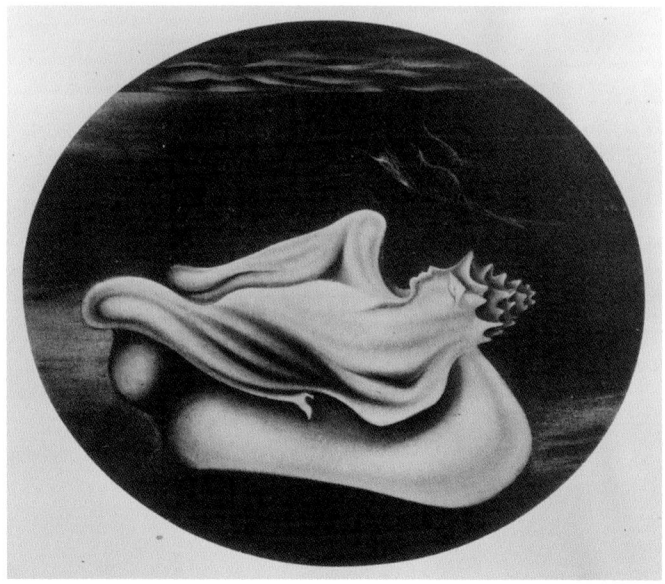

(pl. 18) Jacqueline Lamba, *Les Heures*, 1936, oil on canvas. Ex-collection Lise Deharme; lost

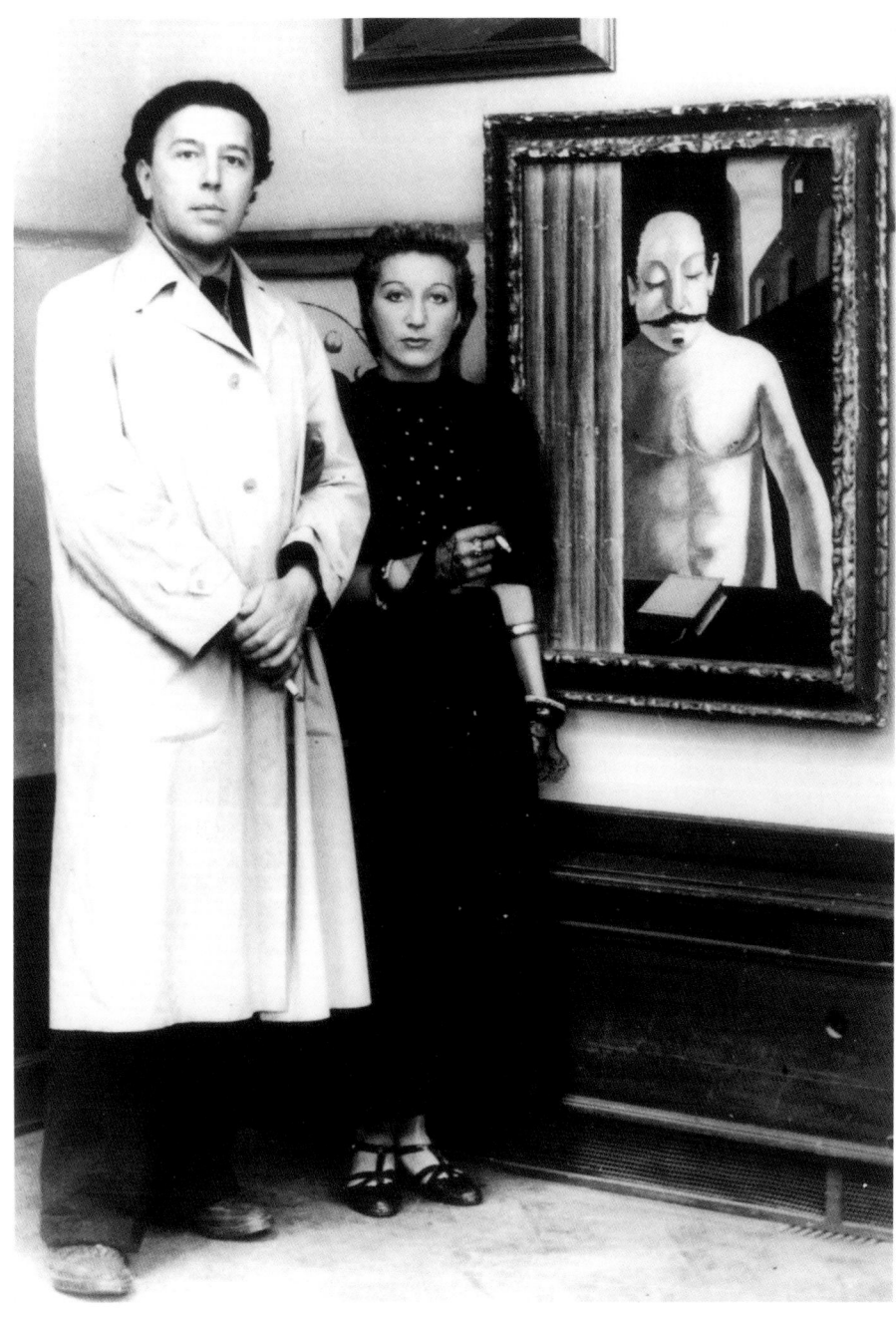

(pl. 19) Jacqueline and André, *International Surrealist Exhibition*, New Burlington Galleries, London, 1936. The painting is *The Child's Brain* (1914) by Giorgio de Chirico

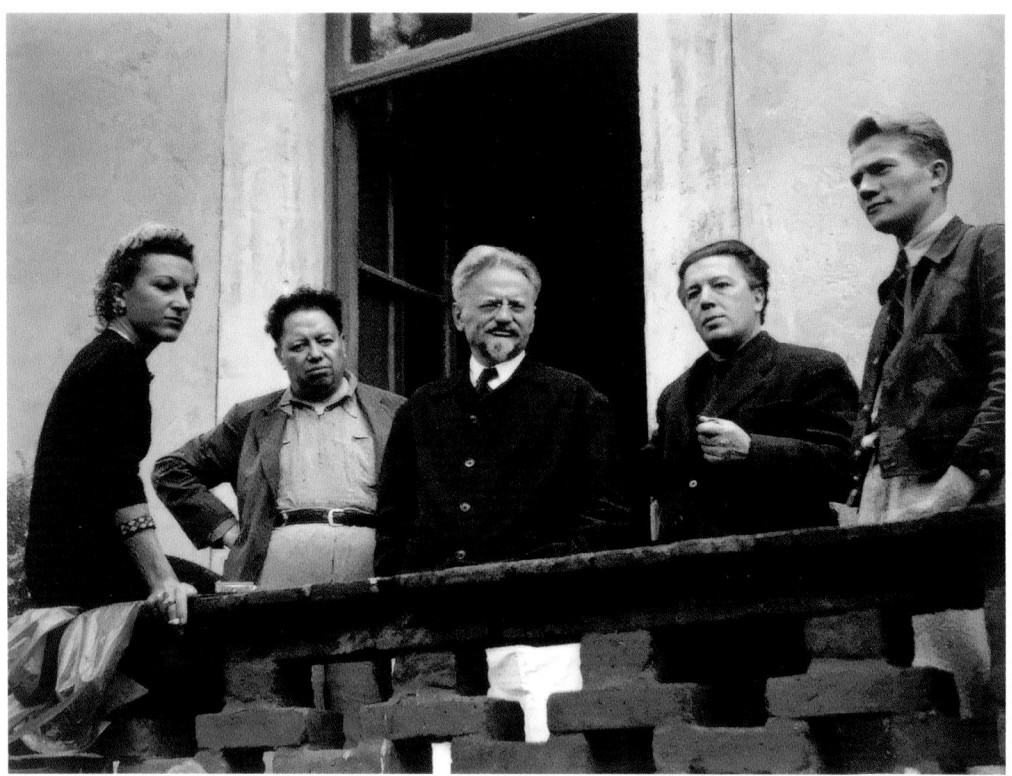

(above)
(pl. 20) Jacqueline, Diego Rivera, Leon Trotsky, André Breton, and Jan van Heijenoort, Mexico, 1938. Photo: Manuel Álvarez Bravo

(opposite)
(pl. 21) Jacqueline and Frida Kahlo, Mexico, 1938. Photo: André Breton

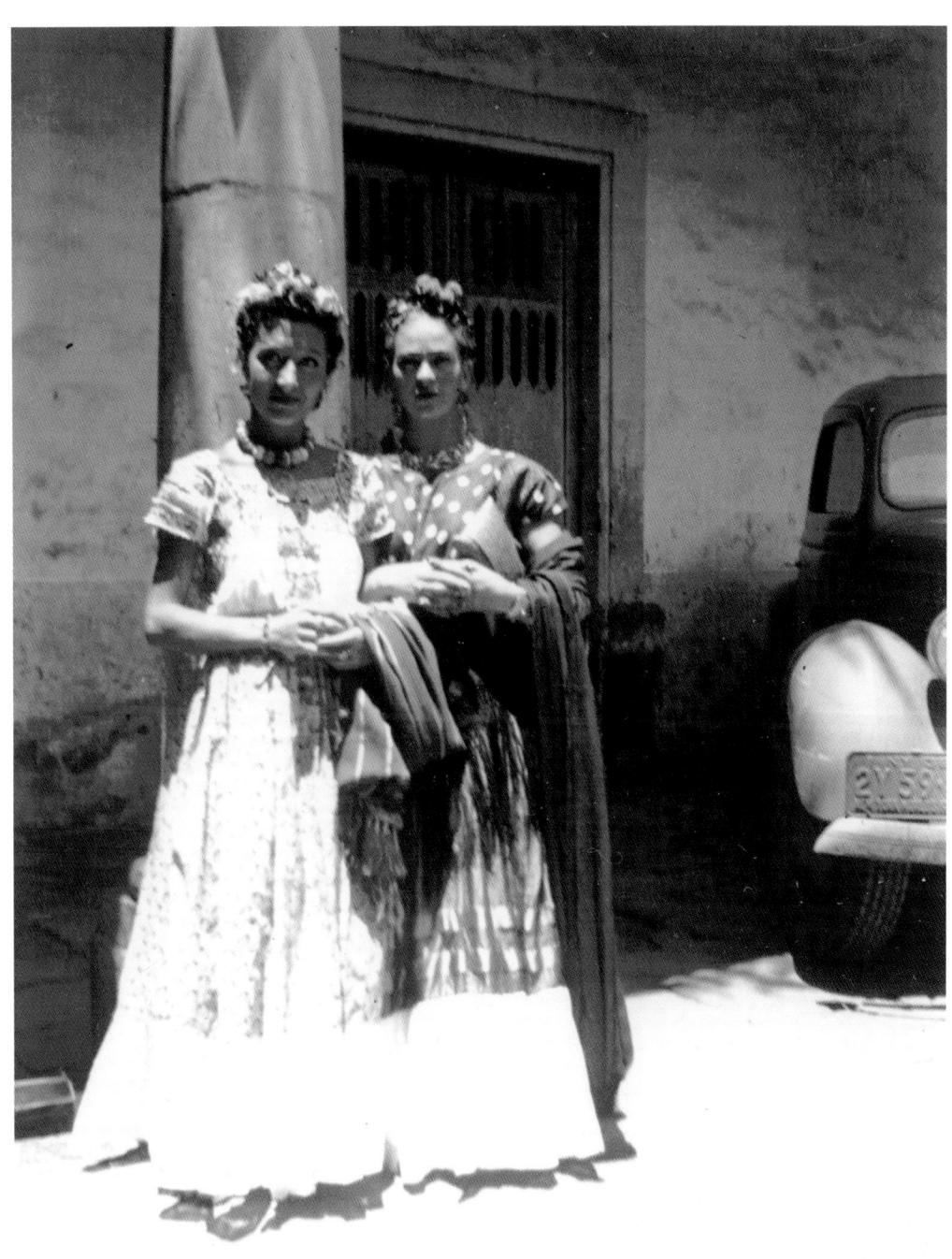

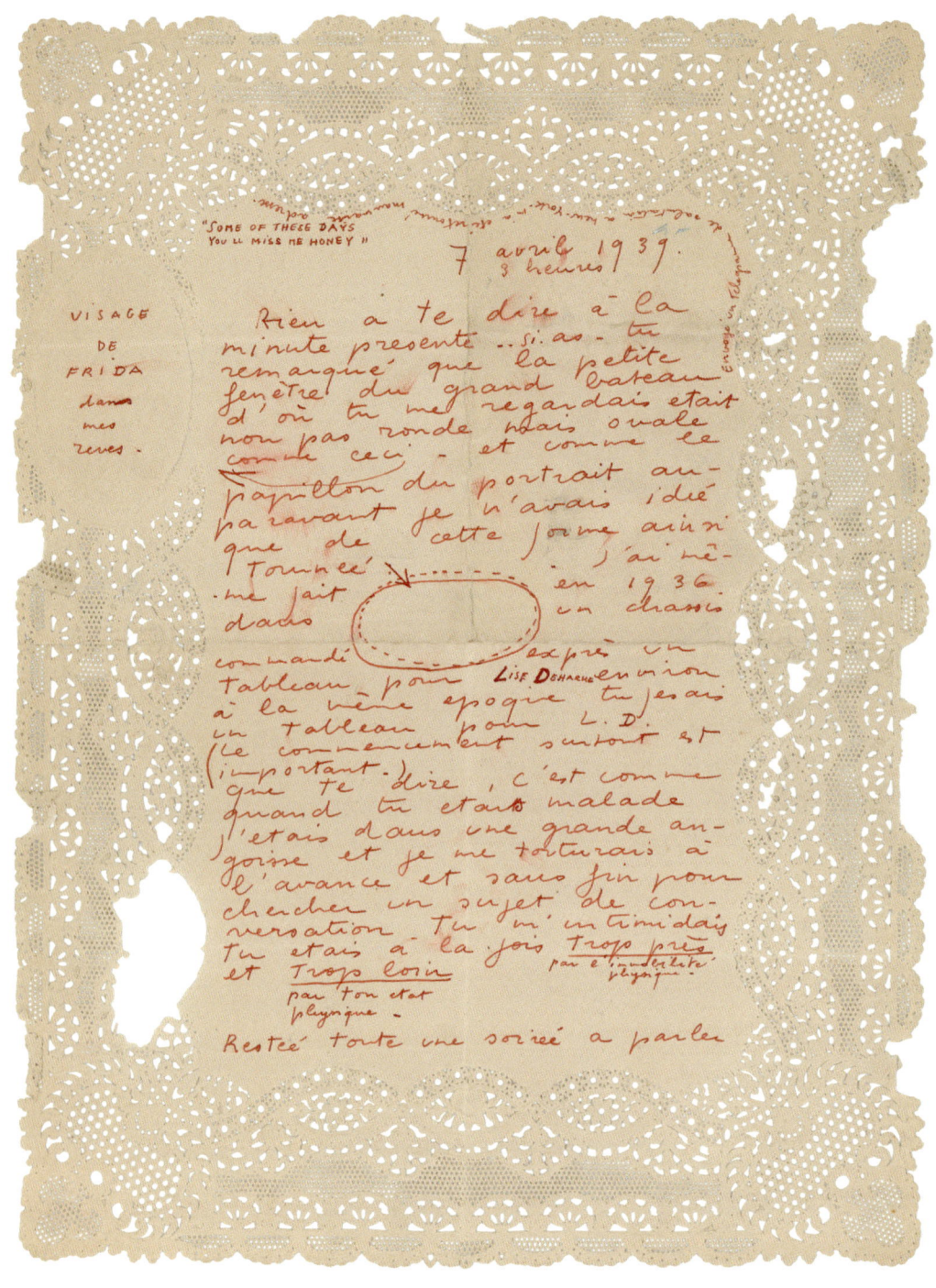

(pl. 22) Jacqueline Lamba, letter to Frida Kahlo written on her departure from France, April 7, 1939

aux paseln de mexique de
Toi, de Diego. Je les aimais
beaucoup ce soir là, j'étais
leur amie.
Plutot plus gentille avec
quelques uns - mais je lutte
contre un état de torpeur en-
valissant - (je pense que tu ne
vas pas te mettre a chercher tous ces
noms dans le dictionnaire)
Dans chaque maison ou tu es
passée il y a un objet. donne-
moi y penses-tu. J'en ai
deja visité quelques unes -
Actuellement
presque tous mes efforts sont con-
centrés pour aller voir un jou
pas plus fou d'ailleurs que
quand nous nous promenions
dans Paris. c'était pourtant
la limite pour ces messieurs spé-
cialistes. malgré tout j'ai une
peur terrible qu'il ne m'ait ou-
blié ils ont du arriver a ça de
puis le temps qu'il est enfermé.
ME VOIS-TU. M'ENTENDS-TU.
a travers tout ce soleil. es-tu bien
oui.
J'en suis sure maintenant
il y a des jours ou je pourrai t'e-
crire de lettres moins imbeciles mais
je te vois tout de même très bien
j'tourne tes yeux d'oiseau de ça
et là, pour ne pas
je m'allonge sur cette feuille pour
te sentir -
Jacqueline
on me telephone de l'asile que je peux voir le fou. Antonin Artaud

LORAZON   CORAZON
SANGRE   MADRE
LABIOS   HABLANTE
ODAGA
V - PALMERA VDE
FUERZA   DEDO

X

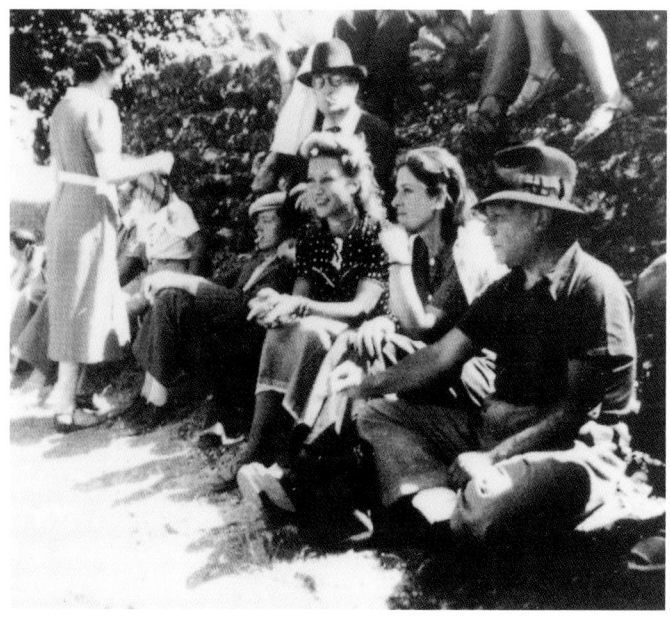

(pl. 23) Pablo Picasso, Jacqueline, Dora Maar, and Jaime
Sabartés at a bullfight in Fréjus, France, 1939

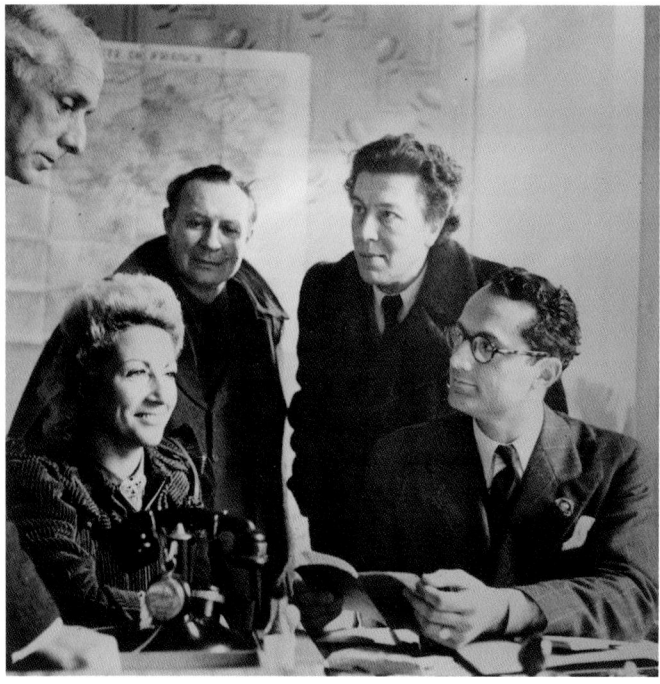

(pl. 24) Max Ernst, Jacqueline, André Masson, André Breton, and
Varian Fry, Air-Bel, Marseilles, 1941

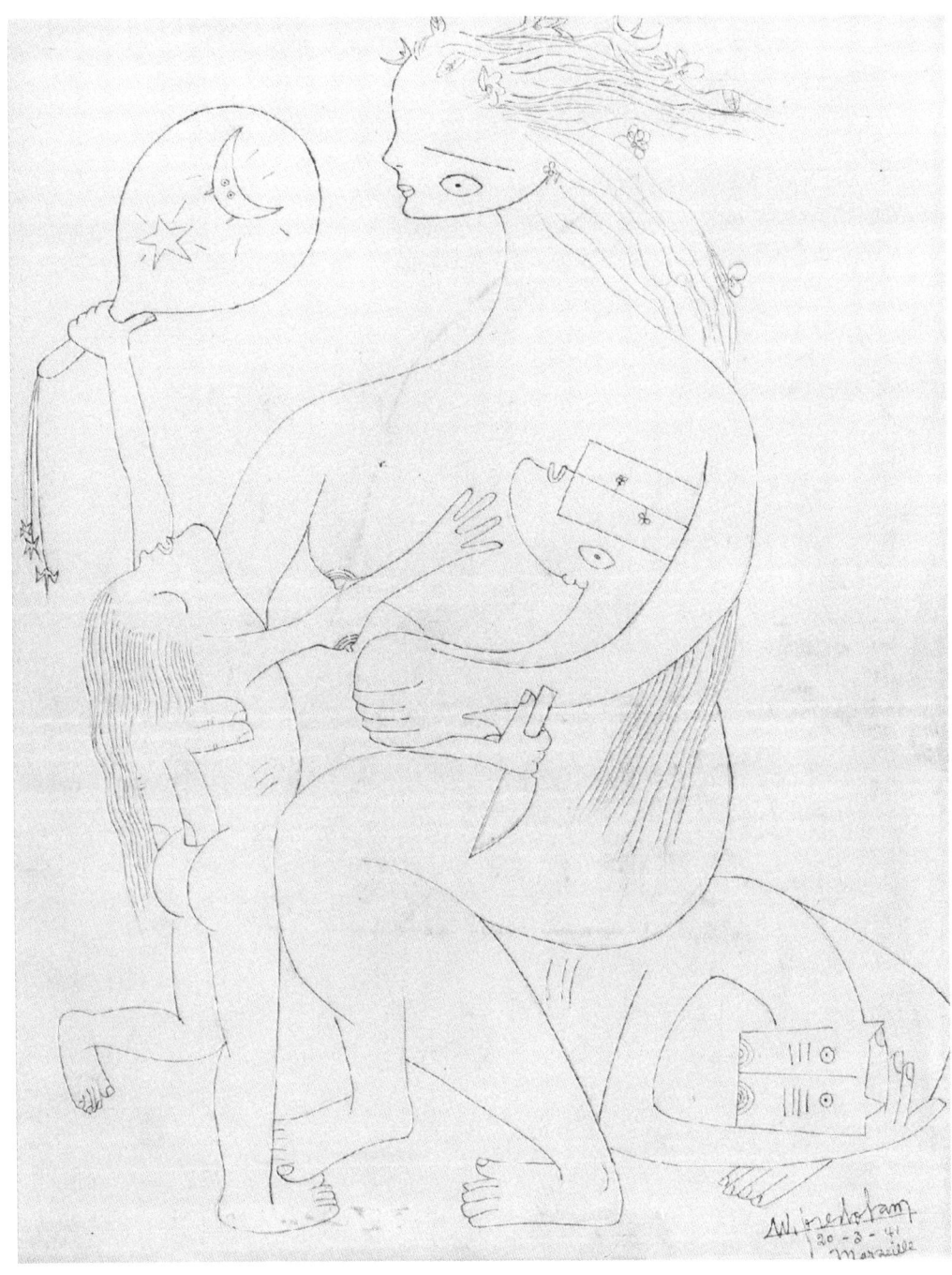

(pl. 25) Wifredo Lam, *Drawing of Jacqueline, Aube and André*, pencil and pen and ink on paper, Air-Bel, Marseilles, s. d. 20/3/41

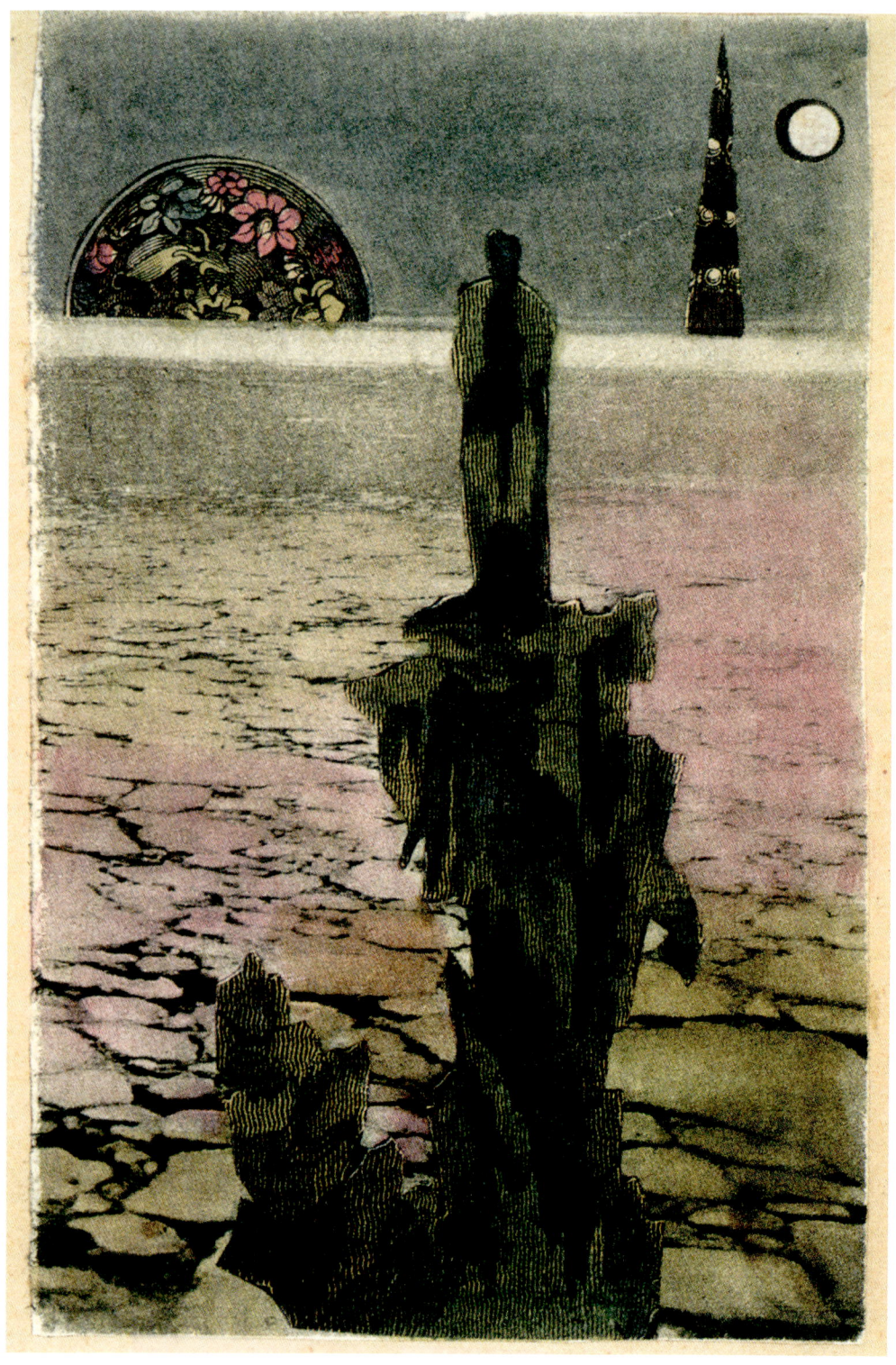

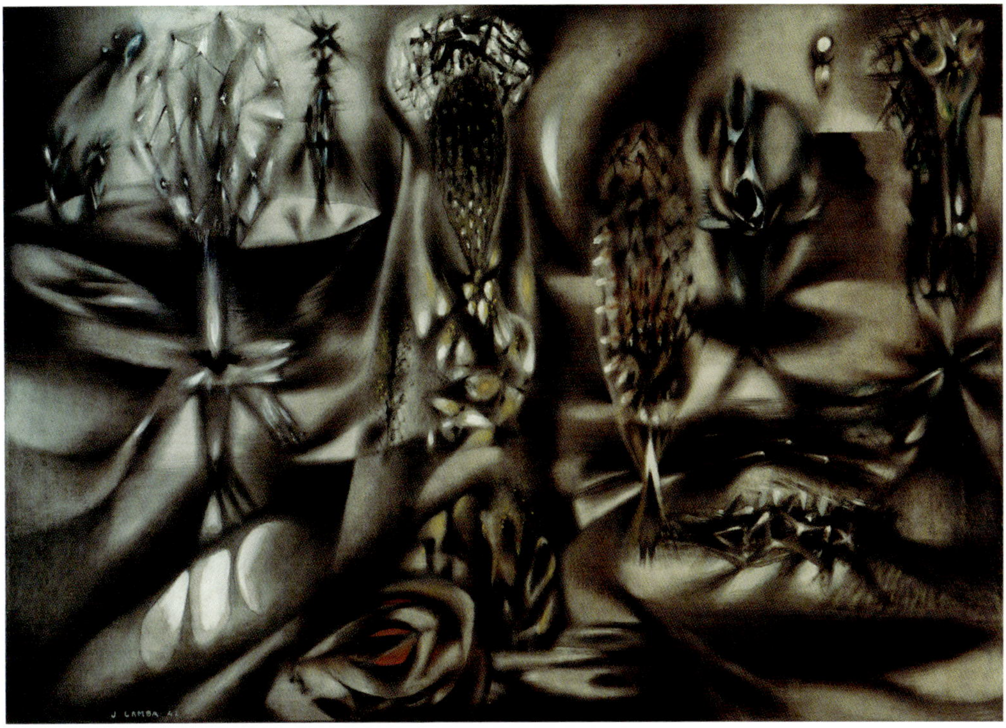

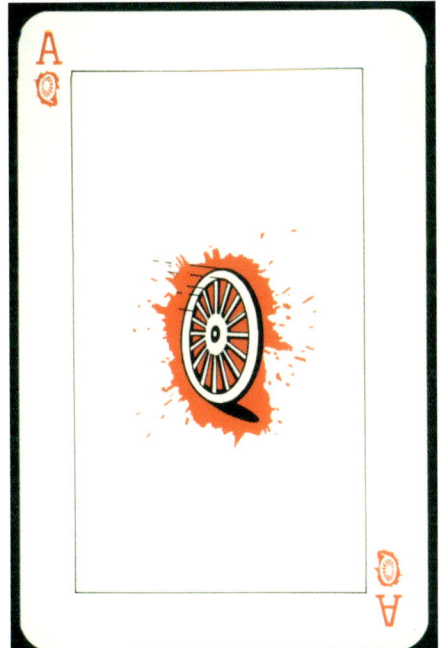

(opposite)
(pl. 26) Jacqueline Lamba, *Collage*, dedicated to Helena Lam, Air-Bel, Marseilles, 1940. Private collection

(above)
(pl. 27) Jacqueline Lamba, *In Spite of Everything, Spring*, 1942, oil on canvas. Private collection

(left)
(pl. 28) Jacqueline Lamba, *The Bloody Wheel of the Revolution*, March 1941. Collection Musée Cantini, Marseilles

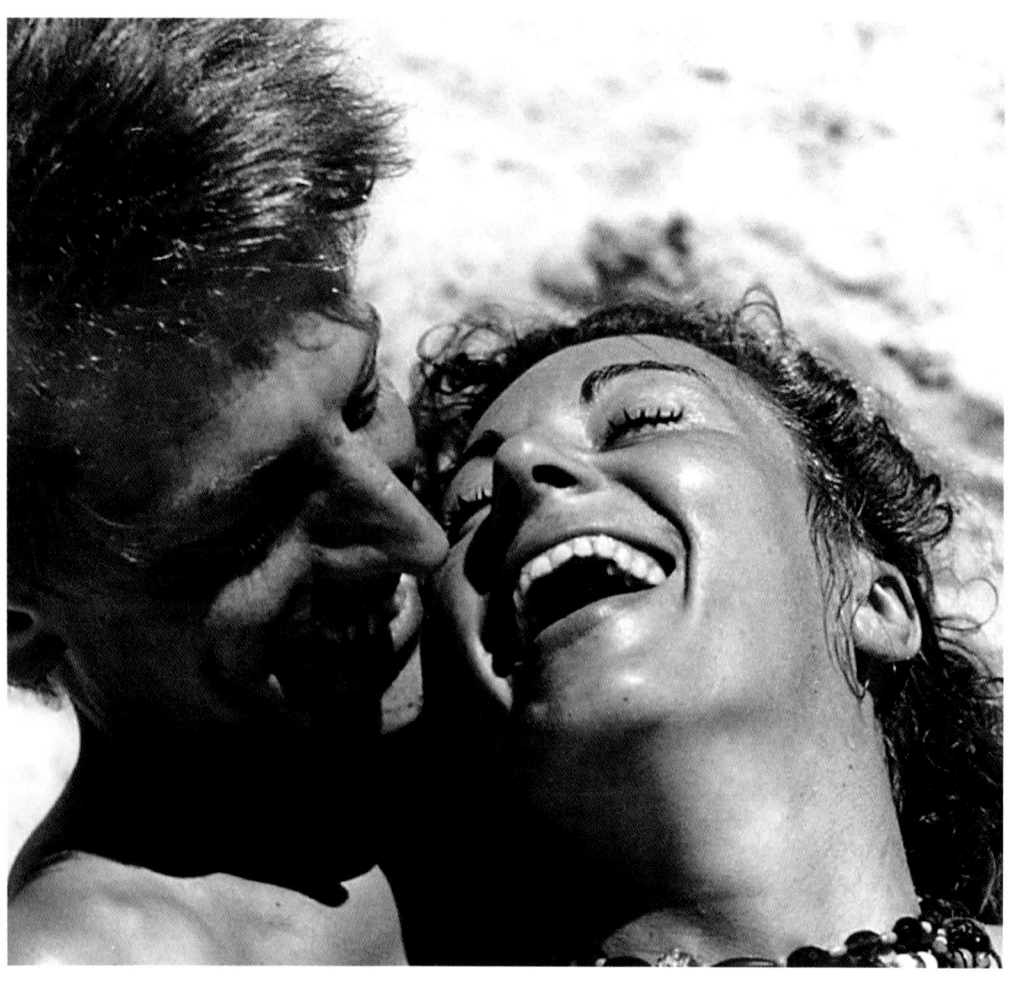

(pl. 29) David Hare and Jacqueline Lamba, ca. 1943

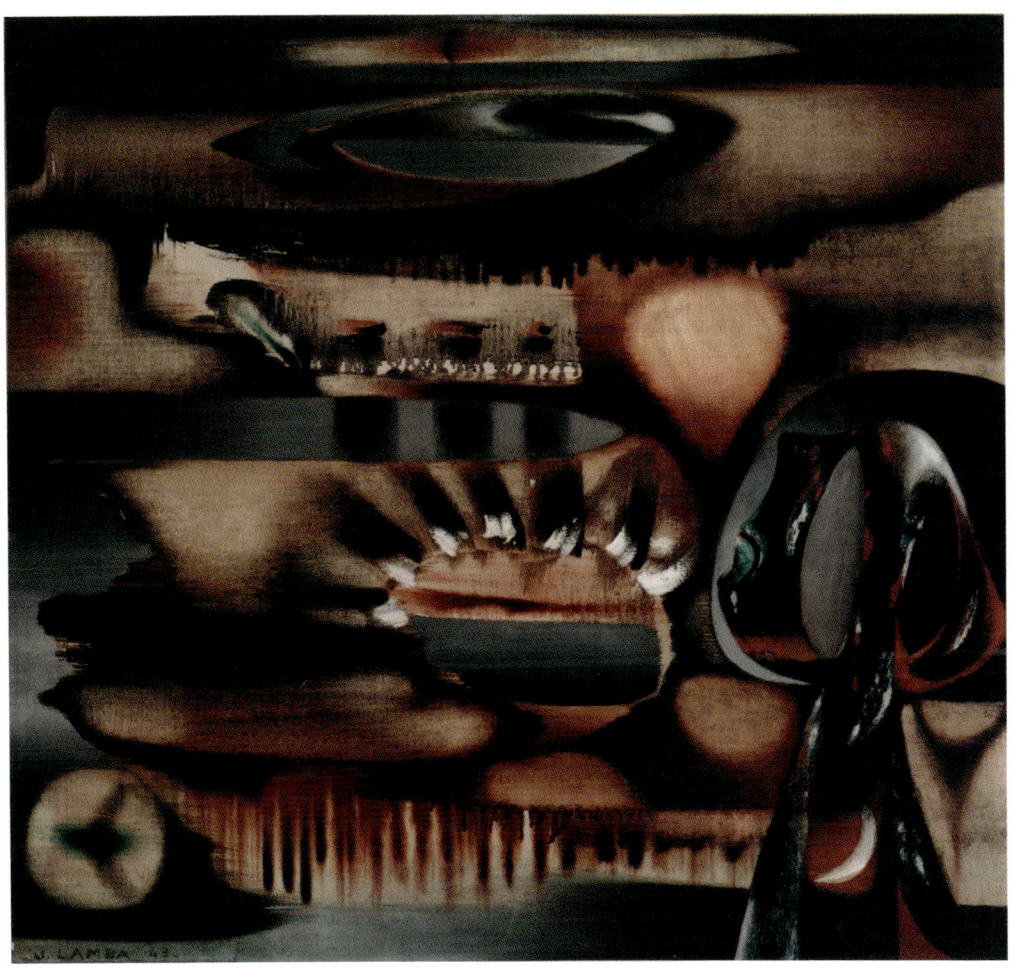

(pl. 30) Jacqueline Lamba, *Behind the Sun*, 1943, oil on canvas. Rowland Weinstein, courtesy Weinstein Gallery, Los Angeles

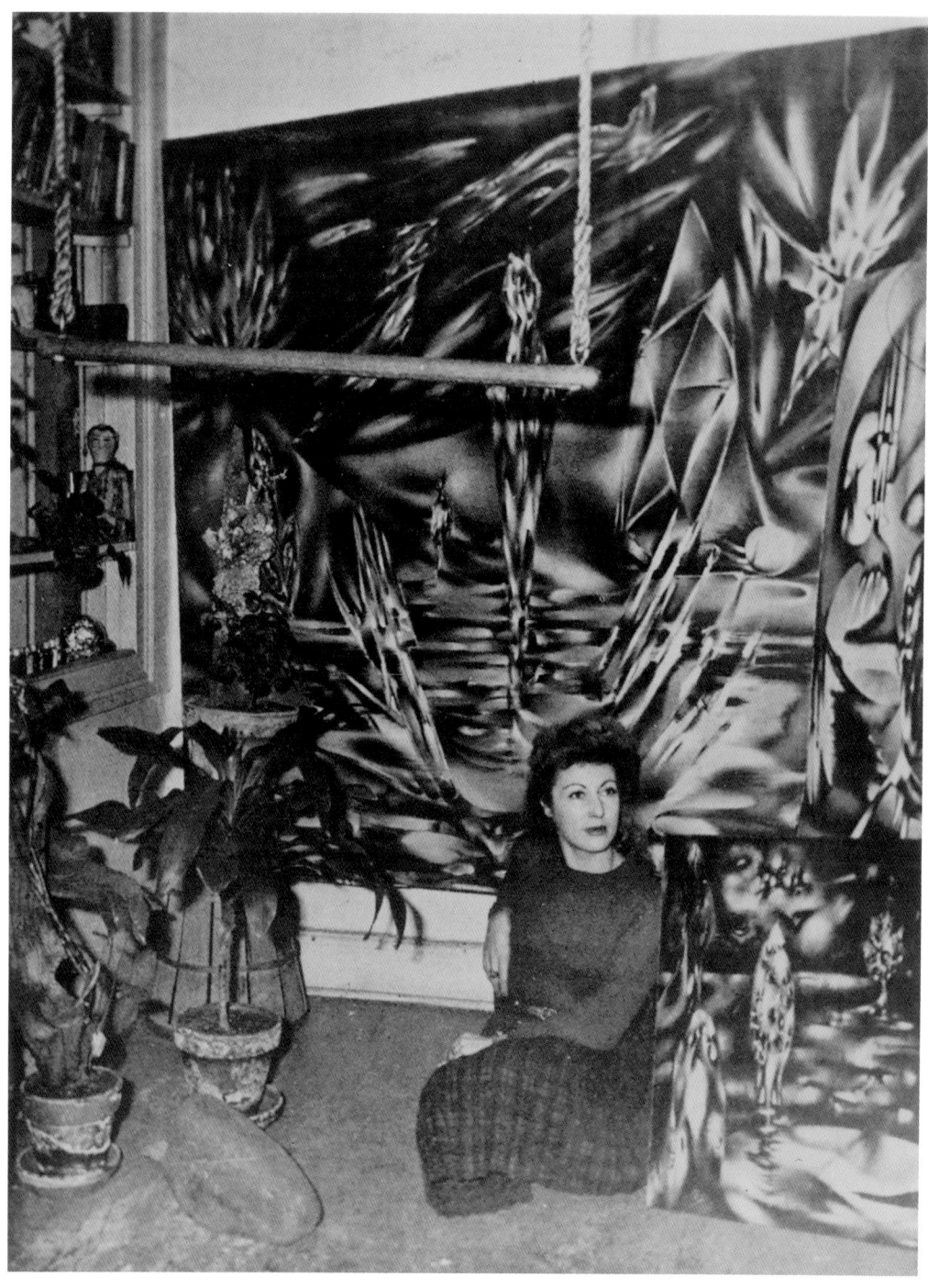

(pl. 31) Jacqueline surrounded by her paintings in the Bleecker Street apartment, Greenwich Village, New York, 1943. Photo: David Hare

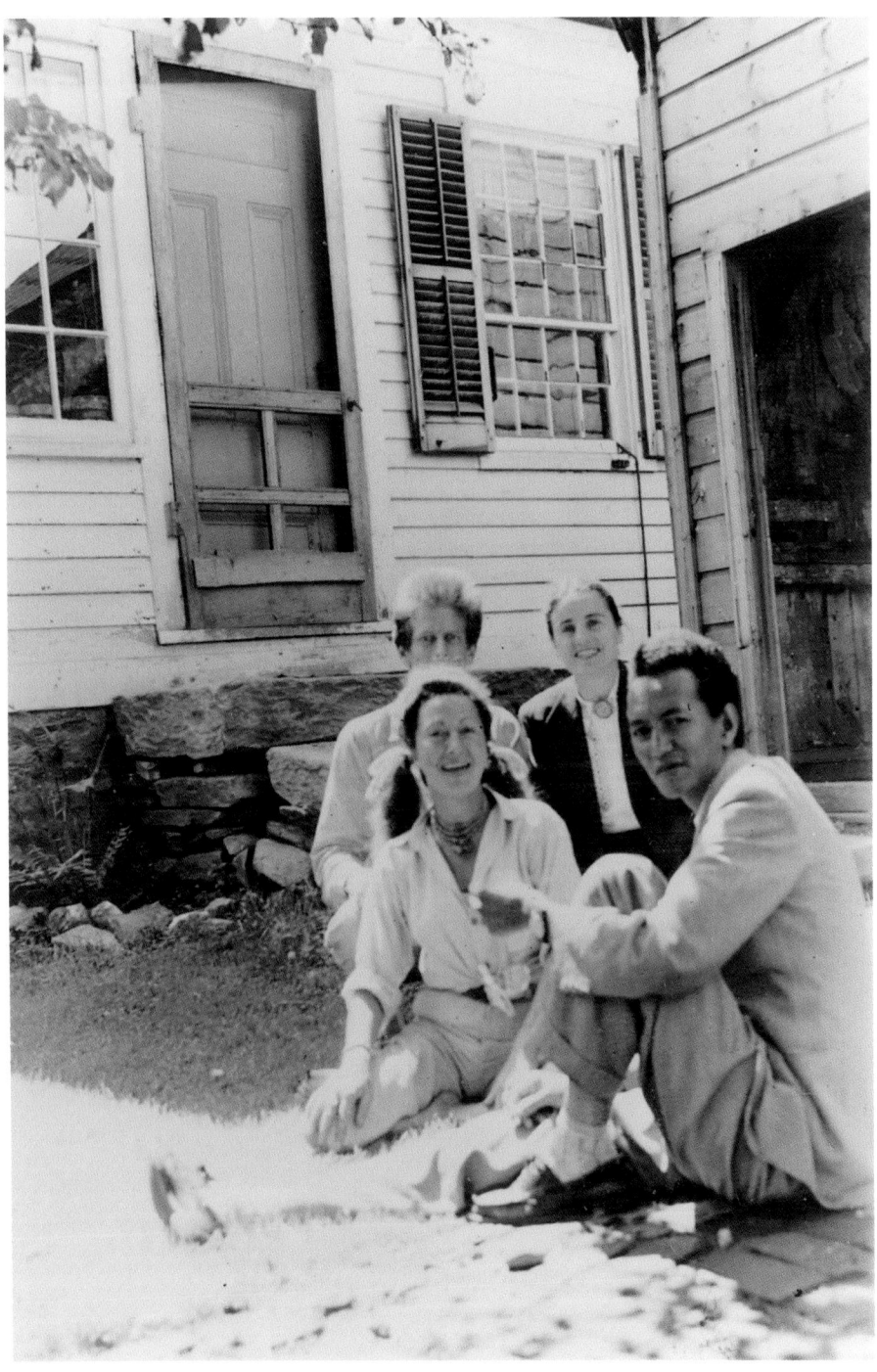

(pl. 32) Back row, David Hare and Helena Lam, front row, Jacqueline Lamba
and Wifredo Lam, Roxbury, Connecticut, ca. 1946

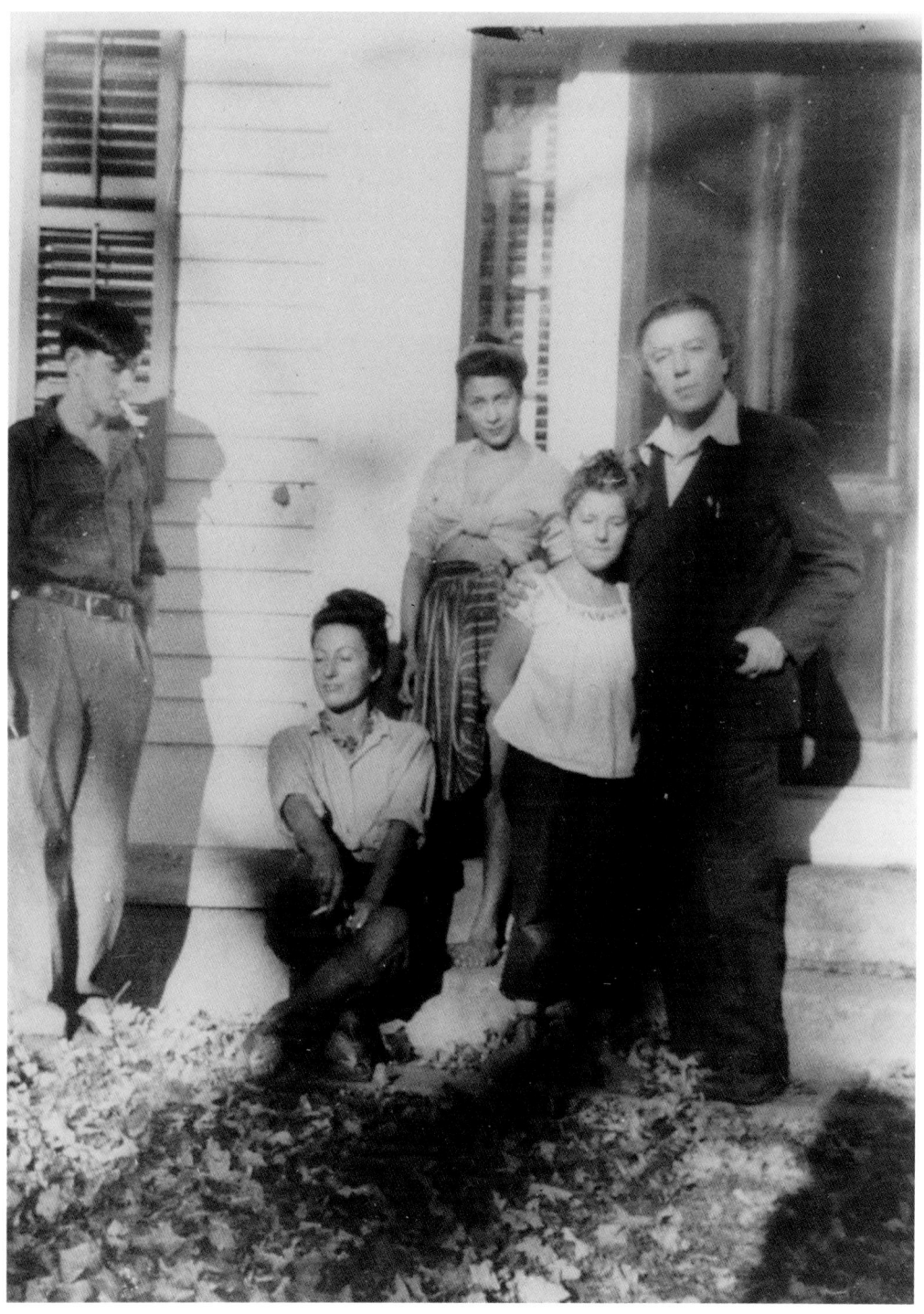

(pl. 33) From left to right, Jacques-Laurent Bost, Jacqueline, Dolorès Vanetti, Aube, and André Breton, Roxbury, Connecticut, 1944. Photo: David Hare

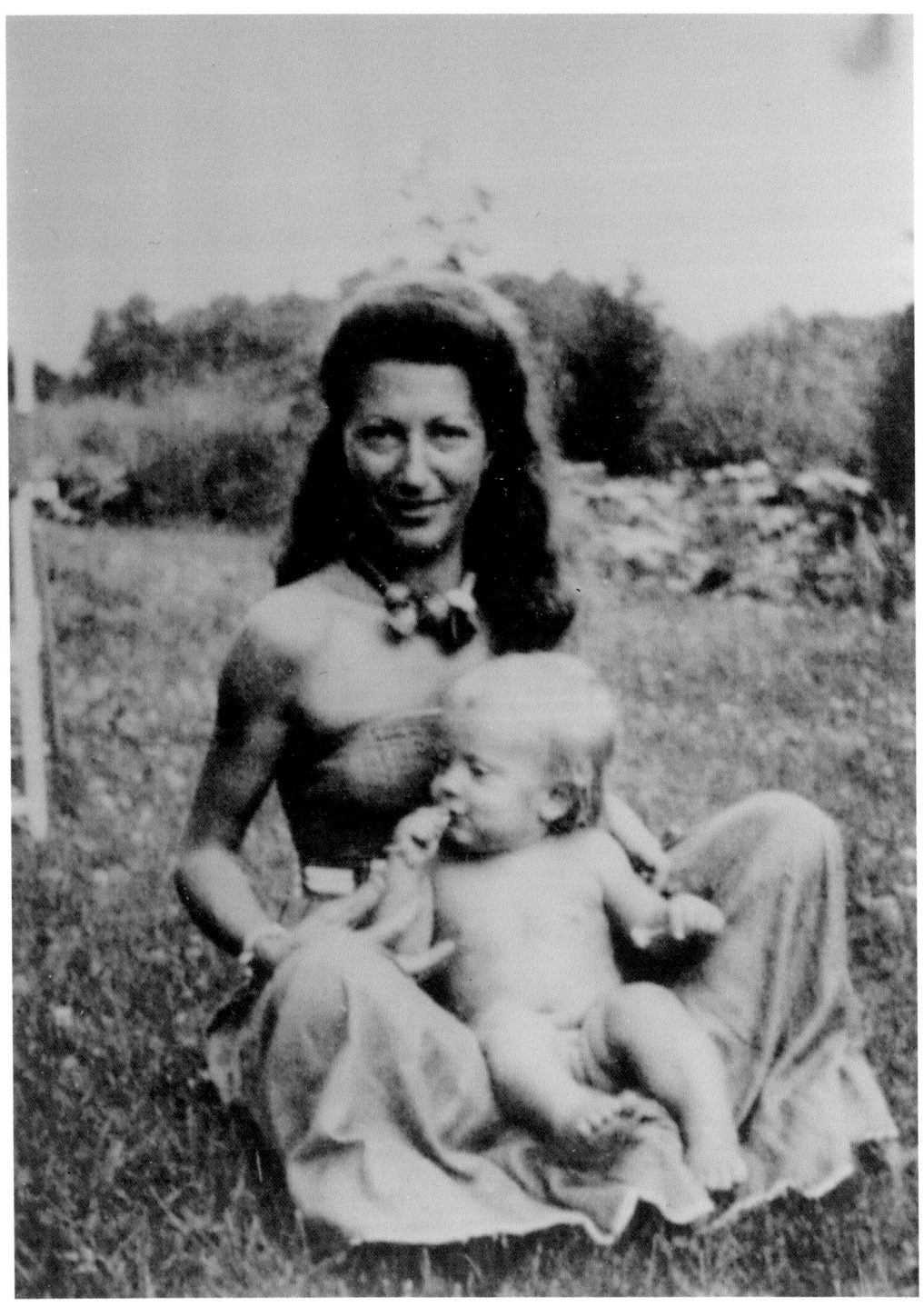

(pl. 34) Jacqueline and Merlin, Roxbury, Connecticut, ca. 1949. Photo: David Hare

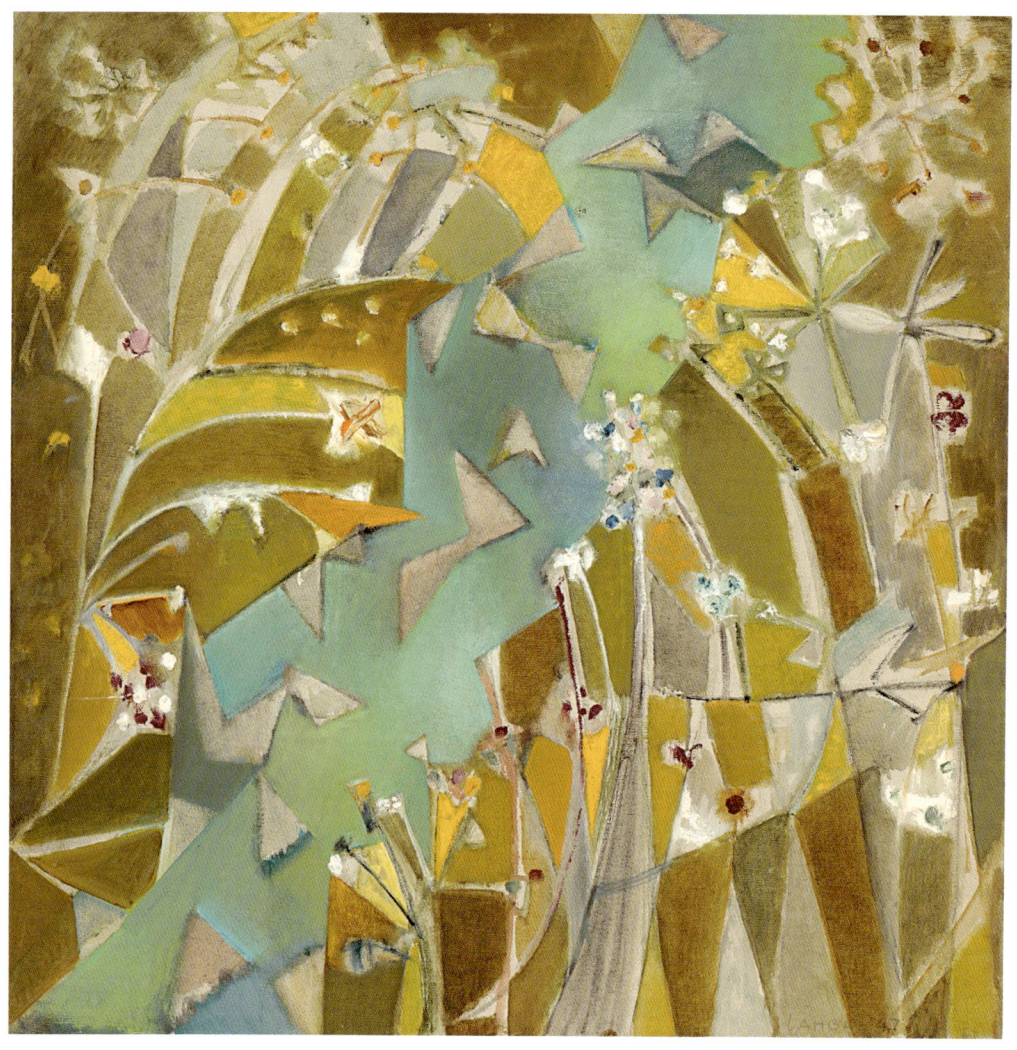

(pl. 35) Jacqueline Lamba, *Rivière*, 1947, oil on canvas. Private collection

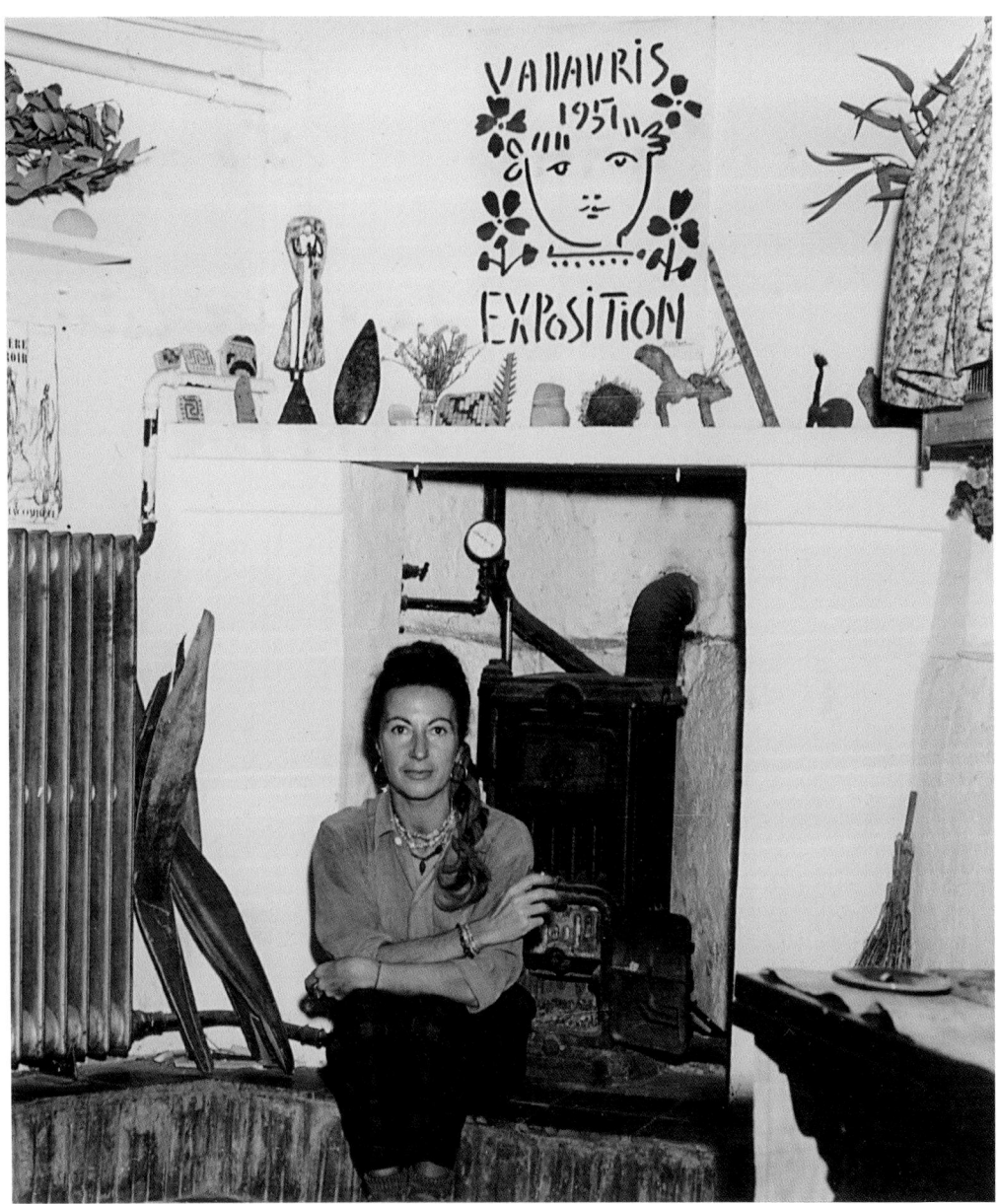

(pl. 36) Jacqueline in Cannes, 1952. In the background is Picasso's poster for the *Vallauris* exhibition in 1951

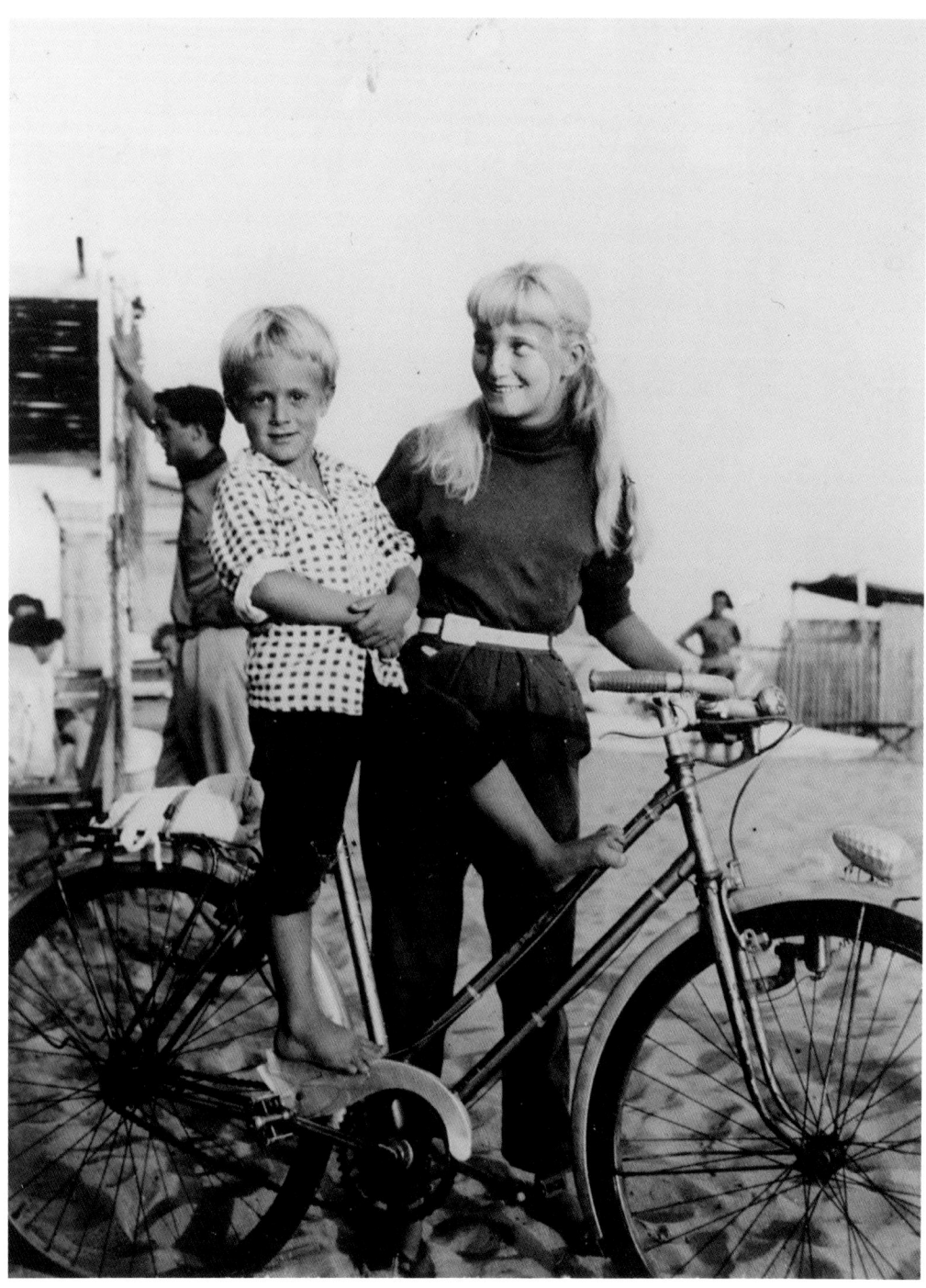

(pl. 37) Merlin with his babysitter, ca. 1955

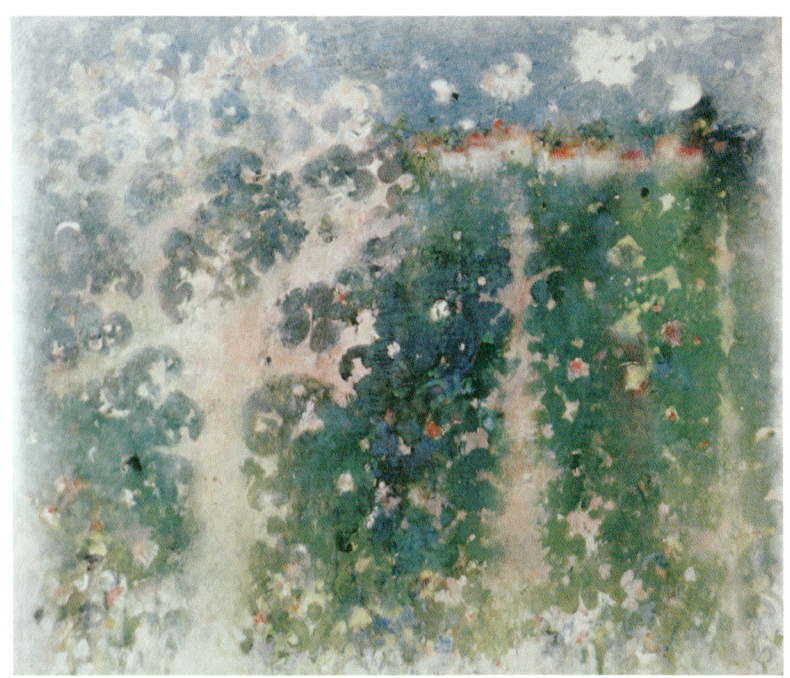

(pl. 38) Jacqueline Lamba, *Biot*, 1962, oil on canvas.
Collection of Patrick Barr, M.D., Dallas

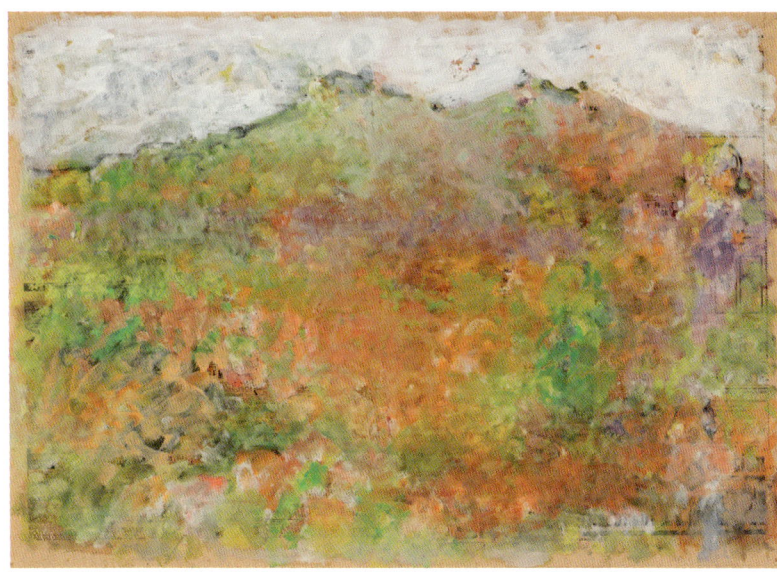

(pl. 39) Jacqueline Lamba, *Simiane*, 1964, oil on paper mounted on canvas.
Private collection

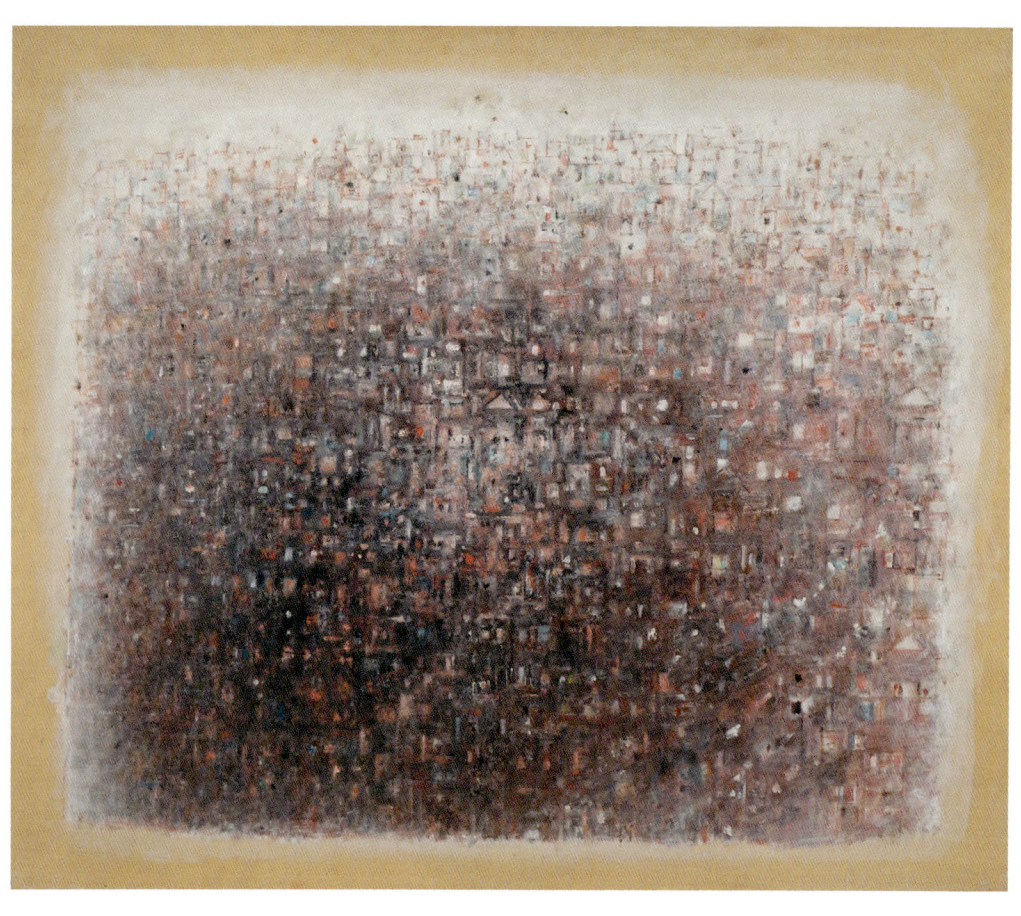

(pl. 40) Jacqueline Lamba, *Paris, Panorama*, 1971. Private collection, courtesy Weinstein Gallery, Los Angeles

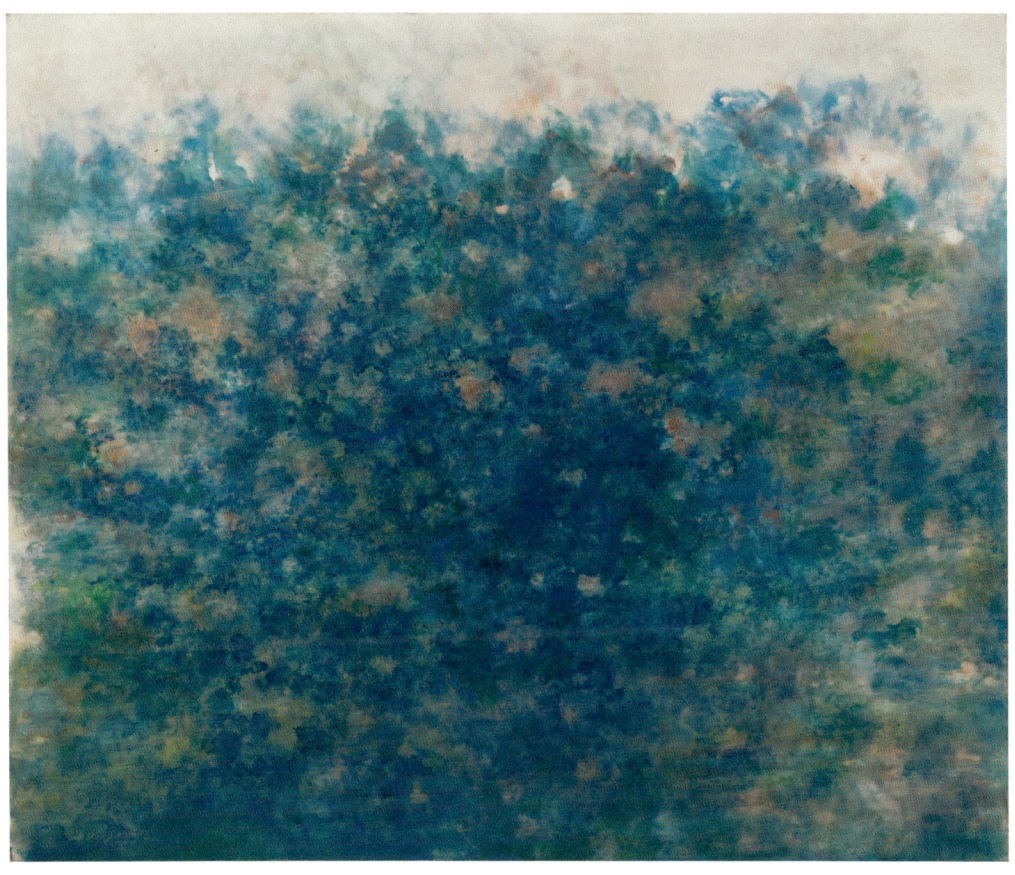

(pl. 41) Jacqueline Lamba, *Nuages, roses et turquoise*, n.d. Weinstein Gallery, Los Angeles

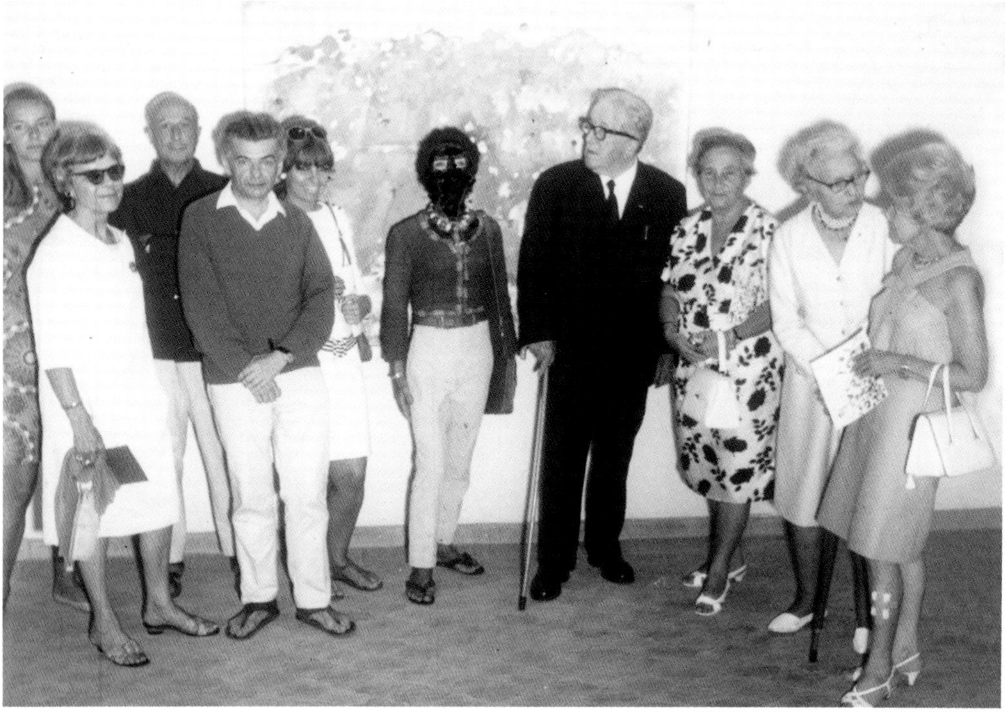

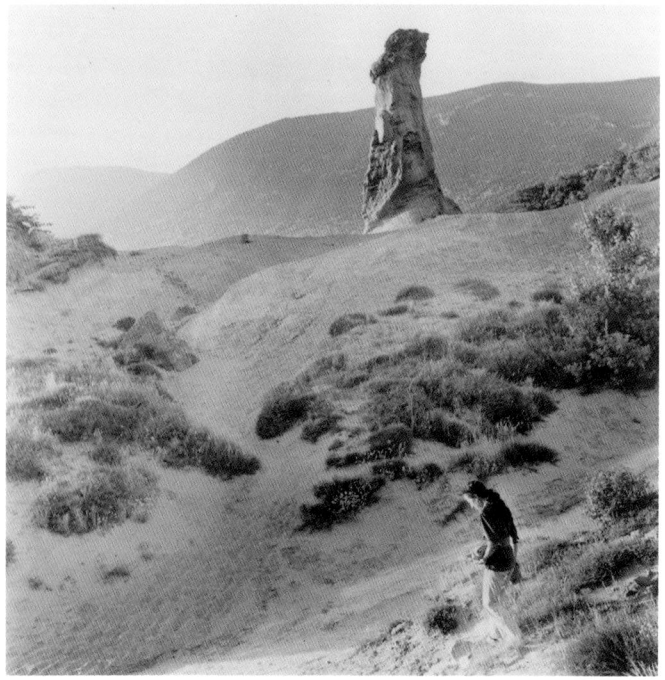

(above)
(pl. 42) Jacqueline, her face blackened, surrounded by friends at the opening of her exhibition at the Picasso Museum, Antibes, 1967

(left)
(pl. 43) Jacqueline in Haute Provence, ca. 1970.
Photo: Henri Cazin

Free, for a Time

Between 1955 and 1976, Jacqueline periodically underwent psychoanalytic psychotherapy, initially under the care of Dr. Gaston Ferdière; afterward with (rheumatologist) Dr. Damoiseau; and she held a professional correspondence with Jacques Lacan, Maar's psychoanalyst.[359] Most likely, she met Ferdière through Claude Cahun, his patient, or in 1935, when he and André participated in the International Congress for the Defense of Culture. Ferdière, a militant leftist and strong supporter of popular education, is best remembered for treating Antonin Artaud. In 1943, when Artaud entered the Rodez asylum, Ferdière, then its director, encouraged him to make art as therapy.

Jacqueline had become a convert to psychoanalysis twenty-five years earlier, after successfully applying Freud's theories to help Huguette. At the time, Surrealists were satisfied with using free association as a tool to make art but less interested in its potential for reflection and personal growth. Not Jacqueline. She considered that conflict and frustration over unmet needs could be expressed in painting but also that, when understood, it could lead to personal freedom. By attending to unconscious information as it surfaced, one could gain insight into the root of the problem, and transform.

Jacqueline told a friend she entered treatment as she turned fifty because her "energy was different. There was little time left, and she wanted to use it to paint."[360] One might never learn what particular issues she worked on while in treatment; however, her narcissistic issues were not resolved. From the time she was young, her sense of self derived from being admired. Beauty provided her with advantages for which she had to do nothing. She told Martica Sawin she "could get what she wanted by being beautiful. She did not get what she needed in her art."[361] Jacqueline had not considered that one day her looks would be gone, and she would be seen as ordinary and treated like anyone else. For the rest of her life, except for moments when reality brought her back, she latched on to her sense of entitlement.

The divorce from David had been a slap from which Jacqueline did not recover. The sting, a constant reminder that David had tired of her. She was not special; there was always someone more attractive, more intelligent. He was spoiled, so the slightest thing that bothered him was easy to discard. If a shirt lost a button, even if it was otherwise in perfect condition, he would throw it out. If Jacqueline's pregnancy was taking attention away from him, that was reason enough for him to take a lover. If that bothered Jacqueline, it was reason enough to discard her.

We have seen that Jacqueline told Dolorès, when David left her for Denise Browne, "Friendship, it's the big revelation for me. All my life, I have benefited from it without really seeing it."[362] Until then, she took friendship for granted, using friends to meet her needs without considering that they, too, had needs, failing to realize they were loyal to her not because she was special but because she was special to them. Like David, unless there was something in the relationship for her, she had no need for it. Without consideration, she, too, discarded those for whom she had no use. Much like Picasso—who she claimed had a similar personality to her own. Thus, it had been as easy for her to discard Esteban Francés, Marianne Clouzot, Dolorès, and Maar when she no longer had use for them. Even Aube, her own daughter. Jacqueline had interpreted their loyalty as a deficit—a form of weakness—in their personalities.

In treatment, Jacqueline realized that these conflicts had been brewing below the surface, and she opened up to Aube about struggling with conflict that hurt in unexpected ways, confronting her demons in the name of healing. "It is absolutely passionate and very painful ... there are terrible moments," she told Aube, who asked, "Why terrible?":

> I didn't understand, I didn't know much about it at age seventeen.
> As far as I was concerned, it was something that was supposed to
> help one live and feel relief, but she was saying that these moments
> were so difficult as to feel unbearable.
>
> Jacqueline replied, "They push you to search for memories
> one cannot find or does not wish to recall, and these memories are
> terribly painful." I suppose they dealt with childhood. She was
> doubly abandoned. Because at birth, they wanted a boy. So she
> was abandoned as a girl. After her birth, she was placed with a wet
> nurse until a year and a half later—the second abandonment.
> The mother rejected her constantly. I believe that when Jacqueline
> spoke about her mother, it was with a certain love. Incredible. It
> was as if there was a complicity between the two. Incredible because
> there was no bitterness.[363]

Aube understood Jacqueline better than Jacqueline understood herself, and even explained her behavior, although no explanation excused rejection, whether intentional or not. Jacqueline had made choices; these were the consequences.

Divorce

On October 29, 1956, Jacqueline wrote in her diary:

> *I have asked for a divorce from David. We had spoken about it about a week ago—he even asked me to wait, that he would make an effort if I could no longer stand it. This particular time I am sure he will go through with it. I had accepted again out of cowardice. This tears me apart. I still love him but more and more badly. I have become hemmed in, sad, persecuted, my jealousy is becoming poisoned food. I see myself sliding down a horrible slope, which has gotten worse these past 7 years, without my being able to see clearly the danger. I cannot concentrate on my work—it is within me. I also say to myself, "You are not a painter, if you were, there would be a thousand ways to get beyond it." I want to save all this, if I am not mistaken. If this is just weakness, perhaps an idea of slow suicide, this is wrong, one must not go on, rekindle the flame ... We have decided for Merlin's sake to stay [together] several months. He has been here just three weeks, still without speaking the language ...*
>
> *The idea of leaving this man makes me ill, what awaits me alone in Paris—it's for that which must be done and without Merlin. Working alone may save me if I put myself fully into it, with all the necessary effort to begin [again]. I know that once I get into it, I will be absorbed by it.[364]*

Three days later, on November 1, she wrote:

> *D. much kinder. It starts again each time that I am to leave—but this time I know quite well that I will not start all over again. I have fully understood, and I am afraid about it. It's terrible; it's like a game that one must not lose. Basically, David is a seducer. Thus in a country where he does not speak the language he is sad because he cannot charm people. If he learned the language, again it would start very nicely for him, but he is always too much in a hurry, it must all happen at once.[365]*

Jacqueline was unaware that David was already involved with Browne, soon to become his third wife; he was done with Jacqueline but had not told her. Eager for a final break, he pretended he would be returning; he had left his belongings at 46 rue Gay-Lussac—the apartment in the Latin Quarter he had bought for her and Merlin the previous year—and never looked back. Thereafter, as stated in the divorce decree that Jacqueline would not sign, which he filed without informing her, he would send her "150 dollars a month when his finances allowed." But between David's investment banker making a costly blunder and Denise giving him endless trouble about money, his finances fluctuated wildly. At those times, Jacqueline was forced to do without. David grew inconsistent about how much he sent her, and she and Merlin had less to live on. Nevertheless, even after Merlin went to college, David continued sending something. Jacqueline was grateful, not only because it lightened her load but also because it annoyed Browne, a fact that brought her great joy. When Therry Frey, David's fourth wife, asked him why he continued to provide for Jacqueline if it was no longer part of the divorce decree, he replied: "Jacqueline does not know how to earn a living. I loved her very much, and I am always going to love her."[366]

The next year, a breakthrough in psychotherapy allowed Jacqueline momentarily to come up for air, feel free from David, and attach to Aube. Ecstatic, Jacqueline wrote to Dolorès on April 28, 1957:

Well, I was waiting for your letter. I took all my time, you see. Your letter adds only to the happiness which came back to me with this adorable spring—the happiness ... that which I am painting, I have found it again, forever. I want to say it no longer depends on events or on people. I have found it within me, for always. Because I have also found again that which I can now look at profoundly—people that I see, that I choose, one by one, with delight in all freedom and without fear now because I demand nothing of them. What they give me overwhelms me. Not to be worried about a show, it all will take place in the fall (September = the comeback) or during the winter. I cannot miss out on anything now, and it is my trade that is precisely what I understood, for three months, to those whom I have called and who came. Real new men: a new friend, oculist, one of the most brilliant and inquiring minds, whom I met, all about him, nothing but new things. Moreover, a young lover, marvelously good and so handsome that I find myself gazing upon him for hours—I have never had that, I have never done that, I am also going to dance very late at night each weekend, and there will be more dances that I don't know perfectly. Work is going well also. I know more and more what I want to say, and I can say it, and I may say it more directly, much more quickly *(that is, by avoiding lots of failures between times). I recognized it and understood on producing them since the past, it goes without saying that others will arrive since <u>one must show</u>. But the certainty that one has passed it already at a certain level gives you a huge assurance, more calm, more confidence in facing new difficulties to come, it is a joy, you know, a marvelous treasure that one owes only to oneself, and it is surely there. I believe in true happiness. I kiss Aube for you and also Yves, her husband whom I like a lot, he works hard 8 hours a day as an engraver retoucher with a printer, who provides for the home including Ubi, the dog and Mimi, the flying squirrel. Aube continues to take her exams and is doing internships in hospital. She is beginning to learn a lot of things, which makes me really proud to be her mother. They have calculated they will be able to raise a child [and] in 2 years' time they want to have three.[367]*

Kiss my dear heart [Merlin], *tell him if he does not know it a thousand times already that I love him, that I think of him, that I await for him with such impatience, and you, a big bouquet of white lilacs.*

Your friend,
Jacqueline[368]

David was right about Jacqueline not knowing how to provide for herself, never having held down a job or learned how to promote her painting. Her misguided sense of entitlement made her see it as beneath her to approach galleries; she expected them to consider her background and seek her out. But what background was there to consider? Very few knew about her, that she had been André Breton's wife, and hence had no idea that she no longer wished to be associated with him. As she grew older, her demands grew more complicated. Her behavior revolved around sustaining her self-esteem; she became less flexible, less interested in compromising, and people did not want to bother. She would admit she was stuck, depending more and more on the kindness of strangers, whom (mostly referred by friends) she permitted to buy her paintings—but only if they jumped through hoops. To a friend, Jacqueline wrote: "Selling one's work is a joy, a little frontal flap of the wings, the certainty of existing for one's self." Yet she lost sales by making it nearly impossible for others to buy. She would only sell a work she had chosen for them, saying she wanted "to keep the best ones for a show."[369] Selling a painting under these circumstances was a way of affirming her self-worth. Not only was she having control over the buyers, but also she was confirming that they were grateful for getting any work she was willing to sell them, even if it was not one of the best.

But Jacqueline was no fool; she was aware of how she came across. Still, she would not compromise. To the same friend, amusedly, she described her interaction with buyers: "I am selling several precious things, in order for life to be less gloomy. This sale of articles is quite amusing, in fact. I know it by heart, including some books, and it is quite funny to see the interest in all its forms, shown by the dealers or other collectors, and I am not so soft as to let them go for nothing. It's a game. I am obviously getting too old, acrimonious, intolerant, etc."[370]

On occasion, Jacqueline might sell a document kept from the time when she was active among the Surrealists, such as a *cadavre exquis* or a signed first edition. These were eagerly sought out by collectors or museums, but sales were few and far between. When she saw herself running out of money, and circumstances forced her to part with works she had been holding on to, she contacted collectors or galleries. These significant objects drew interest. But once she began with irrational demands, she often ended up empty-handed, unable to find a buyer or a gallery to promote her work.[371]

Jacqueline owned the original manuscript of *L'Amour Fou*, which included handwritten notes by Breton and Giacometti, to which she had added her own personal notes, the original photographs. She now wanted to sell it. It was a unique document that any museum would have treasured, but she ended up giving it to Merlin after creating so much dissonance for interested buyers that they walked away rather than deal with her. There were times when she went without eating.[372] Had she been reasonable, she could have fed herself for years with the sale of the manuscript. When word got round that it was on the market, the Pompidou Centre contacted her. Virginia Zabriskie, director of the New York gallery of the same name, accepted Jacqueline's price but requested a 25 percent commission to sell it. Jacqueline refused, even though she knew it was standard procedure. She would not negotiate; it had to be her way. She went hungry.

In 1959, Jacqueline exhibited at the Galerie Saint-Placide, Paris, work unlike any she had shown before. Rather than her characteristic reflective work, her new paintings conveyed despair, her current state of mind. The size of objects was amplified, covering the whole canvas, as with a tree (*Arbre*, Tree, 1959) or flower vase painted rapidly with thick brushstrokes. Reviewers were impressed; rather than describing the mastery of her craft and work, they focused on its emotional content: "passionate," "concerning the deepest secrets of nature," arising "from the female instinct," "out of a violence that reaches out by its sincerity." Spot on was the reviewer for *L'Express* who described Jacqueline's agitation as "Vangoghian passion."[373]

Simiane-la-Rotonde

Despite turning out high-quality work, Jacqueline had a way to go before the summer of 1962, when she finally accessed her creative core. Despite her intense attachment to Merlin, seeing him off to meet David was liberating.[374] Jacqueline yearned to feel free, to find—somewhere within herself—what she had been seeking, impossible to find while he was around.

In Biot, a fortified medieval hilltop village in Provence, between Nice and Cannes, Jacqueline found the madeleine moment she had been waiting for, the childhood memory of merging with nature, "a time in my great youth, six to seven years of age, with my mother ... in Saint Gervais, Chamonix, and surroundings ... there, in the high mountain ... nature entered my being, spring, waterfalls, flowering meadows ..."[375] This took place, she recalled to a friend, "in Switzerland ... my jubilations, the happiness of existing on such an earth, walking all alone to discover everything. I did not love or hate. I was the GODS. The springs, the endless variety of flowers, the perfumed wind had been conceived FOR ME."[376]

In her aloneness, Jacqueline reconnected to the Divine and relived the experience of being one with the universe. In Biot she began painting her signature works—of intense greens, bright reds, translucent pinks, yellows, and blues—but few were privileged to see them first-hand. She entered a visual dimension overlooked by less intuitive painters. Until then, she had painted freely, but in Biot she took her time applying translucent glazes, allowing the bright white canvas to shine through the landscape.

Biot (1962; pl. 38) shows a narrow band of blue sky over a faint suggestion of a town growing along a green wall. Two rivers climb the wall. The borders of one expand, gradually spilling into a pool, while the other meanders upward, stopping short of the houses. The blue and green landscape is painted with fresh colors across the planted fields that surround the water, itself twinkling red, pink, and orange.

Thereafter, for the rest of Jacqueline's productive life, the sense of wonderment experienced in Biot was reproduced in her work. The following year, she painted the ruins of a tenth-century castle perched on the jagged peak above the village of Sainte-Agnès, from the flank of the mountain high above Menton.

Beginning in 1963, then off and on for some seventeen years, Jacqueline painted in the countryside, working on studies and canvases. Henri Laugier, her old friend from the *Recherche Scientifique*, with whom she was having an affair, owned the sixteenth-century manor where she stayed in Simiane-la-Rotonde, a twelfth-century village on a rocky hill in Provence.[377] It overlooked a squared plain that she described as "angled by rays of sunlight, with blossoming flowers of all colors: valerians, stocks, Spanish lilac bushes, hollyhocks bursting into bloom in the sun, and cats sleeping under the moonlight."[378]

Visitors discovered that Jacqueline's monastic schedule was best not disturbed. Pouring herself into her work, she became increasingly attuned to the rhythm of nature and found herself creating images shaped by apperceptions of the landscape. Painted in a state of meditative absorption, her compositions transformed harmonies of color into symphonies of light (pl. 39). With focused attention, she observed how the spirit of light transforms the landscape into a shifting vision, and the fluctuating pitter-patter of the rain reveals its colors and informs about its inner life. In several versions of *Étang Ovale* (Oval Pond, ca. 1975), Jacqueline recorded, one by one, drops of water falling into a pond, rippling out a different message each time they touched the surface.

As Jacqueline suspected, when she surrendered to solitude, wholeness found her. Focused attention meant discovering that each moment has a life of its own and, when observed, teaches about life's richness. Day after day, she followed the same ritual; she woke up early, painted past midday, took long walks, and in the evenings prepared dinner mindfully (pl. 43). These walks gave rise to moments trapped in miniature watercolors copied into small notebooks. In obsessive detail, she transformed *sumi-e* ink calligraphy drawings and asemic texts into mountains or streams. Any of these she might use at a later date and turn into paintings. To bind the writing, white paper became both light source and medium.

This work had been informed by Mark Tobey's unique Abstract Expressionism, influential in the development of French Tachism, in the 1950s.[379] Tobey, who was better known in France than in the United States, had an eye-opening exhibition in 1960 at the Musée des Arts Décoratifs in Paris. His art had developed after embracing the Bahá'í beliefs shared by Jacqueline, beliefs that emphasized oneness with God, an unknowable essence that created the universe. Artists, as extensions of nature, transform nature into art.[380] As Jacqueline's artistic vision deepened under the influence of Tobey's art, her fingerprint style became more contemplative.

Historically, Jacqueline trusted women. It felt natural sharing personal information with them, certain they would know what she meant. Women understand women because, their bodies being different from men's, they experience life differently. As she got older, she adopted a maternal role toward younger women, providing thoughtful advice that she would have wanted from her own mother at their age. Martine Cazin, ceramist and painter from Simiane, admired Jacqueline and her insight:

Jacqueline was for me a great friend and a spiritual mother. If she lived in isolation, she was still listening to others. But unkindly! And she did not forgive the sin of stupidity!

She taught me a great deal: to observe, to see beyond appearances. Her exactness became a permanent lesson. She questioned my work, encouraging me incessantly, and deciphered in it what I myself had not seen.

A hypersensitive and severe person, for me she remained exceptional. At the same time, she was wild and very attentive. Just below the apartment she occupied, there was a terrace where a dog was chained. The sound of the chain dragging on the concrete was intolerable to her. And I had a hard time trying to get her to see that the dog was not unhappy.

She was in awe of children whom she described as "magical beings." She felt wonderment and affection for little Oona [Jacqueline's granddaughter, Aube's adopted daughter].

She spoke little or not at all about her work—and I perhaps was too timid to ask. But meeting after meeting she taught me to see. And, of course, it was all around us, sky, rocks. Among the many that were accumulated on the terrace, there was a stone covered with traces of moss—"An ink portrait of Picasso!" she said. She was searching for the invisible rhythm of things, from which evolved the image of hills. Generally, when I arrived at her place, canvases were turned toward the wall—[a] *secret I respected.*

I recall with joy when my son, who was six or seven at the time, identified the sky in a large canvas stained with tender color.

Jacqueline liked truthfulness in people, detested appearances, lies, social games. She used her time sparingly: all her energy was used for creativity.

I always refused to ask Jacqueline about André Breton: the fact of "being the wife of ..." was an unpleasant thing for her, a form of negation of her Self. Little by little she began to speak to me about it and from it emerged much admiration, and a major conflict. She thought she could not be creative next to him, that he would not allow her. She retained a real bitterness. She suffered at having been forgotten by artistic circles—or being contacted only because of "being the wife of ..."

Almost never she spoke to me about David Hare, if only to mention his great kindness and loyalty during her whole life. And always wore a piece of jewelry that he made for her.

Through Hare she found the freedom to paint that Breton had denied her.

She was very attached to her son, Merlin. She admired his work, and was touched by his wife Debra's affection, whom she liked a lot. Her relationship with Aube was difficult, a reciprocal incomprehension that led to suffering.

She liked music, the cinema, especially art and experimental films, non-commercial films. Once she spoke about an Iranian film while describing light, the wind, silence, all this beauty ...[381]

Another young friend, Dominique Noailles, was a twenty-one-year-old painter whom Jacqueline also met in Simiane in the summer of 1971. Almost immediately, they struck up a friendship in which Jacqueline, protective of Noailles, opened her eyes and showed her a different way of living:

> [Jacqueline] *told me that when you want to be a painter, you have to be alone—no family, no children. I remember very well that she told me she could not stand life with David and the child because one had to stop in order to prepare meals, to take care of the house, because it was necessary to ... One day, she decided to dedicate herself completely to painting.[382]*

When scholar Stephen Robeson-Miller interviewed Jacqueline about Kay Sage, he asked about the recent paintings in her studio, and she informed him that she had "painted Surrealism to please André, abstract art to please David, but now she was painting for herself."[383] To Noailles, she confided that she had struggled to accomplish what she wanted as a painter. It took ten years after leaving David, she said, before she could paint the way she wanted. It was impossible, she explained, until thirteen-year-old Merlin, whom she had raised by herself, returned to his father in the States. "She never regretted the time spent caring for him," Noailles explained. "He adored her with all his soul, as she adored him," but she needed time alone to paint.[384]

Noailles, who painted quickly, marveled at how "Jacqueline could work on one painting for months. Sometimes, she was looking at something in her painting that I could not see ... Light ... she was obsessed [with it], and it took her a long time to paint [it]. She told me she was 'trying to paint light, to paint invisible things ... not palpable, light can't be touched.'"[385] Her brain saw colors that the naked eye could not see, and painted them. Noailles recalled:

Jacqueline lived tortured ... her bedroom, like a monk's cell, was a small space with a narrow bed. There were books nearby. I felt all her readings were to calm [herself], to search, poetry ... She did not speak of her douleur d'âme [painful soul], but it was there. I could see it. I could feel it. She was never relaxed, always in control. And especially, always demanding with words. Each word was thought out. Each word had its meaning. It was incredible. She was very intelligent. And at the same time, there was no lightness. Also, and perhaps, she wanted to tell me in a certain way certain things. But it was the first time in my life that I had met someone who had such absolute awareness ... I think something was burning within, demanding, autocratic. She wanted something unreachable.[386]

Despite Jacqueline being difficult, Noailles recalled her as "kind, she understood people. It's a way to be kind. So if she decides that she loves you ... she is very present with you, listening to you, and if she could give advice, she did. I found that she was very careful with people, very concerned. With people she did not love, she could be quite hard and sharp. She could say very strong words but not cruel. But anyway, she did no harm." Except to herself, as Noailles explained: "She was lost in her absoluteness. She was very demanding. All the time she was thirsty, thirsty ... and what she was doing was not enough ... [she was] insatiable. Her negativity was insatiable."[387]

In her desperate search for self-betterment, Jacqueline became more self-defeating, needing to bend, but refusing to. It had to be what she wanted, how she wanted, or nothing. Through being overcautious, she often got nothing, or not enough, and remained dissatisfied. That summer, Noailles spent several days with Jacqueline. During the day, she painted and they met for meals. In the evening, they went for walks in a rocky area where Jacqueline looked for stones. Noailles recalled:

Jacqueline had made an art of living, every day, in the little everyday things. Each thing was thought through, done conscientiously. For me, [meeting] Jacqueline was an important event, the consciousness of a gesture, the consciousness of what she was doing, even cutting greens, there was always a grand presence in whatever she was doing. It was the first time that I saw a kitchen like hers. The kitchen was another art. Each object had its place. Then later she really wanted me to go visit her in Paris.[388]

From Jacqueline, Noailles learned to focus attention on each task before taking the next step. Indeed, if this friendship was going to take, one had to follow Jacqueline's rituals. After leaving Simiane, when Noailles wanted to speak with Jacqueline, she had to telephone in advance using a code: one call with three rings, then another with one ring; when Jacqueline knew it was a friend, she picked up. Noailles recalled visiting her and discussing Jorge Luis Borges, whom Jacqueline was reading at the time, and the work of Matta and Picasso. She was influenced by Picasso's rhythm of work—he worked incessantly. Sitting in two armchairs, the two women watched in silence the flickering movement of the flames in the kiva fireplace Merlin had built for Jacqueline, after the southwestern pueblo architecture:

> She said to me she was going to have me listen to something: "You have to guess what it is," she said. And she put on this music, and we sat in silence for a long time, and I was trying to discover what it was. It was the first time I heard the song of whales. There! I guessed it. I didn't know I could guess it. I told her, so we had moments like that. I recall the tea ceremony. It was always that thing of picking up the teapot and pouring the tea. Aren't things supposed to be like that? Jacqueline was present [mindful] in everything. And one day, she told me she was going to give me a gift, a very important gift. "A friend of mine gave me this gift and I am giving it to you." And she spoke about this lady without ever revealing her name. And she gave me an Indian skirt quite old and transparent. And so, I received it just like a treasure. I didn't know it was from Frida Kahlo. And she spoke about her, she said she was very impressed because this woman was very ill, and that she painted her dreams, and that it was extraordinary.[389]

Jacqueline liked Noailles's painting and told her that, had she lived in the United States, she would likely earn a scholarship. She advised Noailles on how to live. "All is connected to the body," she explained. Influenced by psychologist Carl Rogers, Jacqueline believed that one could achieve one's potential by working on oneself. She opened up about her psychoanalysis and her marriage to André. People never forgot that she was once married to him: "She said she wanted to exist without André."[390]

Not all their talk was serious. Jacqueline recalled experimenting with peyote in Laugier's home in Antibes, hallucinating colors and flowers. With Noailles, she attended films and exhibitions. But in 1974, when Noailles moved to the south of France, the friendship was interrupted.

Cityscapes

Back from Simiane, Jacqueline began painting cityscapes that reflected her ambivalence toward people. Closeness made her as uneasy as distance made her comfortable. In the countryside, she explored her claustrophobic sense of cities. In *Village-Simiane* (1971), she portrayed the twelfth-century château resting against a rock, trapped within a web of red, black, and green, the disquiet of a caged city. The Paris cityscapes, painstakingly detailed, took months to complete (pl. 40). At some point, desperate for breathing space, she alternated between painting cityscapes and skies in which cumulus clouds of blue, green, and salmon are framed by light (pl. 41). The idea came to her following a trip to Venice, where she discovered "the skies of Tiepolo."[391] To a friend Jacqueline wrote: "I am always in the cities, but now more articulated if not converged. Even if not complete, they are more defined. However, I am anxious to get back to the skies, the mercury skies of Paris."[392]

Triggered initially by the alienating cityscapes of Portuguese artist Maria Helena Vieira da Silva, Jacqueline's pulsating views of Paris became her numinous work. Uninhabited, disappearing, veering toward oblivion, yet alive, they are imbued with spirit, haloed or framed by light. Each shows a step in the transition between evanescence and substance.

Huguette disclosed why Jacqueline's cityscapes were devoid of people: "She had painted few humans and, just like poisonous flowers, they will disappear progressively and completely."[393]

A Princess from Far Away

Aube and her husband, Yves, were eager to have children, so adopting Oona from Korea was a dream come true for them. Jacqueline was looking forward to being a grandmother and became enthralled with this precious girl, to whom she referred as "a princess from a faraway land."[394] Jacqueline's eagerness to babysit could have provided the opportunity to repair her relationship with Aube, but it was not to be. Instead, Jacqueline found ways to criticize Aube or Coco, her new partner.

Jacqueline kept a basket of toys in the studio for Oona when she visited. They spoke mostly about topics that might interest Oona. To stir her curiosity, Jacqueline explained art, Native American culture, or anything else she wanted to know about. Oona recalled a poster of the terracotta army of Emperor Qin Shi Huang's Mausoleum, and the stories Jacqueline told about the soldiers. Throughout the apartment were references to art. Even the refrigerator was concealed behind a reproduction of an angel by Piero della Francesca. To Oona, Jacqueline had "a wonderful personality." They took to each other and Jacqueline freely showed her work to Oona, which Oona loved. Jacqueline cooked special meals for her, Chinese dishes, vegetarian dishes. They did gymnastics and yoga; and because Oona liked horses, Jacqueline often took her to see the ponies in the Luxembourg Gardens.

"Sometimes she would speak about Merlin," Oona recalled, "whom she put on a pedestal, or a little bit aggressively toward Aube. She might say: 'Your mother is a little bit too bossy.'" Oona sensed that "Jacqueline was seething," but she could not figure out why until she concluded, "Jacqueline was torn because she wanted to be both a man and a woman."[395] Oona remembered a blackboard hung outside the bathroom door, on which Jacqueline wrote a quotation of the day, such as, "Life is a fire that reasons," by Antonin Artaud, or, "I recognized happiness by the noise it made when it left," by Jacques Prévert.[396]

A Visit from the Past

Marianne Clouzot also had developed as an artist, her mature style reflecting on space and movement in the manner of Georges Braque's birds in flight, as spirits of prophesy. By remaining in touch with Huguette, she had been kept informed about Jacqueline's life. Each time Jacqueline held an exhibition in Paris, Clouzot attended with genuine interest.

At a difficult juncture in her personal life, "very unhappy at that particular time," Clouzot called on Jacqueline, hoping for a rapprochement with her old friend. She left feeling worse, wounded, struggling to understand what had just happened:

> *I went to see her marvelous apartment on the Boulevard de Bonne Nouvelle, which was of extraordinary beauty. I must admit I was absolutely dazzled by her apartment and by her painting. So I was quite ready to admire her and make new contact, but I felt that she had no need and no desire. Well, for her, it was solitude, which didn't sit well with people, and she had broken up with nearly all her friends, and she had the appearance of being very content, being all alone. She was sufficient unto herself, she looked very well, was not suffering, and painting occupied her entirely. No, I admired her a lot.*
>
> *Her paintings were huge, immense, with little touches of landscapes. I was surprised because it was painting which was very gentle, not at all hard, not at all cutting, as they had been in America. They were on the whole quite gay. So I was altogether surprised because it didn't seem to jive with her personality. She was not pleasant or gay. It was not logical. She really did not correspond at all to the person that she once had been. I believe she was very pacified, very introverted. She lived very much alone and went out alone, it was all very curious. I supposed she had discovered inner peace. All the earlier wanderings in her life had come to an end. It's not a very nice term, but I believe that Breton showed her off in different colors and caused her to drool and sweat. She told me she had separated from him because he had wanted her to do Surrealist painting, but she wanted to do it based on what she wished, even if there was not an elephant on Breton's head. Painting was everything for her.*

At that particular moment, I was in such a state of total loneliness, I tried to bring back the old things and see if I couldn't renew old friendships with her, since she herself was alone. But she was not alone and desired to stay that way. I was completely disabled, and she didn't help me at all, on the contrary. It was indifference, brutality. She was very, very hard, really nasty. I left her immediately.[397]

Jacqueline was difficult with most everyone. The experience of Dominique Noailles was typical. With the skirt she had been gifted, she admitted, "I made a mistake. I cannot recall to whom I gave it away. Perhaps, one day I will find it again. I adored this skirt, as Jacqueline had given it to me saying, 'Here, I'm giving it to you, keep it forever.' And then, one day I wrote to Jacqueline; it had been such a long time since we had seen each other. She told me in her letter, 'I will see you again, if you still have the skirt' ... I was moving a lot. And each time I took the skirt. I wrote a reply but didn't send it. I was angry with her because there were no conditions. She never spoke about conditions. I told her that I had kept the skirt for eleven years—it went with me everywhere—and that I had given it in the same token she had given it to me. I didn't give it to just anyone, and I had not given it in any old way. I gave it away very carefully, for love ... I saw her a week or perhaps a month before her death. I kept saying, 'I will call [my boyfriend] Fabrice [Maze].' I kept saying to him, 'We must go see Jacqueline.'"[398]

Picasso, Ten Years After

Ten years previously, Dolorès had witnessed Jacqueline showing her recent work to Picasso. He studied the paintings and "became silent; he didn't say a word."[399] No one could tell what he was thinking, and no one asked.

Ten years after, Jacqueline showed him paintings she produced since *Biot* (1962–7), with happier results. The medieval Château Grimaldi, where Picasso had painted her and Maar in *Night Fishing at Antibes* one month before the outbreak of war, had been turned into the Picasso Museum the previous year for a show titled *Lamba, Peintures et Dessins* (August 11–October 31, 1967).

Jacqueline was ecstatic—fifty carefully chosen works were exhibited. Between Picasso's approval and critic Yves Bonnefoy's catalogue preface, she felt she had arrived. It was a perfect evening, or nearly so. A recent facelift smoothed her face and made her correct features shine. But for Jacqueline, who would not settle for anything less than perfection, it was not good enough. Plastic surgery made her face look good, but not young. She was photographed surrounded by friends during the vernissage. Once the photograph was in her hands, she covered her face with a black mask (pl. 42).

The exhibition confirmed that Jacqueline had been doing good work. However, interpersonally, she had become more difficult, if that were possible. As a painter, she needed to exhibit regularly, but no one was showing her work. With her recent success, she assumed she would be sought out by galleries, but that did not happen. Even after greeting Matta at an opening of his work, hoping he would ask about her painting, where she was exhibiting, and so on—nothing. He had been at her show at the Château Grimaldi; he was among the lenders. Marie Cuttoli and Alexander Calder, also lenders, were present too. Nothing. Not even Bonnefoy, also a lender. Silence. She could not understand. If her work was good enough to be shown at the Picasso Museum, why was there no interest?[400]

Jacqueline was painting her signature cityscapes when Bonnefoy began planning an exhibition at Paris's Maison de la Culture. Jacqueline was elated. One of her cityscapes was to hang alongside works by Giacometti and Vieira da Silva. But her excitement waned when she saw that the poster featured a drawing of a female nude, which she found "vulgar." When she brought up her concern with Bonnefoy, what began as a dialogue became a power struggle in which neither would yield.[401] As curator, Bonnefoy had the right to choose works and develop the show according to his own desires, and he stood his ground. Jacqueline disagreed. She would neither compromise nor consider that she might be wrong, nor yet concede that there could be other answers. Since it was not going to be as she demanded, she withdrew her painting and thus lost the opportunity to exhibit her work alongside artists whom she admired.

Jacqueline had behaved as if she derived more pleasure from digging in her heels than from participating in the exhibition. Perhaps she felt that by not exhibiting she could shield herself from poor reviews. Regardless, she found it intolerable to be contradicted, as if being told "No" meant something was wrong with her. In the end, it was a pyrrhic victory.[402]

Later, following Jacqueline's death, Bonnefoy was approached by "two or three" people interested in writing about her, requesting interviews. Each time, he refused, explaining that his memory could not be trusted; he did not like giving "pseudo-information, or advancing opinions, whose interpretation I could not control, how they would be used by biographers.

Thus, since I could not be responsible, I made a rule not to respond to requests."[403] After sharing a friendship, surely he recalled a great deal that he could trust not to be misinterpreted, but more likely he did not wish to speak of Jacqueline in anger so he made up an excuse not to. Nevertheless, fair is fair, and it was at his suggestion that the Museum of the City of Paris acquired a painting of hers.

Maintaining the pretense of not needing others, Jacqueline made it known that the Pompidou was the only museum where she would exhibit, nothing less.[404] Fortunately, the Pompidou's director expressed interest in acquiring a painting while considering acquiring the manuscript of *L'Amour Fou*, which she was selling, and asked that she bring two works. She became infuriated: "How dare he!? If he wanted to see her painting, he should make an effort and visit the studio."[405] She didn't follow up, believing that if she had, it would have been demeaning, even though she conceded that it would have given her a greater chance of selling a work to the Pompidou. Again, perhaps, on some level she feared that, after seeing the work, he might not be interested. Then what? She missed out on selling both the manuscript and the painting.

After Laugier's death in 1973, Jacqueline continued to spend most summers in Simiane until 1980, when his family sold the house. In 1973, her friend the painter Jacques Bibonne suggested they take a trip to Toledo, and he, Jacqueline, and Huguette went together. The city and El Greco's paintings were major discoveries. Between 1979 and 1981, Jacqueline lived in San Diego, California, with Merlin and Debra, from where they made road trips to Native American reservations in New Mexico. And during 1982–3, she traveled with them to Switzerland, where Merlin was employed building lightweight aircraft for ULM (Ultralight Aircrafts), simpler and less expensive than traditional airplanes.

Although increasingly isolated, at seventy-one Jacqueline was living as she wanted, taking care of her needs, more selective about whom she spoke with and what about. She avoided going out, saying, "I don't want people to see me the way I look today."[406] However, she remained interested in youth and continued to be helpful whenever scholars and journalists called about André or Surrealism. "Youth is hope," she had replied to an adolescent during the events of May 1968 in France, when he asked—with the arrogance of the young—"Why are you protesting, you're old!" At the time, she was fifty-seven. "Because one needs to protest," she replied.[407] Acknowledgment remained vital to her self-esteem, but she believed "she would not receive recognition as an artist because she was a woman, had been married to André Breton, stopped painting Surrealism, and had a difficult personality."[408] Nevertheless, to her, needing others was an intolerable sign of weakness.

Jacqueline's solitude, which disturbed others, "she claimed as a necessary condition for her work. It was an ascetic conquest."[409] In the summer of 1988, the last that Jacqueline spent in Paris, she wrote to Cazin: "Being alone did not mean my lack of desire to meet people or friends but to be inhabited by one's Self, either to love or to create."[410]

But age does not forgive, and as Jacqueline grew older, she suffered more and more illnesses, the cumulative effect of which—much to her chagrin—made her dependent on others. Finally, she managed to stop smoking her cherished cigarettes, but by then the habit had ravaged her frail body. At seventy-seven, she was having more difficulty climbing the stairs to her fifth-floor apartment. A physical examination by lung specialist Dr. Robert Cartier explained that her weakness had been caused by a silent heart attack; coronary artery disease was causing chest pain. A herniated disk from wear and tear caused chronic back pain.[411] With Cazin, she allowed herself to be vulnerable:

> *I am so often weak and beaten down by illness that I can paint only partially and badly at that. Often I wonder about help. I never will be able to tell you to come to my help. I never do it for Aube, Merlin, or anybody. They are the ones to decide, and my first reflex is that they don't come—I never know what to do about people. For example, telephoning or being telephoned terrifies me—words pronounced in this box are questioned and anyone becomes suspect. There is no body [there] and consequently no soul. Merlin is beginning to understand this for himself.*
>
> *I had a dream last night in which some unknown persons with a long narrow home wanted to rent it to me. You were there to help me in moving the marvelous things I owned. You proposed to help me [but] I hesitated, not liking this place. You proposed also to take care of Tumuc-Umac [her parrot]. I had feelings of regret and guilt at leaving him. I was worried about the dream, which for me symbolized death.[412]*

Jacqueline's financial struggles increased; there were days when she did not have a cent.[413] Merlin, who had been going to college in the States and visited her once a year, was back in France, working in Fontainebleau as assistant to sculptor François-Xavier Lalanne, visiting his mother regularly on his motorcycle. Much to her disabling shame, she broke down and asked for his financial help. She could have asked Aube, who would have helped *avec le coeur dans la main*, with her heart on her sleeve. But Jacqueline's pride would not allow anyone to know that she was struggling, not Aube, of all people. She would rather starve, which she might have, had Aube not rescued her in the nick of time. "Aube has her feet on the ground," Jacqueline confided in a friend, who told Oona.[414]

The Beginning of the End

The more dependent Jacqueline became on Aube, the more she hated her daughter. And there seemed no end to how contemptuously Jacqueline could behave—to suggest that Aube's help was worthless. Nevertheless, Aube remained available by telephone, and, "when Jacqueline wasn't too nasty," she visited.[415]

On a wet day in August 1988, Jacqueline struggled to dial Aube. Her speech was slurred and her words confused, but she managed to ask her to come quickly. Right away, Aube called Huguette to inform her of the problem and took the next train to Paris. Jacqueline had not eaten in days and could hardly walk: "I had the sensation when I entered her home ... like somebody had died three months earlier and no one had been there since."[416]

Jacqueline had seen several doctors about a host of ailments for which she was taking multiple medications. She had been diagnosed as having experienced a mild stroke, and her confusion suggested early signs of dementia. She suffered from rheumatism. The underlying grief she had lived with since early childhood—unrequited love—had finally become disabling. She was living an isolated life, desperate for human contact—unassuaged loneliness. Lonely people with imaginary conditions frequently visit doctors.[417]

When Aube arrived, "There were twelve different medications spread out on the bed and table. I threw everything away and said, 'You're going to rest.' I made her some food. She ate a bit. And I called Dr. Damoiseau, her rheumatologist. He did not make home visits and wanted Jacqueline to be brought to his office. She was in no position to travel but demanded to see Damoiseau."[418] There was a taxi strike, but Aube found a way. The doctor evaluated Jacqueline, instructed Aube to keep her off all previously prescribed medications, and made out a single prescription. As if by magic, after two or three days, she cleared up. Overmedication had caused her confusion. Damoiseau explained that she could no longer live alone.

Aube called Merlin and conveyed the severity of the problem. After he arrived, they discussed options: going to America to live with Merlin and

Debra; staying in her apartment with sitters; or moving into a retirement home. Living with Aube was out of the question. "It is not a very happy episode when you have to put your own mother in a home," Aube said, looking back.[419]

Although initially Jacqueline accepted the idea of moving to Idaho (where Merlin lived) and being cared for by a Quaker sitter during the day, she changed her mind. Meanwhile, getting her down from her fifth-floor apartment to renew her passport became another trial. Afterward, Jacqueline balked at the plan. "I don't want a Quaker. Quakers are very strict and narrow-minded," she concluded without knowing anything about them.[420] She said she wanted to hear French spoken, but she rejected the thought of sitters in her apartment; she did not want strangers eating in her space or using her toilet. Aube reminded her that a person needs to eat and use the toilet, but Jacqueline would not hear of it. The retirement facility it was for her.

Two weeks later, Jacqueline walked into her new, upscale home. Surrounded by a park, on the banks of the Loire in Rochecorbon, Touraine, stood the nineteenth-century Château de la Taisserie, once the property of Madame Tonnelle, wife of General Nicolas Léonard Beker, both of whom were prominent figures during the Napoleonic era. There, Jacqueline could walk the grounds, have visitors, and go out on pass, and she never lacked paper or colors to draw. Aube "took her to movies she chose, to a Chinese restaurant, but all was bad, so I stopped."[421]

La Taisserie had a beautiful view, a landscape surrounded with trees. But Jacqueline did not like to see old or infirm people, so she stopped going downstairs and instead had her meals in her room. She was not happy with her first room, so Aube found one she liked, with a view of a tree.

On November 24, Jacqueline managed to write a couple lines to Cazin: "Martine, I am hospitalized at the Château—in the Indre et Loire area—train to Tours. How are things for you? I think of you tenderly, Jacqueline." Jacqueline asked that she contact Aube in Saché. Cazin took the train, worried that she could not visit often. Jacqueline replied:

> Don't worry yourself about the visits. I am not lonely. But in any case, delivered from A[ube] who has left on summer vacation at Oona's residence—I had really enough of her moods which went from good to especially abominable—thank you for the jasmine [perfume] which is close to its fragrance. I am sad about what you are telling me about your friend's health ...
>
> I don't know why my hand is trembling. It happens often when the subjects are very moving.

She continued with her impressions of the château:

> *It is beautiful. The large linden trees, like a cathedral, are not moving; but just superb. I walk in this garden/park with the sense of a prisoner who is walking in the prison yard.*
>
> *I dream of the flat lands where you live. There are people who live and shout in this horrible house. There are roses outside— they say nothing, just placed there to look chic.*
>
> *Those visiting the mad ones are worse than they are, showing their true colors; pitiable retired persons showing, like Aube, huge cars equipped with a dog.*
>
> *I have a sort of a friend. It does not go far. She is also different = like a flower dressed in white, several words exchanged, nice but discouraging. Only the doctor has an idea of what I could be if he imagines what he does not know ...*
>
> *The best is the gardener who is not French, which isolates him ... and anyway, he is called Argot. He knows how to do everything and everyone acts like a snob toward him because he is a worker. The worst is that I have already said all this. Oh the cold hand, wooden, which comes to perch on you; the mad ones!*[422]

Oona, Coco, and Aube visited frequently in the afternoons. They put together pastries and cakes. When the weather was nice, they went out on to the terrace; if it was not, they stayed in the room. Jacqueline interacted, asked questions, but toward the end she became increasingly absent, listening to the news less and less. Everything slowed down for her. She had been at the château exactly a year when she wrote three lines to Cazin:

> *Alone, yes, alone*
> *Not a word all day*
> *I embrace you tenderly*
> *J.*[423]

Merlin empathized with his mother's situation: "She had a passion for the word—passion for the language. It was very difficult toward the end when she was alone. There were no more dialogues with others, or very little in any case, and I recall that she listened to the radio where she heard people speaking of ideas ..."[424] After struggling to find a word, she explained to Cazin: "I am not stupid. But my reality is now a different one."[425]

Aube was supporting Jacqueline before she entered La Taisserie. Until then, she had survived on what meager sums David sent inconsistently. Aube informed David that he no longer needed to send money; she would be taking over Jacqueline's care. When Jacqueline was in need, to cover her feelings of shame, she had trouble acknowledging the help of others or say thank you. If anything, the conflict she felt at her situation made her behave contemptuously toward those who helped—such as Aube, who visited weekly to be sure her mother's needs were met, even anticipated: "She was mean to me, and I would go and see her alone, sometimes, and I would go back home and just fall apart. It was truly tough, and Oona would give me hell and say, 'Why don't you go away for a week? She has people taking care of her, to attend her, and she is taken care of very well, and that just destroys you, so stop going every week. Why do you do it?'"[426]

Aube had concerns about Jacqueline's health: "That she was ill, I knew it without knowing ... especially in relation to Alzheimer's, she forgot things. There were things regarding her health. We would go on a stroll outside, we tried to walk around the garden. Well, that interested her, of course. She didn't go far ... And I believe she didn't like very much leaving her room. She saw others who were in a worse state than she was, so we stayed for the most part in her room. So, that was it."[427] Oona recalled Jacqueline's constant hostility toward Aube: "Each time she said something, Jacqueline contradicted her, or replied in a disagreeable tone. Once she did it to me, but that was quite rare."[428]

On one occasion, while having tea outside, Jacqueline was hateful to Aube. Oona snapped: "Someone taking care of you, you treat like a dog." She went on, angrily: "I am sick of the way you treat Aube. All the things she does for you, you treat her very badly. I've had enough. If you treat her like that, I will not come back to see you."[429] Jacqueline, seeing that she could no longer speak like that, stood up and walked to her room. They waited, but she did not come back.

Jacqueline grew strangely hostile. She told Aube: "I am pure. You were never baptized."[430] Oona concluded that Jacqueline, jealous of Aube, was settling scores: "Aube learned about life and had succeeded in building something solid with Coco and me. She built a family. Before that, she was married to Yves, who was handsome, very intelligent, a talented painter and writer, whom she loved."[431]

Aube recalled: "One never knew with her, if she was playing, when we would go see her. She would look at me and ask, 'Who are you?' which people with Alzheimer's do. Then, after a while, she would smile and look at me and say, 'You think I don't know, but I know you,' and she would play like that all the time." Sometimes, though, it was unclear whether she was playing: "Once, I put a tray in front of her, and there was a glass and a bottle of water, so I poured her [some], and she didn't like that, [pretending] she couldn't see the glass, which wasn't true. Of course she wasn't blind, she could see the glass. That was a perverse way of bothering you. Well, I don't know if it was perversity or Alzheimer's ..."[432]

No one except Aube understood why she kept coming back to see her mother. Jacqueline's equivocal maternal love had robbed Aube of her childhood. Aube was still hoping to get from her mother the gesture that would validate her, to allow her to feel "a real person."[433] In a letter to Damoiseau in April 1975, as Yves, Aube's husband, was dying of cancer, Jacqueline wrote: "I love Aube."[434] Why tell him but not her daughter?

Jacqueline had never learned about compassion. To the end, she remained incapable of giving or receiving it. She had said as much in her letters to Dolorès, to Frida, to Cazin: "I am incapable of saying anything that might be good to anyone who is in pain." When Clouzot sought her out, "disabled by loneliness," Jacqueline had shown her indifference.

What irony; it would never have crossed Jacqueline's mind that André was the one to thank for her ability to live in La Taisserie during her final days. Fifty years earlier, when she asked for a divorce, he had warned her: "You will get nothing from rue Fontaine."[435] Eager to free herself from him, Jacqueline signed on the dotted line. She regretted it after his death, when, hopeful, she consulted a qualified *notaire* who confirmed that she indeed got nothing. But life has a life of its own, and it makes inexplicable decisions for everyone. Aube sold Magritte's *Ceci est un morceau du fromage* (This Is a Piece of Cheese, 1936–7), an object in André's collection—a bell jar over a painting of a piece of cheese—which paid for Jacqueline's stay at the rest home.

July 20, 1993

Ultimately, Alzheimer's robbed Jacqueline of her memory. As with everything, she fought hard. During her last two years, little by little she stopped reading or writing; she stopped listening to the news and began calling for her father, sometimes mixing the names José and Jesus.[436] Lung cancer sped the process, and heart failure struck the death blow—a tragic end for someone who operated from the heart. Years earlier, she replied to her friend Chrystie Sherman: "If you hear I'm no longer painting, it's because I have died."[437] Indeed, she continued to draw until she could no longer hold a pencil.

The family—Aube, Coco, and Oona—were in Brittany when La Taisserie called. "She's dying. It's going so fast," Aube was told. "And when I arrived, she was dead."[438] Huguette had seen her two or three days earlier. "She didn't suffer long," she recalled.[439] Aube buried Jacqueline in the Saché cemetery, where Yves was also laid to rest. Present at the funeral were Huguette, Merlin and Debra, Aube with Coco and Oona, Dominique Noailles and Fabrice. When Fabrice saw Jacqueline, "looking like an Egyptian goddess wearing an embroidered dress," he broke down.[440] Noailles recalled Merlin and Debra quietly crying in the small chapel, and "Aube placing sunflowers on Jacqueline's grave."[441]

After the funeral, "to pay homage to Jacqueline's life, Aube held a reception at her home in Saché, with a lot of conviviality, to make it the warmest possible situation." Afterward, she sent out death notices.[442]

Jacqueline Lamba
1910–1993
LA NUIT DU TOURNESOL
(The Night of the Sunflower)
The funeral will take place on 23 July in Saché

The death certificate read: "Jacqueline Mathilde Lamba, born 17 November 1910. Lived at Rochecorbon, died 20 July 1993 at La Taisserie." It listed her parents' names, Jane Adele Pinon and José Lamba, and mentioned that she had divorced André Breton. She was eighty-two years old.

Afterword

When Aube asked Fabrice to clean out the studio, he requested permission to film the place as it looked when Jacqueline left it, five years earlier. He and Dominique replaced the dead plants and set pots of thyme, bay leaves, and laurel on the tables, alongside potted morning glories and other flowers Jacqueline favored. After filming, they began to empty the studio. Initially, Aube found it difficult to be there, so Fabrice and Dominique began the work. Earlier, Aube had stumbled across a portrait that Jacqueline had painted of her when she was in her twenties: "It had a tear through the middle. It was terrible because she obviously trashed it, but she kept it."[443] Dominique found a box containing Aube's school notebooks and childhood drawings: "Aube was very moved that Jacqueline kept those boxes with things belonging to her little one. It was really the limit ... Aube suffered a lot, and I don't know why or how. Aube does not cry, she contains herself."[444]

Merlin was uninterested in keeping the appointment books, but Aube wanted them. One opened to a photograph of an adolescent Merlin; another, to one of Aube in profile. On a third, Jacqueline had inscribed: "When you are bad to your children, you are bad to yourself."[445]

Dominique listened to Aube's description of placing Jacqueline in a retirement home, how Merlin and Debra said goodbye tearfully. When Aube was asked why, despite a life of repeated rejections, she was unstinting about keeping alive the memory of Jacqueline and interest in her painting, she thought of her mother's determination to rise out of her darkness into the light. She replied: "*C'est mon devoir de memoire*" (It's my duty to remember).[446]

Notes

1 Letter from Jacqueline Lamba to Enrico Donati dated June 12, 1954. Donati papers, folder 5, letters from Jacqueline Lamba and David Hare, Getty Research Institute, Los Angeles. Henceforth, Donati papers.

2 Some information in this text has been drawn from previous publications of mine on Jacqueline Lamba.

3 The primary source on Jacqueline's early years and family history is her older sister, Huguette Lamba, interview with the author in Paris, October 1999, and her written reminiscences to the author. I am deeply grateful for Huguette's patience with my endless questions. Henceforth, Huguette interviews.

4 Interview with Debra Patla in Victor, ID, September 1999. Henceforth, Patla interview.

5 Dolorès Vanetti-Ehrenreich, friend and confidante of Jacqueline, provided information about Jacqueline's family of origin, marriage to David Hare, and sources of creativity; interview with the author, April 1999, in New York. Henceforth, Vanetti interview.

6 Aube Breton-Elléouët, Jacqueline's daughter, could not have been more generous and helpful. She opened her archives and allowed me to peruse them freely; she wrote letters of introduction for libraries and research centers, to grant me access to André Breton documents. Interviews with the author, October 10, 1999, and April 10, 2002, in Paris. Henceforth, Aube interviews.

7 Strange coincidence, but Hippolyte Maindron (1801–1884) had also been a sculptor.

8 James Thrall Soby, *Modern Art and the New Past*, with an introduction by Paul J. Sachs, Norman, OK (University of Oklahoma Press), 1957, pp. 122–3.

9 James Lord, *Giacometti: A Biography*, New York (Noonday Press) 1983, p. 155.

10 Ibid., pp. 155–6.

11 Mark Polizzotti, *André Breton: Revolution of the Mind*, New York (Farrar, Straus and Giroux) 1995, p. 404. Henceforth, Polizzotti.

12 Ibid.

13 Eileen Agar, *A Look at My Life*, London (Methuen) 1988, pp. 120–21.

14 Ibid.

15 Telephone interview with Ethel Baziotes, October 4, 2000. Ethel and her husband, painter William Baziotes, were friends with the Hares. Henceforth, Baziotes interview.

16 Telephone interview with Therry Frey, David's fourth wife, October 15, 2000. Henceforth, Frey interview.

17 Vanetti interview.

18 Interview with Ernestine Lassaw, wife of sculptor Ibram Lassaw, April 1999, in East Hampton, New York. Henceforth, Lassaw interview 1999.

19 Huguette interviews.

20 Oona Elléouët interviews with the author, October 10, 1999, and April 10, 2002, in Paris. Henceforth, Oona interviews.

21 Jacqueline Lamba, undated note to herself. Aube archive.

22 Huguette interviews.

23 Interview with Marianne Clouzot, who, with her sister Marie Rose, was childhood friends with Jacqueline and Huguette. Their friendship with Huguette lasted until the end of their lives. I'm deeply grateful to Marianne for meeting with me several times and providing segments of her diaries relevant to Jacqueline, October 1999, in Paris. Henceforth, Clouzot interview.

24 Huguette archive.

25 Huguette interviews.

26 Aube interviews.

27 Huguette interviews.

28 Ibid.

29 Ibid.

30 Ibid.

31 Copies of these articles for the *Bulletin de L'Union des Agriculteurs d'Egypte* are in the Merlin Hare archive.

32 Samir W. Raafat, *Cairo, the Glory Years: Who Built What, When, Why and for Whom* ... Alexandria (Harpocrates Publishing) 2003, pp. 89–90.

33 Article about the accident in Merlin Hare's archive.

34 Huguette interviews.

35 Ibid.

36 Ibid.

37 Clouzot interview.

38 Vanetti interview.

39 Clouzot interview.

40 On October 10, 1996, film director Teri Wehn Damisch interviewed Jacqueline in her Paris studio for a documentary on Air-Bel. I thank Merlin Hare for lending me the recording. Henceforth, Damisch interview.

41 Vanetti interview.

42 Quoted in Martica Sawin, *Surrealism in Exile and the Beginnings of the New York School of Painting*, Cambridge, MA (MIT Press), 1995, p. 306.

43 Martica Sawin, telephone interview with the author, August 26, 2000. Henceforth, Sawin interview.

44 Clouzot interview.

45 Ibid.

46 Ibid.

47 Leon Trotsky, *To the Memory of Sergei Essenin* (January 1926), quoted in André Breton, "Political Position of Today's Art" (1935), in *Manifestoes of Surrealism*, Ann Arbor, MI (University of Michigan Press), 1972, p. 228.

48 Damisch interview.

49 Ibid.

50 Marianne Clouzot met Dora at l'Union Centrale des Arts Décoratifs. Clouzot interview.

51 Wallace Fowlie (translator, introduction, and notes); Seth Whidden (updated, revised, and foreword), *Rimbaud, Complete Works, Selected Letters: A Bilingual Edition*, Chicago and London (University of Chicago Press) 1966, p. 305. Henceforth, *Rimbaud*.

52 Ibid.

53 Aube archive.

54 Damisch interview.

55 Jacqueline to filmmaker Fabrice Maze in a letter dated January 15, 1968.

56 Damisch interview.

57 Louis Chavance, "Le Décorateur et le Métier," *Du Cinéma: Revue de critique et de recherches cinématographiques*, First Series, no. 1 (December 1928), pp. 19–23, illus. p. 19.

58 André Delons, "Chronique des film perdues," *Du Cinéma*, First Series, no. 2 (February 1928), pp. 46–9, illus. p. 48.

59 Clouzot interview.

60 Huguette's diagnosis was likely hysterical hypochondriasis caused by the event she witnessed. This can resemble a catatonic state and resolves itself without leaving sequelae. But catatonia, a type of schizophrenia, is incurable.

61 Clouzot interview.

62 Ibid.

63 Antinea, descendant of the rulers of Atlantis, was a sex-starved queen who had a warrior to procure her lovers, whom she drugged and held captive. She wanted 120 sex slaves but managed to trap just 53—one of whom escaped.

64 Clouzot interview.

65 Ibid.

66 Spanish painter (1904–1977), friend of Marianne Clouzot's, protégé of Picasso, who introduced him to his circle of friends. Pruna's work is associated with the neoclassical style that created pre-Surrealism.

67 Clouzot interview.

68 Ibid.

69 At this time, Jacqueline had the first of several abortions. Vanetti interview.

70 Damisch interview.

71 Ibid.

72 Ibid.

73 André Delons, *Au Carrefour du Grand Jeu et du Surréalisme*, Limoges (L'Atelier Graphique à Limoges) 1988, pp. 75–7 (here translated from the French by Maurice Elton).

74 Jacqueline Lamba, "A Revolutionary Approach to Life and the World," in Penelope Rosemont (ed.), *Surrealist Women: An International Anthology*, Austin (University of Texas) 1988, p. 77.

75 Breton confided in Aube information about his childhood that he would not have shared with others. Aube interviews.

76 André Breton, quoted in Jean-Paul Sartre, *The War Diaries, November 1939–March 1940*, translated from the French by Quentin Hoare, New York (Pantheon Books) 1984, p. 20.

77 Aube interviews.

78 He was a witness at Breton's wedding to Simone Kahn.

79 Ricardo Nirenberg, "Paul Valéry and Some of His Contemptors," in *off course*, www.albany.edu/offcourse; www.offcourse.org, ISSN 1556-4975.

80 Helena Holzer (Lam), interview with the author on February 2, 2002, Saarbrücken, Germany. Helena befriended Jacqueline at Air-Bel, where she stayed with painter Wifredo Lam, soon to be her husband. Also, they were Jacqueline and David's friends in the United States. Henceforth, Holzer interview.

81 Leonora Carrington, interview with the author, May 12, 2002, in New York. Henceforth, Carrington interview.

82 Aube interviews.

83 Vanetti interview.

84 Marcel Jean, *The History of Surrealist Painting*, New York (Grove Press) 1960, p. 260.

85 Polizzotti, p. 25.

86 Simone de Beauvoir, *The Prime of Life*, New York (Harper-Colophon Books) 1976, p. 278.

87 Pierre Mabille was the go-to physician among the Surrealists. He attended Jacqueline during her pregnancy with and delivery of Aube.

88 Translated from the French by Mary Ann Caws for the *London Review of Books*, XXXIII/17, September 8, 2011.

89 André Breton, *Mad Love*, New York (Farrar, Straus and Giroux) 1995, p. 41. Henceforth, *Mad Love*.

90 Huguette recalled that when she brought up André's age, Jacqueline became angry and uninvited her to the wedding. Huguette interviews.

91 Damisch interview.

92 Jacqueline Lamba in an undated note to herself in Fabrice Maze's archive.

93 After returning from exile, Jacqueline learned that André destroyed all her art left at rue Fontaine.

94 Damisch interview.

95 Catalogue of the exhibition in the Museum of Modern Art, *Antonin Artaud, Works on Paper*, ed. Margit Rowell, New York (Harry N. Abrams) 1996), p. 44, illus.

96 Reproduced in Jaime Moreno Villarreal, *Frida en París, 1939*, Madrid (Turner Publicaciones SL) 2021, p. 23. Henceforth, *Frida in Paris*.

97 Hôpital de Ville-Évrard, a public psychiatric hospital in Neuilly-sur-Marne, opened in 1875 for indigent patients. Camille Claudel was interned there in 1913. Artaud was hospitalized between 1939 and 1943; he died of an accidental overdose of chloral hydrate in 1948.

98 Ronad Hayman, *Artaud and After*, Oxford, London and New York (Oxford University Press) 1977, p. 123.

99 Damisch interview.

100 Ibid.

101 Charles Duits, *André Breton, a-t-il-dit passe*, Mayenne (L'Imprimerie Floch) 1991, p. 103. Henceforth, Duits.

102 I thank Gordon Onslow Ford for providing the until now unknown information about Picasso's portraits of Jacqueline, and Fariba Bogzaran for interviewing Gordon for me. Among the portraits that Picasso painted in 1934–5, some are of Jacqueline and some are of Marie-Thérèse Walter. In the latter's portraits, the features are soft and sensuous. In Jacqueline's portraits, they are strong and angular. Historians often mistake the two women for each other because both were about the same age and blonde. In the Picasso literature, scholars often identify the women in the double portraits as Dora Maar and Walter. This was disproved by photographs the artist took of Maar and Jacqueline side by side during the years when the portraits were done, Maar wearing a garland of flowers next to Jacqueline, as they appear in the paintings. Authors have been mistaken when Jacqueline and Aube traveled with Picasso and Maar, referring to them as Marie-Thérèse and Maya, her daughter with Picasso. Aube interviews.

103 Vanetti interview.

104 Polizzotti, p. 415.

105 Paul Éluard, *Letters to Gala*, New York (Paragon Press) 1989, p. 220. Henceforth, Gala letters.

106 Marguerite was married to Alfred Rosmer, author of *Lenin's Moscow*, 1953. On very friendly terms with Lenin and Trotsky, he

stood by the original aims and principles of Communism but also saw many problems from the period. Breton likely knew her from his early days, when he was a member of the Communist Party.

107 André Breton, *Oeuvres complètes*, Paris (Gallimard) 1999, vol. III, p. 137.

108 *Mad Love*, p. 11.

109 J.E. Cirlot, *A Dictionary of Symbols*, New York (Philosophical Library) 1981, p. 35.

110 *Mad Love*, p. 47, and George Melly and Michael Woods, *Paris and the Surrealists*, New York (Thames and Hudson) 1991, p. 19. See also C.J.S. Thompson, *The Lure and Romance of Alchemy*, New York (Bell) 1990, pp. 87–90. Flamel lived on rue Notaire, near the former belfry of the church Saint-Jacques-de-la-Boucherie, which was built in the sixteenth century and pulled down in 1802.

111 Damisch interview.

112 The correspondence from André Breton to Jacqueline Lamba was donated by her to the Jacques Doucet Literary Library, Paris. I thank Aube for facilitating my access to it. André destroyed the letters from Jacqueline to him.

113 Arturo Schwarz, "Entrevista a Jacqueline Lamba," in *El Encuentro de Breton y Trotsky en México*, compiled by Ariane Díaz, Buenos Aires (Ediciones IPS) 2016, pp. 308–9. Henceforth, Lamba–Schwarz interview.

114 Huguette interviews.

115 Exquisite corpses is a game in which several participants contribute in turn to a collaborative artwork or story without seeing or reading the previous submission or submissions. Only when the last player has finished is the whole creation revealed.

116 Not to be confused with *La Femme blonde* (1930), a painting of the same name in Charles Ratton's collection.

117 "Breton expressed his disdain for the mimetic (bourgeois or social realist) as a socially defensive maneuver in a contrasting pair of objects—'heads' that Jacqueline and he made in 1936— 'The Great Paranoiac' and 'Le Petit Mimétique.'" See Jack J. Spector, *The Gold of Time: Surrealist Art & Writing 1919–39*, New York (Cambridge University Press) 1997, p. 153.

118 Paul C. Ray, *The Surrealist Movement in England*, Ithaca, NY, and London (Cornell University Press) 1971, p. 137. Henceforth, Paul C. Ray.

119 Interview with Martine Cazin, potter-painter friend of Jacqueline, in Paris, October 1999. Henceforth, Cazin interview 1999.

120 Picasso made several portraits of Jacqueline with green hair.

121 Glasgow *Daily Record*, June 11, 1936, courtesy of the Scottish National Gallery of Modern Art.

122 Paul C. Ray, p. 139.

123 Ibid., p. 152.

124 Ibid., p. 160.

125 Shell of *Strombus gigas* (now *Aliger gigas*).

126 *Mad Love*, p. 53.

127 Ibid., p. 13.

128 For an understanding of the relationship between Breton and Éluard, see Jean-Charles Gateau, *Paul Éluard ou Le frère voyant 1895–1952*, Paris (Editions Robert Lafont) 1994, pp. 230–57.

129 Jacqueline wrote to Maar after Breton received a letter from Éluard expressing his sadness, which the Bretons found "idiotic," and to which Breton replied angrily with a letter that Jacqueline tore up—with permission. Letter dated August 18, 1937, courtesy of Victoria Combalía.

130 The poem "November 1936," about the bombing of Madrid by the Nazis, who also tried to block the distribution of food supplies, was published in *L'Humanité* on December 17, 1936.

131 Georges Hugnet, *Pleines & déliés, témoignages et souvenirs 1926–1972*, Paris (Éditions Guy Gauthier) 1972, pp. 402–7.

132 Cazin interview 1999.

133 A recent discovery is a painting by Jacqueline also titled *La Femme blonde* (1930), oil on wood, 17¾ x 19¾ in. (45 x 50 cm), initially owned by Charles Ratton, at the time of publication of the present volume in the collection of Guy Ladrière.

134 Collection Daniel Filipacchi, Paris. In France, in this context, the word "friend" suggests more than friendship.

135 Translated by Henry Winfield.

136 Polizzotti, p. 442.

137 Gala letters, p. 230.

138 Historian Antony Beevor maintained, in his *The Spanish Civil War*, London (Orbis) 2002, that Durruti was not assassinated as it was believed, but died when a companion's machine gun went off by mistake and a bullet pierced his heart.

139 Aube, age two and a half, was left in the care of Rose and André Masson.

140 Lamba–Schwarz interview, p. 301.

141 Ibid., p. 302.

142 Ibid., pp. 301–9.

143 For a thorough understanding of how Surrealism developed in Mexico and Breton's visit, see Luis Mario Schneider, *México y el surrealismo (1925–1950)*, Mexico City (Arte y Libros) 1978.

144 For a description of how Breton interpreted the Surrealist mindset while in Mexico, see Salomon Grimberg, "Mexico Reflected in André Breton's Mirror," in *Surrealism in Mexico*, exh. cat., April 26–June 28, 2019, New York (Di Donna Galleries) 2019, pp. 26–37.

145 André Breton, "Frida Kahlo de Rivera." Reproduced in the catalogue *Frida Kahlo and Tina Modotti*, London (Whitechapel Art Gallery) 1982, pp. 35–6.

146 "Diálogo de André Breton con Rafael Heliodoro Valle," reproduced in the catalogue *Los Surrealistas en México*, Mexico City (INBA/MUNAL/SEP), 1986, pp. 102–6.

147 The groundwork research on the life and work of Frida Kahlo was done by Hayden Herrera. All subsequent research follows her *Frida: A Biography of Frida Kahlo*, New York (Harper & Row) 1983. Henceforth, Herrera, *Frida*.

148 The painting has been dated 1938, but in a letter dated 1934 that Frida Kahlo wrote to Alejandro Gómez Arias, and that he gave to Raquel Tibol, she describes working on the painting. See Salomon Grimberg, *Song of Herself*, London (Merrell Publishers) 2008, p. 57. Henceforth, *Song of Herself*.

149 Letters from André Breton and/or Jacqueline Lamba, here reproduced, unless otherwise stated, private archive.

Breton's requests made in the letter to Rivera were not fulfilled. The excuse was that Rivera did not reply to letters. But the reason was the repeated negative experiences that Frida had with André, including the late delivery of the text for the Julien Levy catalogue, and problems concerning Frida's stay at the Bretons' home and her exhibition.

150 Jacqueline is referring to becoming pregnant in Mexico and the abortion she had upon returning to France.

151 For a comprehensive description of Frida Kahlo's trip to New York and Paris, see Herrera, *Frida*.

152 Frida Kahlo to Diego Rivera in a letter in the Frida Kahlo Museum.

153 Frida met Michel Petitjean, two years her junior, through Marcel Duchamp. He worked at Charles Ratton's gallery, where Breton intended originally to present her exhibition.

154 *Frida in Paris*, p. 55.

155 Letters from Frida Kahlo to Nickolas Muray are in the Archives of American Art, Washington, DC. I thank Mimi Muray for providing me with copies.

156 *Xochitl* in the Aztec language means flower, something fragile, a nickname that Frida embraced and used to refer to herself when communicating with Muray.

157 Frida Kahlo, *Diario*, Mexico City (La Vaca Independiente) 1994, n.p. Henceforth, Kahlo letter.

158 Quoted in Victoria Combalía, *Dora Maar*, Barcelona (Circe) 2013, p. 125. Henceforth, Combalía.

159 Ibid., p. 125.

160 For his recollection of the stay at Chémilieu, see Gordon Onslow Ford, *Mirando en lo profundo/Seeing in Depth*, exh. cat., Santiago de Compostela (Fundación Eugenio Granell) 1998, chronology, pp. 154–6. Henceforth, Onslow Ford.

161 Ibid., pp. 70–73.

162 Ibid., p. 70.

163 Stephen Robeson Miller (ed.), "Kay Sage, Château de Chémilieu (1939)," in *Kay Sage: The Biographical Chronology and Four Surrealist One-Act Plays*, New York (Gallery of Surrealism) 2011, pp. 83–4.

164 Andreas Neufert, ed. Gordon Onslow Ford, *Bilder/Paintings*, Munich (Höcherl Verlag) n.d., pp. 64–8.

165 Roberto Matta, interview with Federica Matta for the author, July 25, 2000, in Paris.

166 Ibid.

167 Undated letter from Dora Maar to Jacqueline in a private archive.

168 Gordon Onslow Ford, interview with Fariba Bogsaran for the author.

169 Onslow Ford, p. 67.

170 Pregnant again, Jacqueline was having trouble finding a physician to perform the abortion. Dr. Pierre Mabille, generally sought by the women of Surrealism in such cases, was unavailable.

171 Combalía, p. 199.

172 Aube interviews.

173 Combalía, p. 204.

174 Frida confided to Ella and Bertram Wolfe that her affairs were intended to get back at Diego. See Bertram D. Wolfe, *A Life in Two Centuries: The Autobiography of Bertam D Wolfe*, New York (Stein and Day) 1981, p. 587.

175 Nickolas Muray, letter to Frida Kahlo dated April 6, 1940, Frida Kahlo Museum, reproduced in Salomon Grimberg, *I Will Never Forget You*, Munich (Schirmer/Mosel) 2004, p. 36.

176 Damisch interview.

177 Ibid.

178 Daniel Bénédite, *La Filière Marseillaise, Un chemin vers la Liberté sous l'occupation*, preface by David Rousset, Paris (Éditions Clancier Guénaud) 1984, p. 123. Henceforth, Bénédite.

179 Varian Fry, *Surrender on Demand*, preface by Warren Christopher, Boulder, CO (Johnson Books), 1945, p. 113. Henceforth, Fry.

180 Damisch interview.

181 Ibid.

182 Jean Gemähling, interview with the author, April 8, 2002, Paris.

183 Bénédite, p. 120.

184 Fry, p. 117.

185 Serge's wife, Liuba Russakova Kibalchich, diagnosed as schizophrenic, stayed in France, in the Rodez asylum under the care of Dr. Gaston Ferdière. Telephone interview with the author, September 26, 2000.

186 Damisch interview.

187 Ibid.

188 Ibid.

189 Breton gave the original drawings to Delanglade to redraw the set and give it a uniform appearance.

190 Holzer interview.

191 Brigitte Benkemoun, *Finding Dora Maar, An Artist, An Address Book, A Life,* translated from the French by Jody Gladding, Los Angeles (Getty Publications) 2020, p. 43. Huguette returned to Paris and was helped by Maar at Jacqueline's request. She had a baby girl, Brigitte, who died in infancy. Henceforth, *Finding Dora Maar.*

192 Mary Jayne Gold, *Crossroads Marseilles 1940: A Memoir*, New York (Doubleday) 1980, pp. 267–9.

193 Kahlo letter. The section referring to their conversation about Trotsky's death is scratched out but legible.

194 Bénédite, p. 150.

195 Holzer interview.

196 Ibid.

197 *Poems of André Breton: A Bilingual Anthology*, trans. and ed. Jean-Pierre Cauvin and Mary Ann Caws, Austin (University of Texas Press) 1982, pp. 130–55. Henceforth, *Poems of André Breton*.

198 Damisch interview.

199 Claude Lévi-Strauss in a letter to the author dated April 3, 2002.

200 Holzer interview.

201 Jacqueline wrote to Varian Fry in a letter dated "mardi 29 Juin 1941," in the Rare Book and Manuscript Library of Columbia University, New York.

202 Letters from Jacqueline to Maar dated October 18, 1941, reproduced in the Dora Maar Estate sale catalogue *Les Livres de Dora Maar, autographes et documents*, Paris (PIASA; Maison de la Chimie) 1998, p. 12. Henceforth, Maar letter, PIASA.

203 Duits, pp. 99–100.

204 Maar letter, PIASA.

205 Claude Francis and Fernande Gontier, *Simone de Beauvoir: A Life, a Love Story,*

London (St Martin's Press) 1987, p. 241. Henceforth, *Simone de Beauvoir: A Life.*

206 Vanetti interview.

207 *Simone de Beauvoir: A Life*, p. 242.

208 Baziotes interview.

209 Carolyn Burke, *Becoming Modern: The Life of Mina Loy*, Berkeley (University of California Press) 1977, p. 380.

210 Anna Balakian, *André Breton: Magus of Surrealism*, New York (Oxford University Press) 1970, p. 173.

211 Anaïs Nin, *The Diary of Anaïs Nin, Volume Three, 1939–1944*, ed. and with a preface by Gunther Stuhlmann, New York (Harcourt, Brace, Jovanovich) 1969, p. 144.

212 Mary Ann Caws (ed. and intro.), *Joseph Cornell, Theater of the Mind: Selected Diaries, Letters, and Files*, New York and London (Thames and Hudson) 1993, p. 99. In maritime law, flotsam and jetsam are debris in the water that often result from a shipwreck. Flotsam is not deliberately thrown overboard; jetsam is thrown overboard by the crew of a ship in distress.

213 Dominique Noailles, interview with the author, July 2000, in Paris. Henceforth, Noailles interview.

214 Susanna Wilson, interview with the author, June 14, 2002, Newcastle, Maine. I thank her also for providing me with the original issues of *VVV Almanac* and access to her archives. Henceforth, Wilson interview.

215 Vanetti interview.

216 Aube interviews.

217 Carrington interview.

218 Ibid.

219 André Thirion, *Revolutionaires without Revolution*, New York (Macmillan) 1975, p. 175.

220 Gérard Roche (ed.), *André Breton Benjamin Péret Correspondance 1920–1959*, Paris (Éditions Gallimard) 2017, p. 141. Henceforth, AB–BP Letters.

221 Vanetti interview.

222 Wilson interview.

223 In 1941, David produced a color portfolio, *Pueblo Indians of New Mexico, as they are today: twenty photographs*, introduced by Dr. Clark Wissler, curator of anthropology at the Museum of Natural History in New York.

224 Duits, p. 95.

225 Vanetti interview.

226 David took nude photos of Jacqueline and made prints from the heated negatives. One of these was among the originals included in the *VVV Portfolio*.

227 Carrington interview.

228 Polizzotti, p. 512.

229 AB–BP Letters, pp. 149–50.

230 Polizzotti, p. 512.

231 AB–BP Letters, pp. 152–3.

232 Jacqueline Lamba, interview with the author, August 1987, in Paris. Henceforth, Lamba interview.

233 Wilson interview.

234 Jane Gunther interview.

235 Ibid.

236 Ibid.

237 Suzy suffered from bipolar disorder.

238 Patla interview.

239 Baziotes interview.

240 Frey interview.

241 *Rimbaud*, p. 280.

242 Duits, p. 115.

243 *Poems of André Breton*, p. 169.

244 Duits, p. 116.

245 Ibid.

246 The reference here is to *la rose trémière*, the hollyhock mentioned in the work of influential French Romantic poet Gérard de Nerval (1808–1855).

247 Duits, p. 115.

248 Julien Levy, *Memoir of an Art Gallery*, New York (G.P. Putnam's Sons) 1977, p. 280.

249 Vanetti interview.

250 Duits, p. 89.

251 André Breton, *Young Cherry Trees Secured against Hares*, trans. Edouard Roditi, Ann Arbor (University of Michigan Press) 1969.

252 See Angelica Zander Rudenstein, *Peggy Guggenheim Collection, Venice*, New York (Abrams) 1985, p. 789.

253 Jacqueline to Huguette, postcard dated May 26, 1946. Huguette Lamba archive.

254 Jacqueline to Huguette, postcard dated July 18, 1946. Huguette Lamba archive.

255 Ibid.

256 Sawin interview.

257 This oil on canvas, 23¼ x 26½ in. (59 x 67.3 cm), n.d., is lost. The San Francisco

Museum of Modern Art (SFMoMA) deaccessioned it (date unknown) through Butterfields auction house. Acct. #46.3172. The Museum kept an image not available for reproduction.

258 *Rimbaud*, p. 133.

259 In a letter Mougouch Gorky wrote Jeanne Reynal on May 5, 1944, she describes visiting Matta's studio: "We sat & looked & discussed his ideas. They are cockeyed if I may say—he behaves more & more like a spoilt boy who wants to masquerade as [the Marquis] de Sade. He has done some huge drawings v. well executed of ladies & gents doing push push in a most ungentlemanly way gents masturbating with one hand & slitting a throat with ze other all v. realistic—he was aching for me to be repulsed or vomit but I couldn't react that strongly because the realism—though not pornographic—was too graphic to move me anyway. He then tried to tell me that this was man—man as he really was—a cruel beast quite empty—I felt like saying my dear child but did not—Breton hates them & likened them to scars—to which Matta say yes but I find scars v. exciting." See Matthew Spender (ed.), *Arshile Gorky Goats on the Roof: A Life in Letters and Documents*, London (Ridinghouse) 2010, pp. 229–30. Henceforth, Spender.

260 Sidney Janis, *Abstract and Surrealist Art in America*, New York (Reynal and Hitchcock) 1944, p. 126.

261 Lamba interview.

262 Mougouch Gorky, interview with the author in London. Henceforth, Mougouch interview.

263 Isabelle Waldberg to Patrick Waldberg in a letter from New York, April 15, 1944. Quoted in Michel Waldberg (ed.), *Patrick Waldberg Isabelle Waldberg Un Amour acéphale Correspondance 1940–1949*, Paris (Éditions de la Différence) 1992, pp. 190–92. Henceforth, Waldberg.

264 Mougouch Gorky to Jeanne Reynal in a letter dated April 1944, in the Matthew Spender papers in the Mulhall Achilles Library, Whitney Museum of American Art.

265 The line is drawn from *Fata Morgana*, the love poem Breton wrote for Jacqueline at Air-Bel about their fragile relationship and his need to hold on to her. When Laila, queen of the night, appears to him, he asks her to heal his wounds, but suddenly she disappears. Throughout the poem he repeats the phrase "So close yet so far."

266 Vanetti interview.

267 Translated by Lionel Abel.

268 Maude Riley, "Fifty Seventh St. in Review," *Art Digest*, April 15, 1944, p. 19.

269 Howard Devree in the *New York Times*, April 16, 1944, p. 159.

270 Waldberg, pp. 205–6.

271 A character in Alfred Jarry's play *Ubu Cocu*.

272 A member of the French Resistance, awarded Commander of the Legion of Honor in 2002.

273 Waldberg, pp. 216–17.

274 Kahlo letter; a copy of the photograph she used for Jacqueline's portrait is in Aube's archive.

275 See Salomon Grimberg, *Frida Kahlo: The Still Lifes*, London (Merrell Publishers) 2008, pp. 86–91. Henceforth, *The Still Lifes*.

276 Mougouch Gorky recalled that Jacqueline wrote to her from Mexico, but "misplaced the letters." Mougouch interview.

277 Waldberg, p. 273.

278 Frey interview.

279 In an undated *France Soir* review in Jacqueline Lamba's archive, "Jacqueline Lamba explores the unknown spaces of painters."

280 Letter dated October 19, 1944, from Jeanne Reynal to Mougouch Gorky, in the Matthew Spender papers in the Mulhall Achilles Library, Whitney Museum of American Art.

281 Arturo García Bustos, interview with the author in Mexico City.

282 Cristina Kahlo, daughter of Antonio, interview with the author in Mexico City.

283 See Frida Kahlo's clinical history in *Song of Herself*, pp. 104–19.

284 Carrington interview.

285 *The Still Lifes*, pp. 91–4.

286 Newspaper clipping in the archive of the Galería de Arte Mexicano, Mexico City.

287 Aube interviews.

288 *The Still Lifes*, pp. 96–8.

289 According to Dolorès Vanetti, the customs officers quizzed Jacqueline about her sex life. Although Dolorès was not specific, the author understood her to imply that the questioning had been about whether she was into S & M.

290 Pierre Matisse Archives, Morgan Library, New York.

291 Vanetti interview.

292 Wilson interview.

293 I thank Dr. Richard Fullington, ex-director of the Museum of Natural History, Dallas, for identifying each insect and its life cycle in each painting.

294 Spender, p. 251. Spelling and punctuation of the letter left as Mougouch wrote it.

295 Vanetti interview.

296 Dieter Schwarz, *Sonja Sekula 1918–1963*, with biography by Roger Perret, Winterthur (Kunstmuseum Winterthur) 1996, p. 67.

297 Ibid., p. 69.

298 Ibid.

299 David Hare, in Nancy Foote, "Who Was Sonia Sekula?," *Art in America*, LIX/5 (September–October 1971), p. 79.

300 Ibid.

301 Ibid.

302 Aube interviews.

303 Baziotes interview.

304 Lassaw interview 1999.

305 Ibid.

306 Letter from Patrick Waldberg to E.L.T. Mesens, dated July 4, 1945, E.L.T. Mesens papers, Correspondence 1942–7, box 5, folder 7, Getty Research Institute, Los Angeles.

307 As reported in the *New York Times*.

308 Vanetti interview.

309 Before moving in with Jacqueline, David lent the house to the Gorkys. He was resisting paying Suzi's dentist bill even though it was he who injured her. At a party, he was frantically whirling a glass bottle with his finger stuck in its neck. As Suzi warned him it could slip out and hurt someone, it came loose, knocking out her two front teeth. Wilson interview. The letter, transcribed as David wrote it, is in Susanna Wilson's archive.

310 Holzer interview.

311 Ibid.

312 Ibid.

313 Aube interviews.

314 Ibid.

315 Ibid.

316 Ibid.

317 Ibid.

318 Ibid.

319 Ibid.

320 Simone de Beauvoir, *America Day by Day*, trans. Carol Cosman, foreword by Douglas Brinkley, Berkeley, LA, and London (University of California Press) 1990, pp. 339–41.

321 Letter from Jacqueline Lamba to Enrico Donati, dated June 10, 1947, Donati papers, folder 5, letters from Jacqueline Lamba and David Hare.

322 Vanetti interview.

323 AB–BP Letters, letter 98, dated Paris, 8 July, 1947, p. 255.

324 Aube interviews.

325 Sylvia Bataille had married psychoanalyst Laurence Bataille in 1928, when she was twenty; she separated from him in 1934 and divorced him in 1946. In 1938, she became the companion of psychoanalyst Jacques Lacan.

326 Aube in a letter to the author dated "3/5/25."

327 Undated letter from David Hare to Enrico Donati (August 1947), Donati papers.

328 Hazel Rowley, *Simone de Beauvoir and Jean-Paul Sartre: Tête-à-Tête*, New York (HarperCollins) 2005, p. 157. De Beauvoir writes to Sartre about the nervous collapse they caused Bianca Bienenfeld, "suffering an intense and dreadful attack of neurasthenia, and it's our fault," having harmed her by making her their lover.

329 Simone de Beauvoir, *After the War, Force of Circumstance, 1, 1944–1952*, with a new introduction by Toril Moi, New York (Paragon House) 1992, p. 122.

330 *Simone de Beauvoir: A Life*, p. 241.

331 Simone de Beauvoir, *A Transatlantic Love Affair: Letters to Nelson Algren*, New York (The New Press) 1999, p. 75.

332 Undated note from Jacqueline to Huguette. Huguette archive.

333 Aube interviews.

334 Ernestine Lassaw, telephone interview with the author, September 9, 2000.

Henceforth, Lassaw interview 2000.

335 Martica Sawin telephone interview with the author.

336 Aube interviews.

337 Mary Abbott, interview with the author in New York.

338 Ibid.

339 Quoted in *Wikipedia*, "Mary Abbott (artist)," ref. 8, Danielle Krysa, *A Big Important Book (Now with Women): Profiles of Unstoppable Female Artists—and Projects to Help You Become One* (first edn.), Philadelphia (Running Press) 2018.

340 Vanetti interview.

341 Aube archive.

342 Letter in the Aube archive.

343 Aube interviews.

344 Ibid.

345 Hayden Herrera, interview with the author in New York.

346 Quoted from *Art News* (October 1949), p. 4, in Barry Schwabsky, "Hidden Harmonies," online.

347 Letters from Jacqueline to Dolorès Vanetti. Henceforth, Vanetti archive.

348 Lassaw interview 1999.

349 Baziotes interview.

350 Vanetti archive.

351 Antonina Vallentin, "Notes on Exhibitions," *Les Temps Modernes*, March 1952, no. 77, pp. 1706–7.

352 Aube interviews.

353 Frey interview.

354 Hare's dazzling career, for which Jacqueline was fundamentally responsible, lost its vision after he left her.

355 Vanetti archive.

356 Marcelle Ferry (Lila) had an affair with André in the early 1930s, before he met Jacqueline.

357 Interview between Merlin Hare and Fabrice Maze, New York, December 2002. Fabrice Maze archive (henceforth, Maze archive). Henceforth, Merlin–Maze interview.

358 Ibid.

359 Jacqueline's correspondence with Lacan and Damoiseau in a private archive. In her 1978 daily planner she wrote, "Left psychoanalysis [with Ferdière]14-1-1976."

360 Noailles interview.

361 Sawin interview.

362 David met Denise in 1956.

363 Aube archive.

364 Vanetti archive.

365 Ibid.

366 Frey interview.

367 Yves's premature death abruptly ended the couple's plans for the future. In a letter to Dr. Damoiseau, dated April 19, 1975, Jacqueline wrote: "Aube's husband is dying. I love Aube." Private archive.

368 Vanetti archive.

369 Letter from Jacqueline to Martine Cazin, July 17, 1980. Henceforth, Cazin archive.

370 Ibid.

371 Telephone interview with Paul Destribats, avant-garde book and manuscript collector, in Paris, ca. 2000.

372 Cazin interview 1999.

373 *L'Express*, April 30, 1959.

374 Also, what might have contributed to her sense of freedom was David's marriage to Denise in that year.

375 Letter from Jacqueline to Debra Patla and Merlin Hare dated February 9, 1982 in their archive.

376 Ibid., June 6, 1986.

377 Vanetti interview.

378 Jacqueline Lamba, note to herself in Fabrice Maze's archive.

379 Vanetti interview.

380 Letter from Mark Tobey to Arthur L. Dahl, reproduced in the exhibition catalogue, *Mark Tobey, Paintings from the collection of Joyce and Arthur Dahl,* shown at the Stanford Art Gallery, Stanford University, June 17–August 20, 1967, p. 9.

381 Martine Cazin interview in Paris, November 12, 2002; henceforth, Cazin interview 2002.

382 Noailles interview.

383 Stephen-Robeson Miller, telephone interview with the author.

384 Noailles interview.

385 Ibid.

386 Ibid.

387 Ibid.

388 Ibid.

389 Ibid.

390 Ibid.

391 They were painted from the balcony of her fifth-floor apartment at 8 boulevard de Bonne Nouvelle, or the fourteenth-floor

apartment of her friend pianist Colette
Maze, at 6 boulevard de Grenelle.
392 Cazin interview 1999.
393 Ibid.
394 Ibid.
395 Oona interviews.
396 Jacqueline's note to herself; Aube archive.
397 Clouzot interview.
398 Noailles interview.
399 Vanetti interview.
400 Jacques Bibonne, interview with
    the author, October 1999, in Paris.
    Henceforth, Bibonne interview.
401 Ibid.
402 Ibid.
403 Letter from Yves Bonnefoy to the author,
    dated March 28, 2002.
404 Lamba interview.
405 Bibonne interview.
406 Sawin interview.
407 Lamba interview.
408 Aube interviews.
409 Letter from Jacqueline to Martine Cazin,
    dated July 8, 1988. Cazin archive.
410 Letter to Martine Cazin, dated
    August 7, 1988. Cazin archive.
411 Lamba's medical records, Aube archive.
412 Letter from Martine Cazin to the author,
    dated October 1, 2000.
413 After Jacqueline's death, Aube "read in
    her address book, she sent Merlin most of
    the money she gave her after the sale of
    André's atelier. To friends, she asked for
    clothes, she said because she was poor.
    They would call asking her how could
    she abandon her mother that way."
    Aube interviews.
414 Oona interviews.
415 Ibid.
416 Ibid.
417 In an undated note to herself, Jacqueline
    wrote in black ink and underlined in
    blue, yellow, and red, "The attraction for
    doctors: the one that saved my two eyes,
    age two and allowed me to paint; then
    another at ten years old, my intelligence
    or my life through my ears; then another,
    that gave me my life; then another who
    brought me back to life, not without
    having tried, but it stayed." Private
    archive.
418 Ibid.
419 Aube interviews.
420 Ibid.
421 Aube interviews.
422 Cazin interview, 1999.
423 Note to Martine Cazin dated August 31,
    1989. Cazin archive.
424 Merlin–Maze interview.
425 Cazin interview, 1999.
426 Aube interviews.
427 Ibid.
428 Oona interviews.
429 Ibid.
430 Aube interviews.
431 Oona interviews.
432 Aube interviews.
433 Ibid.
434 Letter in a private archive.
435 Lamba interview.
436 Fabrice Maze, interview with the author,
    1999.
437 Jacqueline to Chrystie Sherman in a
    postcard dated October 1, 1973, Paris.
    Sherman archive.
438 Aube interviews.
439 Huguette interviews.
440 Fabrice Maze to the author, 1999.
441 Noailles interview.
442 Ibid.
443 Aube interviews.
444 Noailles interview.
445 Aube archive.
446 Aube also produced a documentary,
    *Jacqueline Lamba, Painter, Painting to the
    Very End of the Sky*, made by Fabrice Maze,
    for "Phares," a series of documentaries
    focusing on Surrealist artists.

Index

Acknowledgments

When I began working with Jacqueline Lamba, I was unaware she screened her phone calls. If the ringing did not match the expected code, she would not answer. I thank her for picking up when I first called—without knowing the rules. In retrospect, I see it as a fortunate coincidence—a *hasard objectif*—an invitation to work together.

Since divorcing André Breton, Jacqueline had done all she could to build a life separate and apart from him, although history would not let go. For years, she consistently helped scholars write about him and other Surrealists. She never said no.

During her self-effacing process from Surrealism, when painting was her main focus, she had done little to document her extraordinary life, and others did not help. By the time I approached her, in 1986, Jacqueline was in her seventies and not one single scholar had expressed interest in writing about her life or work. Art historians asked about Breton or other figures in Surrealism but were uninterested in how hundreds of exquisite paintings in the studio—visions of light—were quietly produced during the previous twenty-four years, while Jacqueline was developing her unique iconography. When I volunteered to present her work in a museum exhibition, she replied with her characteristic bluntness that after showing at the Picasso Museum in Antibes, where she had been directly involved in choosing the paintings, she had no interest in exhibiting anywhere other than at the Beaubourg. Nevertheless, Jacqueline generously provided the information I needed, and more.

This biography of Jacqueline Lamba became a reality thanks to Georgiana Colville, who first suggested I write about her life and work, and introduced me to Aube Breton-Elléouët. Aube and Merlin Hare, her half-brother, paved the way for me to bring well-deserved acknowledgment to Jacqueline Lamba, the person and the painter, in this biography and the traveling retrospective, May 3, 2001–February 21, 2002, including the accompanying publications. I am grateful to Huguette Lamba, Jacqueline's sister; Debra Patla, Jacqueline's daughter-in-law; and Oona Elléouët, her granddaughter, who provided memories and family documents to help develop an understanding of Jacqueline's complex life. Fabrice Maze, documentary filmmaker, devoted to Jacqueline Lamba since childhood—the best friend to have—generously shared with me letters and other documents, gathered over a lifetime, that would not have survived without his devotion, and that I could not have accessed without his continuous help. Marianne Clouzot, Jacqueline's childhood friend, kept diaries throughout their adolescence, in which she described Jacqueline's early years.

Mary Abbott, Ethel Baziotes, Helena Benitez, Jacques Bibonne, Leonora Carrington, Martine Cazin, Enrico Donati, Anne Egger, Arturo García Bustos, Therry Frey, Jean Gemähling, Mougouch Gorky, Jane Gunther, Cristina Kahlo, Ernestine Lassaw, Claude Lévi-Strauss, Roberto Matta Echaurren, Dominique Noailles, Gordon Onslow Ford, Vlady Serge, and Chrystie Sherman brought to life key moments in Jacqueline's life. Dolorès Vanetti, friend and confidante, educated me about Jacqueline's personal struggles and the iconographic sources of her creativity. I thank Federica Matta and Fariba Bogzaran for providing interviews with Roberto Matta Echaurren and Gordon Onslow Ford, respectively. Martica Sawin, generous with her time, helped in countless ways, including contacting Susanna Wilson Coggeshall, who, until then, had been unwilling to speak about the Surrealists exiled in New York, and who became a friend; and Tomlin Coggeshall, her son, who provided copies of Susanna's archive and introduced me to Mary Abbott. Scholars to whom I am indebted are Josefina Alix, Arsène Bonafous-Murat, Yves Bonnefoy, Henri Cazin, Whitney Chadwick, Victoria Combalía, Siobhan Conaty, Katharine Conley, Guy Delacour, Paul Destribats, Estela Duarte, Sheila Eisenberg, Jean Gemähling, Jean-Michel Goutier, Hayden Herrera, Jean Paul Kahn, Roseanne Livingston, Steve Lucas, Charlotte Mays, Walter Meyerhoff, Martine Monteau, Masayo Nonaka, Paul Resika, Stephen Robeson-Miller, Helen Rusotto, Arturo Schwarz, Marcel Verzeano, Thomas Windholz, and Amy Winter.

Priceless research assistance came from Ann Potter and Judy Throm, Archives of American Art, Washington, DC; Bernard R. Crystal, Varian Fry Papers 1940–1967, Columbia University Libraries, Rare Book & Manuscript Library; Richard Fullington, ex-Director of the Museum of Natural History, Dallas; Mark Henderson, Getty Research Institute, Los Angeles; Ziva Haller, The Israel Museum, Jerusalem; Robert Parks, Pierre Matisse Gallery Archives, The Morgan Library and Museum, Department of Literary and Historical Manuscripts, New York; Philippe Arbaïzar, Bibliothèque nationale de France; Fatima Dilme, Yves Peyré, and Rémi Froger, Directeur, Bibliothèque littéraire Jacques-Doucet; Ann Simpson, Senior Curator Archive & Library, and Logan Sisley, Penrose Archive, Archive and Library Assistant, Oscar Román, Director, Galería Oscar Román, Mexico City; Scottish National Gallery of Modern Art, Edinburgh; and Carol Rusk, Librarian, Whitney Museum of Art, New York. And those collectors who provided documents and information and requested anonymity.

Elsa Honig Fine, Publisher, and Margaret Barlow, Editor, of the *Woman's Art Journal*, respectively, were responsible for producing the special number dedicated to Jacqueline Lamba and the catalogue that accompanied the Jacqueline Lamba retrospective exhibition I curated, and presented by Natalia Fernández Segarra, Directora, Fundación Eugenio Granell, Santiago de Compostela; Helen Harrison, Director, Pollock-Krasner House and Study Center, East Hampton; Dr. William Jeffett, Senior Curator, Salvador Dalí Museum. A very special debt of gratitude to Dr. Katherine Crum, Director Mills College Art Museum, who, with knowledge, understanding, and saintly patience, was pivotal in organizing the show, negotiating difficult loans, and securing grants from the Florence Gould Foundation and the New York Council for the Arts to provide funding for the exhibition.

Eric Berlin, I thank for proofreading an early version of the manuscript and making valuable comments.

I thank Professor Maurice Elton for impeccable French translations; André Gomes for generously providing photographs taken at Villa Air-Bel; and Jean-Claude Georges for invaluable assistance during my research in Paris.

Deepest gratitude goes to Marcel and David Fleiss, Directors of the Galerie 1900–2000 administrators of the André Breton and Jacqueline Lamba estates. And to Rowland Weinstein, Director, and Kendy Genovese, Managing Director & Curator, of Weinstein Gallery. Their vision, enthusiasm, and tireless help were behind Jacqueline Lamba's exhibition in San Francisco and helped to make this publication a reality.

Salomon Grimberg
Dallas, Texas, 2026

Photo Credits

Salomon Grimberg writes on various aspects of the creative process. He co-edited Frida Kahlo's *Das Gesamtwerk* (1988), co-authored Remedios Varo's catalogue raisonné (1994), and has written numerous articles and essays for museum exhibition catalogues. He has curated shows on Leonora Carrington, Frida Kahlo, Nickolas Muray, and the 2001 traveling retrospective exhibition *Jacqueline Lamba: In Spite of Everything, Spring*. He is the author of *Frida Kahlo, The Still Lifes* (Merrell, 2008), *Frida Kahlo Song of Herself* (Merrell, 2008), *Frida Kahlo, I Will Never Forget You* (2004), and *Nickolas Muray, Portrait of a Photographer* (2013). He is contributing editor of the *Woman's Art Journal* and is working on the authorized catalogue raisonné of Leonora Carrington's paintings.

First published 2026 by Merrell Publishers
Limited, London and New York

Merrell Publishers Limited
70 Cowcross Street
London EC1M 6EJ

merrellpublishers.com

A catalogue record for this book is available from
the Library of Congress.
British Library Cataloguing-in-Publication data:
A catalogue record for this book is available
from the British Library.

ISBN 978-1-8589-4726-6

Produced by Merrell Publishers Limited
Designer: Roger Fawcett-Tang
Project editor: Henry Russell
Picture researcher: Nick Wheldon
Proofreader: Rosanna Fairhead
Indexer: Vicki Robinson

Printed and bound in Europe

Front jacket image: Jacqueline Lamba in profile,
ca. 1934

The Publishers wish to thank Rowland Weinstein
for his generous financial sponsorship of the
book, without which this publication would not
have been possible.

A note on the translations
Unless otherwise stated in the endnotes,
translations from the French are by
Maurice Elton or the author; translations
from the Spanish are by the author unless
otherwise indicated.